P9-CQI-355

The Research Foundation of
The Institute of Chartered Financial Analysts

Board of Trustees

Stocks, Bonds, Bills, and Inflation: Historical Returns (1926-1987)

Roger G. Ibbotson
Yale University and
Ibbotson Associates

Rex A. Sinquefield
Dimensional Fund Advisors

Stocks, Bonds, Bills, and Inflation: Historical Returns (1926-1987)

The Research Foundation of
The Institute of Chartered Financial Analysts

This publication is designed to provide accurate and authoritative
information in regard to the subject matter covered. It is sold with the
understanding that the publisher is not engaged in rendering legal,
accounting, or other professional service. If legal advice or other expert
assistance is required, the services of a competent professional should be
sought.

*From a Declaration of Principles jointly adopted by a Committee of the
American Bar Association and a Committee of Publishers.*

For reprint information, please contact

Permissions Editor
8 South Michigan Avenue, Suite 707
Chicago, Illinois 60603
(312) 263-3434

Library of Congress Cataloging-in-Publication Data

Ibbotson, Roger G.
   Stocks, bonds, bills, and inflation : historical returns
(1926-1987) / Roger G. Ibbotson, Rex A. Sinquefield.
     p.   cm.
   Bibliography: p.
   ISBN 1-55623-140-7. — ISBN 1-55623-231-4 (pbk.)
   1. Stocks—Prices—United States. 2. Securities—Prices—United
States. 3. Stock price forecasting. I. Sinquefield, Rex A.
II. Institute of Chartered Financial Analysts. Research Foundation.
III. Title.
HG4915.I2 1989
332.63'222'0973—dc20   89-7840
                                                 CIP

Susan S. Brennan, *Production Editor*
Ellen D. Goldlust, *Editorial Assistant*
Joni L. Tomal, *Editorial Assistant*
Diane B. Hamshar, *Administrative Assistant*

Printed in the United States of America
1 2 3 4 5 6 7 8 9 0 V 6 5 4 3 2 1 0 9

Mission

The mission of the Research Foundation is to identify, fund and publish research material that:

- expands the body of relevant and useful knowledge available to practitioners;
- assists practitioners in understanding and applying this knowledge; and
- enhances the investment management community's effectiveness in serving clients.

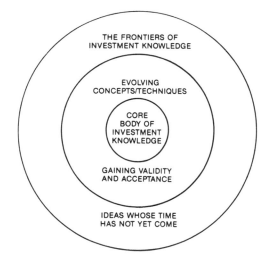

The Research Foundation of
The Institute of Chartered Financial Analysts
P.O. Box 3665
Charlottesville, Virginia 22903

Table of Contents

Exhibits

Foreword

For more than a decade, the Research Foundation of the Institute of Chartered Financial Analysts has had the high privilege of being involved in the development of a standard reference work, commonly dubbed "Ibbotson and Sinquefield," but more formally called *Stocks, Bonds, Bills, and Inflation (SBBI)*. No one can be in the investment business for very long without referring to *SBBI;* it is *the* reference source for every serious financial analyst. It has perspicuity; its presentation is lucid, systematic, and coherent; and it is the beginning of performance benchmarks.

This edition of *SBBI* continues and adds to the knowledge base of investment practitioners. The asset classes covered are those that dominate contemporary investing. Newly added are intermediate-term (five-year) government bonds, as well as two notably practical chapters.

The first new chapter examines how to estimate and use the cost of capital. Those analysts who have wrestled with these knotty and sensitive issues in such arenas as public utility rate making or valuation of damages in liability suits will value the authors' approaches.

The second new chapter is an important addition because it provides insights about forecasting the probability distributions of returns on assets and portfolios. As valuable as yesterday's returns are, we live in a world of tomorrows, and we must find a way to refine our ability to forecast, within reasonable probabilistic bounds, expected returns and their associated risks.

The full measure of *SBBI's* importance to financial analysts lies in its blend of theory and practice. But *SBBI's* value will never be discovered until it is fully tasted and digested. *Bon Appetit!*

Charles A. D'Ambrosio, CFA
Research Foundation of the
Institute of Chartered Financial Analysts

Acknowledgments

We would like to thank the many colleagues who helped us with this version, as well as previous editions of *Stocks, Bonds, Bills, and Inflation,* published by the Financial Analysts Research Foundation. We owe a great debt to James H. Lorie and Lawrence Fisher, who founded the Center for Research in Security Prices (CRSP) at the University of Chicago and provided the foundation for the type of empirical research in finance found here. Mr. Fisher, along with Thomas S. Coleman of the State University of New York at Stony Brook (currently on leave and with the Bank of Boston), also provided the five-year Treasury-bond-yield data for 1926-33. We thank Yale University and Dimensional Fund Advisors, Inc., for their generosity in providing us with the resources to prepare this edition, and CRSP, for providing the data without which this analysis would not have been possible.

Laurence B. Siegel served for many years as the principal editor of periodical updates of this publication and made many improvements, including the addition of the five-year Treasury series. He continues to serve in an editorial role. At Ibbotson Associates, Katie B. Weigel is now principal editor of the updates and has reorganized the entire book; Kimberly A. Maselli is assistant editor of the updates; Paul D. Kaplan provided assistance at many stages of editing, production, and graphic display; and Tze-Wah Chan programmed the analysis with great skill and speed. Marvin B. Waring and Margaret A. Corwin, Managing Directors of Ibbotson Associates, provided encouragement and help.

Rolf W. Banz of Dimensional Asset Management Ltd. (London) contributed the small-stock series used for most of the period covered in this book. Stephen P. Manus, of the American National Bank of Chicago, updates the common stock return series, as he has for many years. Yasushi Hamao, of the University of California at San Diego, has participated in long discussions about the methods used.

At Dimensional Fund Advisors, we thank Jeanne Cairns Sinquefield for caretaking of the data over many years, and for insisting that we compute income returns correctly, a change that was long overdue. Ramakrishnan Chandrasekar, Cem Severoglu, and Henry Otto (who is now with Brandywine Asset Management) have carefully scrutinized fixed-income and other data and have caught many errors. We, of course, are responsible for any that remain.

Eugene F. Fama, of the University of Chicago and a director of Dimensional Fund Advisors, has provided continual guidance and intellectual stimulation. David G. Booth, Co-Chair of Dimensional Fund Advisors, provided both encouragement and resources needed to produce this book.

Because this is the fourth edition of *Stocks, Bonds, Bills, and Inflation* intended for general publication, we would like to recognize those who had an impact on earlier editions, including Merton Miller, Eugene F. Fama, Fischer Black, and Myron Scholes. The staff and officers of the Research Foundation of the Institute of Chartered Financial Analysts were helpful throughout the production of the book and their help is hereby acknowledged. We would also like to express our thanks to the many other contributors to our ideas and research over the years, who are too numerous to name here.

Roger G. Ibbotson
Rex A. Sinquefield

1. Introduction

Who Should Read This Book?

Stocks, Bonds, Bills, and Inflation: Historical Returns (1926-1987) is a history of the returns of the capital markets in the United States from 1926 to 1987. It will be useful to several types of readers.

Foremost, anyone who is serious about investing must appreciate capital-market history. Such an appreciation, which this book provides, is valuable both to individual and institutional investors. For graduate and undergraduate students of finance, economics, and business, *Stocks, Bonds, Bills, and Inflation* is both a source of ideas and a reference. Other readers who will benefit from this publication include teachers; practitioners and scholars in finance, economics, and business; portfolio strategists; and security analysts.

Chief financial officers and, in some cases, chief executive officers of corporations will also find this book useful. People who are concerned with the cost of capital may apply the findings directly. More generally, economic historians may find it valuable to study the details revealed in more than six decades of capital market returns.

To all of these readers, the authors provide two resources. The first is the data. The second is a thinking person's guide to using historical data to understand financial markets and the decision-making process. This guide is necessary to answer the questions raised by the historical record. This book illustrates the authors' method of appreciating the past—only one of many possible techniques, but one grounded in real theory. In setting forth their appreciation, the authors enable the reader to think about the past and about financial markets.

Previous Work

In 1976, *The Journal of Business* published the authors' two companion papers on security returns (Ibbotson and Sinquefield January 1976 and July 1976). In the first paper, we presented historical data on the returns from stocks, government and corporate bonds, U.S. Treasury bills, and consumer goods (inflation). We described how the return on a security is the sum of two or more component returns.

In the second paper, we analyzed the time-series behavior of the component returns and the information contained in the U.S. government bond yield curve to obtain inputs to a simulation model of future security price behavior. We forecasted security returns through the year 2000 using the methods developed in the two papers.

The response to these works showed that historical data are fascinating in their own right. Both security and component historical returns have a wide range of applications in investment management, corporate finance, academic research, and regulation of industry.

Subsequent works—the 1977, 1979, and 1982 monographs of the Financial Analysts Research Foundation and, later, Ibbotson Associates' *Stocks, Bonds, Bills, and Inflation Yearbooks*—updated and further developed the historical data and forecasts.

In 1981, we began tracking a new asset class, small-company stocks. This class consists of those issues listed on the New York Stock Exchange (NYSE) which rank in the ninth and tenth (lowest) deciles when sorted by capitalization (price times number of shares outstanding), plus non-NYSE issues of comparable capitalization. This asset class has been of extraordinary interest to researchers and investors in recent years because of its high long-term returns.

In This Edition

With this edition, the authors continue to make changes and improvements. Another asset class, intermediate-term (five-year) government bonds, is added. Monthly and annual total returns, yields, income returns, and capital appreciation returns are presented. Yields on long-term government bonds are also presented. A new chapter (Chapter 8) examines the relation between firm size and return in greater detail, presenting and analyzing the returns on all 10 deciles of the NYSE, sorted by market capitalization.

The present volume updates the historical data. The motivations continue to be (1) to provide a convenient and useful history of security market returns and (2) to discern the relations among the various returns by examining their components: inflation, real interest rates, risk premiums, and other premiums.

A few other changes distinguish this edition. The chapters have been reorganized and exhibits added. The Questions and Answers section of previous editions has been converted to two chapters focusing on the use of historical data. Chapter 9 discusses the formation of estimates of the cost of capital. The forecasting of probability distributions of returns on assets and portfolios is addressed in Chapter 10.

Finally, this edition incorporates two new or revived calculation methods. First, the method of calculating series differences, or derived series (component and inflation-adjusted series) is different from that used in the 1982 edition of this book. In the 1982 edition, derived series were obtained by subtracting two monthly basic series. Returns on derived series C, defined as series A minus series B, were calculated as follows.

$$C = A - B.$$

In this volume, derived series are calculated by division. Returns on derived series C are related to series A and B as follows:

$$(1 + C) = (1 + A) / (1 + B),$$

where series A, B, and C are in decimal form (i.e., 5 percent is indicated by 0.05). Thus, C is given by

$$C = (1 + A) / (1 + B) - 1.$$

This method is referred to as "geometric subtraction."

The formulation corresponds to that which we used in our original (1976) monograph. It rectifies many of the problems arising from annualization or other compounding of series differences, and simplifies the calculation of summary statistics on the derived series. All exhibits relating to derived series reflect this calculation method.

Second, annual income returns are now calculated as the sum of the 12 monthly income payments, divided by the beginning-of-year price. In previous editions, the 12 monthly income returns were linked (compounded) to form an annual return. This change applies to annual income returns on common stocks and long- and intermediate-term government bonds.

The Data Series

The series presented here are total returns and, where applicable or available, capital appreciation returns, income returns, and yields for

(1) Common Stocks, represented by the Standard & Poor's 500 Stock Composite Index (S&P 500);

(2) Small Company Stocks, represented by the fifth capitalization quintile of stocks on the NYSE for 1926-81 and the performance of the Dimensional Fund Advisors (DFA) Small Company Fund thereafter;

(3) Long-Term Corporate Bonds, represented by the Salomon Brothers long-term, high-grade corporate bond total return index;

(4) Long-Term Government Bonds, measured using a one-bond portfolio with a maturity near 20 years;

(5) Intermediate-Term Government Bonds, measured using a one-bond portfolio with a maturity near five years;

(6) U.S. Treasury Bills, measured by rolling over each month a one-bill portfolio containing, at the beginning of each month, the bill having the shortest maturity not less than one month; and

(7) Consumer Price Index for All Urban Consumers (CPI-U), not seasonally adjusted.

In addition, the 10 deciles of the NYSE sorted by market capitalization are studied, making a total of 17 asset classes for which returns are presented.

2.   The Long-Run Perspective

Motivation

This study examines U.S. capital market returns for the 62-year period 1926-87. Using such a long period enables us to assess the basic relations among asset classes, between risk and return, and between nominal and real (inflation-adjusted) returns. This period, we hope, is long enough to include most of the major types of events that investors may expect to experience. Such events include war and peace, growth and decline, inflation and deflation, and less dramatic events that likewise affect asset returns.

In finance, we study the past to make inferences about the future. Although the actual events that occurred from 1926 to 1987 will not be repeated, the event-types of that period will probably recur. Some say that the past tells us little because one period or another is "unusual"—for example, the depression of 1929-32 or World War II. This logic is suspect: all periods are unusual. For example, two of the most "unusual" events of the century took place in the last decade. One was the inflation of the 1970s and early 1980s; the other was the stock market crash of October 1987. If historical event-types (not specific events) tend to repeat themselves, a study of long-run capital market returns may reveal a great deal about the future. (See Chapter 10.)

Historical Returns on Stocks, Bonds, Bills, and Inflation

Exhibit 1 shows graphically the growth of a dollar invested in common stocks, small-company stocks, long-term government bonds, Treasury bills, and inflation over the period from the end of 1925 to the end of 1987. The crash of 1987 appears as a downward "blip" in the two stock series. All results assume reinvestment of dividends on stocks or coupons on bonds and ignore taxes. We ignore transaction costs except in the small-stock index starting in 1982.

The cumulative index values each start at $1.00 at year-end 1925. The vertical scale is logarithmic, so that equal distances represent equal percentage changes anywhere along the axis. The graphs vividly show that common stocks and small-company stocks were the big winners over the entire 62-year period. If $1.00 had been invested in common stocks at year-end 1925 and all dividends were reinvested, the dollar investment would have grown to $347.96 by year-end 1987. If $1.00 were invested in small-company stocks over the same period, the dollar investment would have grown to $1,202.97.

This phenomenal growth was not without substantial risk. In contrast, long-term government bonds (with a constant 20-year maturity) exhibited much less risk, but grew to only $13.35.

The virtually riskless strategy over the past 62 years (for those with short-term time horizons) has been to buy U.S. Treasury bills. Treasury bills have tracked inflation with the result that their real (inflation-adjusted) return is near zero for the entire 1926-87 period.

EXHIBIT 1
WEALTH INDEXES OF INVESTMENTS IN
U.S. CAPITAL MARKETS
(1926-1987)
(YEAR-END 1925 = 1.00)

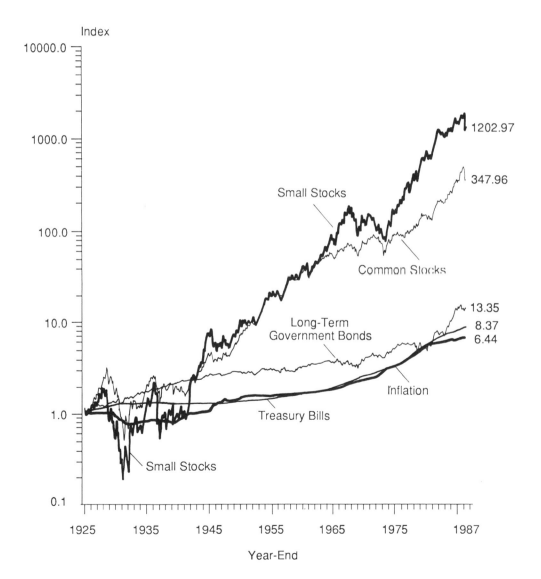

Common Stocks

As noted above, an index of common stock total returns, initialized on December 31, 1925 at $1.00, closed 1987 at $347.96. This was a yearly all-time high level, although far below the August 1987 monthly peak, when the S&P 500 total-return index closed at a level of $459.86.

The inflation-adjusted S&P 500 total-return index also reached its all-time monthly high level of $72.06 in August 1987. This index closed the year much lower but still at a yearly all-time high level of $54.05.

Small-Company Stocks

Over the long run, small-company stocks have far higher returns than the S&P 500. The small-stock total-return index closed 1987 at $1,202.97. This represents a compound annual growth rate of 12.1 percent, the highest of any of the asset classes studied. Rolf W. Banz was the first to document the superior performance of small stocks (Banz 1981).

The small-stock performance in excess of the performance of large-company stocks exhibits long waves of high and low returns. In the late 1920s and early 1930s, small-company stocks fared far worse than large-company stocks. From 1932 to 1945, small stocks boomed; then, from 1946 to 1957, they lagged large stocks again. Starting in 1958, small stocks beat larger issues fairly consistently, with the biggest gains in small stocks occurring after 1974. From mid-1983 to late 1987, small stocks once again lagged their larger counterparts.

Long-Term Government Bonds

The long-term government bond total-return index, constructed with an approximately 20-year maturity, closed 1987 at a value of $13.35. This compares with the all-time high of $14.23 recorded at the end of February 1987. Long-term government bonds have had positive historical returns entirely because of income; the long-term government bond capital appreciation index fell to $0.66 at year-end 1987, about 50 percent below its all-time high.

Intermediate-Term Government Bonds

Over the 1926-87 period, intermediate-term government bonds outperformed long-term government bonds. A dollar invested in intermediate-term bonds at year-end 1925, with coupons reinvested, grew to $17.89 by year-end 1987, compared to $13.35 for long-term government bonds. The compound annual total return for intermediate-term government bonds is 4.8 percent.

The superior performance of intermediate-term bonds was caused by the rise in bond yields over the period. Intermediate-term bond prices are less sensitive to yield changes than are long-term bonds; therefore, as yields rose, intermediate-term bonds suffered less than longer-term issues. Intermediate-term bonds also outperformed Treasury bills because the intermediate issues had higher yields without offsetting price declines.

U.S. Treasury Bills

A dollar invested in U.S. Treasury bills at the end of 1925 grew to $8.37 by year-end 1987, a compound annual growth rate of 3.5 percent. Treasury bills tend to track inflation, so that the average inflation-adjusted return on Treasury bills—the real riskless rate of return—was near zero (0.5 percent). Treasury bill returns followed distinct patterns throughout this period.

Patterns in Treasury Bill Returns

During periods of deflation (for example, the late 1920s and early 1930s) Treasury bill returns were near zero but not negative, because no one intentionally buys securities with negative nominal yields. (Cash, which has a zero nominal yield, is always preferable to a security with a negative nominal yield. Investors do, however, intentionally buy securities with negative real yields when such securities offer the best yield available. This may occur in times of high inflation.) Beginning in the early 1940s, the yields (returns) on Treasury bills were pegged by the government at low rates while inflation was high.

Treasury bills tracked inflation after March 1951, when the U.S. Treasury-Federal Reserve Accord allowed Treasury bill yields to float freely. The tracking pattern weakened starting about 1973. Real riskless returns were unusually negative in the 1970s and unusually positive in the 1980s.

Inflation

The compound annual inflation rate over the 1926-87 period was 3.0 percent. The inflation index, initiated at $1.00 at year-end 1925, grew to $6.44 by year-end 1987. All of this increase took place in the postwar period. The years 1926-33 were marked by deflation, but consumer prices rose to their 1926 levels by the middle of 1945. After a brief postwar spurt of inflation, prices rose slowly over most of the 1950s and 1960s. Then, in the 1970s, inflation reached a pace unprecedented in peacetime, peaking at 13.3 percent in 1979. (On a month-by-month basis, the peak inflation rate was a breathtaking 24.0 percent, stated in annualized terms, in August 1973.) The 1980s saw a reversion to more moderate, though still substantial, inflation rates averaging about 4 percent per year.

Summary Statistics of Total Returns

Exhibit 2 presents summary statistics for the annual total returns on each asset class over the entire 62-year period. The data summarized in these exhibits are described in detail in Chapters 3 and 6.

Note that in Exhibit 2, the arithmetic mean returns are always higher than the geometric mean returns. The difference between these two means relates directly to the variability of the series. For Treasury bills, the two means appear to be the same because of rounding, but the arithmetic mean is, in fact, higher than the geometric mean (see Chapter 6).

The histograms to the right in Exhibit 2 show the frequency distribution of returns on each asset class. The height of the common-stock histogram in the range between +10 and +20 percent, for example, shows the number of years that common stocks had a return in that range.

Riskier assets, such as common stocks and small-company stocks, have wide histograms, reflecting the broad distribution of returns from very poor to very good. Less risky assets, such as bonds, have narrow histograms, indicating the tightness of the distribution around the mean of the series. The histogram for Treasury bills is "one-sided," lying almost entirely to the right of the vertical line representing a zero return; that is, Treasury bills experienced almost no negative returns on a yearly basis. The inflation histogram shows both positive and negative annual rates. Although deflationary months and even quarters have occurred recently, the last negative annual inflation rate was in 1954.

EXHIBIT 2
BASIC SERIES: SUMMARY STATISTICS
OF ANNUAL RETURNS
(1926-1987)

Series	Geometric Mean	Arithmetic Mean	Standard Deviation	Distribution
Common Stocks	9.9%	12.0%	21.1%	
Small Company Stocks	12.1	17.7	35.9	
Long-Term Corporate Bonds	4.9	5.2	8.5	
Long-Term Government Bonds	4.3	4.6	8.5	
Intermediate-Term Government Bonds	4.8	4.9	5.5	
U.S. Treasury Bills	3.5	3.5	3.4	
Inflation Rates	3.0	3.2	4.8	

-90%   0%   90%

3. Description of the Basic Series

This chapter describes the construction of the returns on the seven basic asset classes and portrays the market results graphically. We form annual returns for each asset by compounding monthly returns. In all cases, with the exception of small-company stocks starting in 1982, we assume no taxes or transactions costs. As explained below, returns for small-company stocks starting in 1982 reflect the performance of an actual, tax-free investment and therefore reflect transaction costs but not taxes.

Common Stocks

Total Returns

The common-stock total-return index is based on the S&P's Composite Index. This index is a readily available, carefully constructed, market-value-weighted benchmark of common stock performance. Market-value-weighted means that the weight of each stock in the index, for a given month, is proportionate to its price times the number of shares outstanding (i.e., market capitalization) at the beginning of that month. Currently, the S&P Composite includes 500 of the largest stocks (in terms of stock market value) in the United States; prior to March 1957, it consisted of 90 of the largest stocks.

EXHIBIT 3
COMMON STOCKS: RETURNS, RETURN INDEXES, AND YIELDS
(1926-1987)

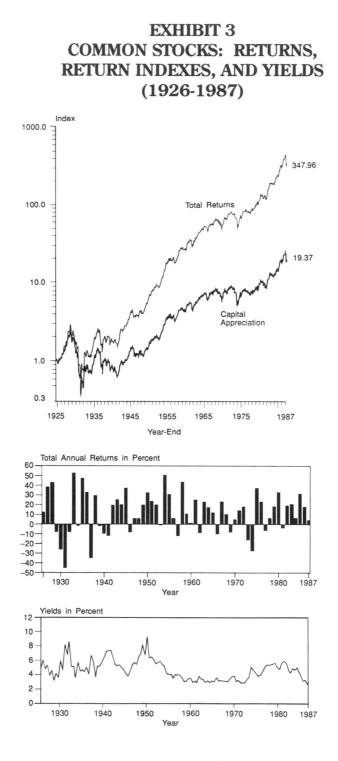

The total return for a given month is equal to the capital appreciation plus income for that month.

Capital Appreciation

The capital appreciation component of the common stock total return is the change in the S&P 500-stock index (or 90-stock index) as reported in the *Wall Street Journal* from 1977 to 1987, and in Standard & Poor's *Trade and Securities Statistics* from 1926 to 1976.

Income

For 1977-87, income equals realized dividends and is provided by the American National Bank and Trust Company of Chicago. American National Bank and Trust obtains monthly income numbers from Wilshire Associates, Santa Monica, California, and makes occasional minor modifications. These modifications typically are made when a company pays a dividend in the form of another company's stock; such payments are rare. American National Bank and Trust treats such payments differently from Wilshire.

We assume that dividends accumulate over the month, and we then invest them on the last trading day of the month in the S&P index at the day's closing level. For 1926 through 1976, quarterly dividends are extracted from rolling yearly dividends reported quarterly in Standard & Poor's *Trade and Securities Statistics,* and are then allocated to months within each quarter using proportions taken from the 1974 actual distribution of monthly dividends within quarters.

Results

A dollar invested in common stocks at year-end 1925, with dividends reinvested, grew to $347.96 by year-end 1987; this represents a compound annual growth rate of 9.9 percent (see Exhibit 3). Capital appreciation alone caused a dollar to grow to $19.37 over the 62-year period, representing a compound annual growth rate of 4.9 percent. Total annual returns ranged from a high of 54.0 percent in 1933 to a low of -43.3 percent in 1931. The average annual dividend yield was 4.8 percent.

Small Capitalization Stocks

NYSE Fifth Quintile Returns (1926-1981)

To represent the equities of smaller companies from 1926 to 1980, we use the historical series developed by Rolf W. Banz. This is composed of stocks in the ninth and tenth (smallest) deciles (i.e., the fifth quintile) of the NYSE where the stocks on the NYSE are ranked by capitalization (price times number of shares outstanding) and each decile contains an equal number of stocks at the beginning of each formation period.

The ninth and tenth decile portfolio was first ranked and formed as of December 31, 1925. This portfolio was "held" for five years, with value-weighted portfolio returns computed monthly. Every five years through December 31, 1980, the portfolio was rebalanced (i.e., all of the stocks on the NYSE were re-ranked, and a portfolio of those falling in the ninth and tenth deciles was again formed). Banz's method avoids survivorship bias by including the return after the delisting from the NYSE. (Survivorship bias is the optional bias caused by studying only stocks which have survived bankruptcy, takeover, and so forth.)

For 1981, Dimensional Fund Advisors, Inc. updated the returns using Banz's methods. The data for 1981 are significant to only three decimal places (in decimal form) or one decimal place when returns are expressed in percent, so that the trailing zeroes are superfluous for that year.

DFA Small Company Fund (1982-1987)

Beginning in 1982, the small-company stock return series is the total return, net of all expenses, of the Dimensional Fund Advisors (DFA) Small Company Fund. The fund is, in effect, a live market-value-weighted index of the ninth and tenth deciles of the NYSE, plus stocks listed on the American Stock Exchange (AMEX) and over-the-counter (OTC) with the same or less capitalization as the upper bound of the NYSE ninth decile. Through 1987, the Fund did not purchase stocks if they were smaller than $10 million in market capitalization (although it holds stocks that fall below that level). The portfolio does not buy bankrupt companies but will retain companies that become bankrupt. At least twice yearly, DFA recomputes size boundaries.

The portfolio retains stocks until they rise into the seventh NYSE decile or higher. Beginning in 1982, the portfolio's performance represents after-transaction-cost returns, as contrasted with before-transaction-cost returns for the other asset classes and for pre-1982 small company stocks.

As of year-end 1987, the DFA Small Company Fund contained approximately 1,895 stocks, with an average capitalization of about $38 million. The upper bound of the ninth decile at that time was about $74 million.

Results

A dollar invested in small-company stocks at year-end 1925 grew to $1,202.97 by year-end 1987 (see Exhibit 4). This represents a compound annual return of 12.1 percent over the past 62 years. Total annual returns ranged from a high of 142.9 percent in 1933 to a low of -58.0 percent in 1937.

EXHIBIT 4
SMALL-COMPANY STOCKS:
RETURNS AND RETURN INDEXES
(1926-1987)

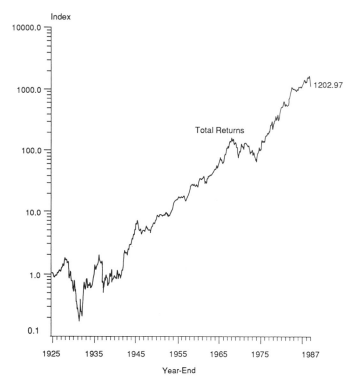

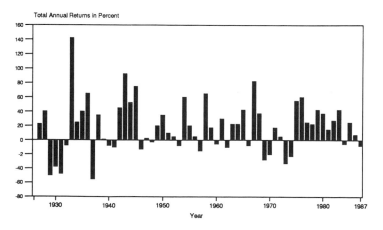

Long-Term Corporate Bonds

Because most large corporate bond transactions take place over the counter, the natural source of data is a major dealer. Salomon Brothers has constructed the Long-Term High-Grade Corporate Bond Index. This monthly index is used from its inception in 1969 through 1987. The index includes nearly all Aaa- and Aa-rated bonds. If a bond is downgraded during a particular month, its return for the month is included in the index and the bond is then removed from future portfolios.

In 1985, Salomon Brothers introduced a Broad Index, which some people consider to be a replacement for the Long-Term High-Grade Corporate Bond Index. We continue to use the Salomon Brothers Long-Term High-Grade Corporate Bond Index.

For the period 1946-68, the Salomon Brothers' Index, using Salomon Brothers' monthly yield data, was backdated, with a methodology similar to that used by Salomon Brothers for 1969-87. For the period 1925-45, S&P's monthly High-Grade Corporate Composite yield data were used, assuming a 4 percent coupon and a 20-year maturity.

Monthly capital appreciation returns for 1926-68 were calculated from yields assuming (at the beginning of each monthly holding period) a 20-year maturity, a bond price equal to par, and a coupon equal to the yield. The conventional present-value formula for bond price for the beginning and end-of-month prices was used (Ross and Westerfield 1988). The monthly income return is assumed to be one-twelfth of the coupon. Total returns are equal to capital appreciation plus income.

EXHIBIT 5
LONG-TERM CORPORATE BONDS:
RETURNS AND RETURN INDEXES
(1926-1987)

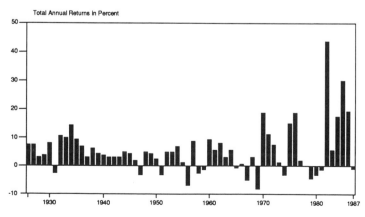

Results

A dollar invested in long-term high-grade corporate bonds at the end of 1925 grew to $19.78 by year-end 1987. The compound annual return is 4.9 percent (see Exhibit 5).

Long-Term Government Bonds

Total Returns

The total returns on long-term U.S. government bonds over 1926-76 come from the Government Bond file at the Center for Research in Security Prices (CRSP), Graduate School of Business, University of Chicago. Each year, we "buy" a one-bond portfolio containing a bond with a term of approximately 20 years and a reasonably current coupon, and which avoids potential tax benefits, impaired negotiability, or special redemption or call privileges. Where callable bonds are necessary, we assume that the term of the bond is a simple average of the maturity and first call dates minus the current date. The bond is "held" for the calendar year and monthly returns are recorded.

From 1977 to 1987 we used the same method with data from the *Wall Street Journal*. For example, the bond used in 1987 is the 10 percent issue of May 2005/2010 (that is, first callable in 2005 and maturing in 2010).

Total returns for 1977 through 1987 are calculated as the change in the flat price. The flat price is the average of the bond's bid and ask prices, plus the accrued coupon. (For the purpose of calculating the return in months when a coupon payment is made, the change in flat price includes the coupon.) The accrued coupon is equal to zero on the day a coupon is paid, and increases over time until the next coupon payment, according to this formula:

$$A = fC \qquad (1)$$

where

A   =   accrued coupon;

C   =   semiannual coupon rate; and

f   =   <u>number of days since last coupon payment</u>
number of days from last coupon
payment to next coupon payment

Prior to January 1985, the number of half-months instead of the number of days was used to calculate f in equation (1). This gives acceptable results, because coupons typically are paid on the 15th of the month; to obtain greater accuracy, the calculation method was converted to days between dates.

Yield

The yield on the long-term government bond series is defined as the internal rate of return that equates the bond's price (the average of bid and ask, without adding the accrued coupon) with the stream of cash flows (coupons and principal) promised to the bondholder. For years when a noncallable bond was used, the yield is calculated as if the bond were held to maturity; that is, the yield to maturity is reported. When a callable bond was used, the reported yield is the yield to first call if the bond was selling above par; otherwise the reported yield is the yield to maturity. The yield is calculated as a semiannually compounded rate, then multiplied by two to convert to an annual rate, and expressed as a percentage.

Income, or Yield, Return

The income return (or yield return) for a given month is assumed to be equal to the previous month-end yield after conversion to a monthly rate. For the period 1926-76, the income return for a given month is calculated as the total return minus the capital appreciation return (see below). For 1977-87, the income return (I_t) in month t is calculated as:

$$I_t = 1 + \left(\frac{y_{t-1}}{2}\right)^{\frac{1}{6}} - 1 \qquad (2)$$

where

y_{t-1} = bond's previous month-end yield to maturity or yield to first call, as explained above, stated as an annual rate in decimal (not percent) form.

The term "income return" is used here to mean the yield return. In other contexts, the same term is sometimes used to mean the current yield (coupon divided by price).

Return in Excess of Yield, or Capital Appreciation

For 1926-76, we obtain the return in excess of yield (labeled capital appreciation) from the CRSP Government Bond File. For the period 1977-87, we calculate the return in excess of yield as the total return minus the income return for each month.

The term capital appreciation is sometimes used to mean the price change on a bond, as it does for a stock. Here, a bond's capital appreciation is defined as the total return minus the income (yield) return—that is, the return in excess of yield. This definition omits capital appreciation or depreciation that comes from the movement of a bond's price toward par (in the absence of interest-rate change) as it matures. Stated another way, our measure of a bond's capital appreciation captures changes in bond price caused by changes in the interest rate.

Results

A dollar invested in long-term government bonds at year-end 1925, with coupons reinvested, grew to $13.52 by

EXHIBIT 6
LONG-TERM GOVERNMENT BONDS:
RETURNS, RETURN INDEXES, AND YIELDS
(1926-1987)

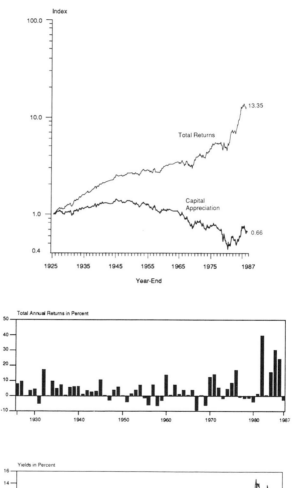

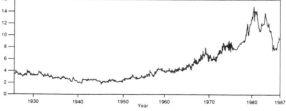

year-end 1987; this represents a compound annual return of 4.3 percent (see Exhibit 6). Returns from the capital appreciation component, however, caused a dollar to decrease to $0.66, representing a compound annual return of almost -0.7 percent. Total annual returns ranged from a high of 40.4 percent in 1982 to a low of -9.2 percent in 1967. The average yield to maturity (or yield to first call, where applicable) was 4.9 percent.

Intermediate-Term Government Bonds

Total Return

Total returns of the intermediate-term government bonds over the 1934-86 period come from the CRSP Government Bond File. We calculated returns for 1987 from *Wall Street Journal* prices, using the coupon accrual method described above for long-term government bonds.

As with long-term government bonds, we form one-bond portfolios. Each year, we choose the shortest noncallable bond with a maturity not less than five years. This bond is "held" for the calendar year, and monthly returns are recorded. (Bonds with impaired negotiability or special redemption privileges are passed over, as are partially or fully tax-exempt bonds starting in 1943.) If, for a given year, a noncallable bond with a maturity between five and eight years does not exist, we choose a callable bond, giving preference to bonds selling below par. Where callable bonds are necessary, we assume that the term of the bond is the term to maturity. The series consists entirely of noncallable bonds starting in 1955.

Over the period 1934-42, almost all bonds with maturities near five years were partially or fully tax exempt. Such bonds are used in this period, with the same selection rules as for the later period described above. Personal tax rates were generally low in that period, so that yields on tax-exempt bonds were similar to yields on taxables.

Over 1926-33 period, there were few or no bonds suitable for construction of a series with a five-year maturity. For this period, we use estimates of five-year bond yields (Coleman et al. 1988). The estimates reflect what a "pure play" five-year Treasury bond, selling at par and with no special redemption or call provisions, would have yielded had one existed. Estimates are for partially tax-exempt bonds for 1926-32 and for fully tax-exempt bonds for 1933.

We convert monthly yields to monthly total returns by calculating the beginning and end-of-month "flat" prices for the hypothetical bonds. We "buy" the bond at the beginning of the month at par (i.e., the coupon equals the previous month-end yield), assuming a maturity of five years. We then "sell" it at the end of the month, with the flat price calculated by discounting the coupons and principal at the end-of-month yield, assuming a maturity of 4 years and 11 months. The flat price is the price of the bond including coupon accruals, so that the change in flat price represents total return. We assume that monthly income returns are equal to the previous end-of-month yield, stated in monthly terms. We form monthly capital appreciation returns as total returns minus income.

Yield

The yield reported for intermediate-term government bonds for the 1934-86 period was obtained from the CRSP Government Bond File. It is the semiannually compounded yield to maturity (or yield to first call where the bond is callable and selling above par), multiplied by two to form an annual rate, and stated in percent. Yields for 1926 through 1933 are estimates from Coleman et al. (1988). The yields for 1987 are calculated from *Wall Street Journal* prices. The yield is the internal rate of return that equates the bond's price with the stream of cash flows (coupons and principal) promised to the bondholder.

Income and Capital Appreciation

For the period 1934-86, capital appreciation (return in excess of yield) is taken directly from the CRSP Government Bond File. The income return is calculated as the total return minus the capital appreciation return. For the period 1926-33, the income and capital appreciation components of total return are generated from yield estimates as described above under "Total Return" for that period. Income and capital appreciation returns for 1987 are calculated from *Wall Street Journal* prices.

Results

A dollar invested in intermediate-term government bonds at year-end 1925, with coupons reinvested, grew to $17.89 by year-end 1987. This represents a compound annual return of 4.8 percent (see Exhibit 7).

Returns from the capital appreciation component caused a dollar to increase only to $1.12 over the 62-year period, representing a compound annual return of approximately 0.2 percent. This result differs from what might be expected: because yields rose on average over the period, capital appreciation on a hypothetical intermediate-term government bond portfolio with a constant five-year maturity would be negative. This positive average return is explained at the end of this chapter.

Total annual returns ranged from a high of 29.1 percent in 1982 to a low of -2.3 percent in 1931. The average yield to maturity (or yield to first call, where applicable) was 4.5 percent.

EXHIBIT 7
INTERMEDIATE-TERM GOVERNMENT BONDS:
RETURNS, RETURN INDEXES, AND YIELDS
(1926-1987)

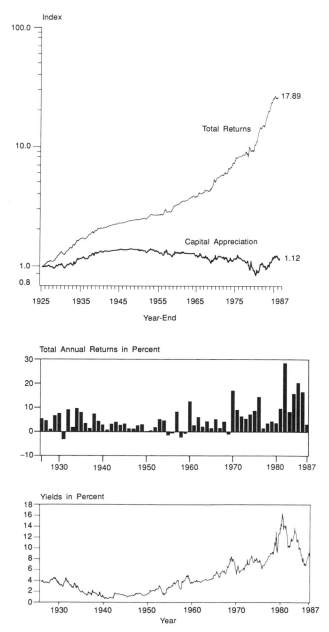

United States Treasury Bills

For the U.S. Treasury bill index, data from the CRSP U.S. Government Bond File were used through 1976; the *Wall Street Journal* is the source thereafter. Each month a one-bill portfolio containing the shortest-term bill having not less than one month to maturity is constructed. (The term to maturity of the bill when originally issued is not relevant.) To measure holding period returns for the one-bill portfolio, the bill is priced as of the last trading day of the previous month-end and as of the last trading day of the current month.

The price of the bill (P_t) at each point in time (t) is given as:

$$P_t = (1 - rd/360) \qquad (3)$$

where

r   =   yield on the bill at that time (the average of bid and ask quotes, converted to decimal form), and

d   =   number of days to maturity.

The total return on the bill is then the month-end price divided by the previous month-end price, minus one.

Results

A dollar invested in U.S. Treasury bills at year-end 1925 grew to $8.37 by year-end 1987; this represents a compound annual return of 3.5 percent (see Exhibit 8). Total annual returns ranged from a high of 14.7 percent in 1981 to a low of 0.0 percent in 1938. The average yield over the period was 3.5 percent.

Inflation

The Consumer Price Index for All Urban Consumers, not seasonally adjusted (CPI-U NSA) is used to measure

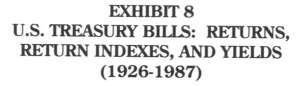

EXHIBIT 8
U.S. TREASURY BILLS: RETURNS,
RETURN INDEXES, AND YIELDS
(1926-1987)

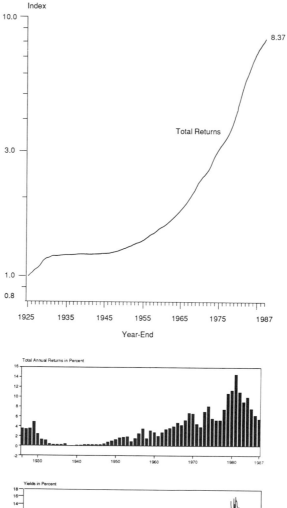

inflation, which is the rate of change of consumer goods prices. Unfortunately, the inflation rate as measured by the CPI is not measured over the same period as the other asset returns. All of the security returns are measured from one month-end to the next month-end. CPI commodity prices are collected during the month. Thus, measured inflation rates lag the other series by about one-half month. Prior to January 1978, we used the CPI (as contrasted with CPI-U), not seasonally adjusted. Both inflation measures are constructed by the U.S. Department of Labor, Bureau of Labor Statistics, Washington, D.C.

Results

A basket of consumer goods costing a $1.00 at year-end 1925 would have cost $6.44 by year-end 1987 (see Exhibit 9). Of course, the exact contents of the basket would have changed over time. This increase represents a compound annual inflation rate of 3.0 percent over the past 62 years. Inflation rates ranged from a high of 18.2 percent in 1946 to a low of -10.3 percent in 1932.

Why Was Capital Appreciation on Intermediate-Term Government Bonds Positive?

The capital appreciation component of intermediate-term government bond returns causes $1.00 invested at year-end 1925 to grow to $1.12, a compound annual rate of 0.2 percent. This is surprising, as yields rose on average over the period.

An investor in a hypothetical five-year constant-maturity portfolio, with continuous rebalancing, suffers an 18.95 percent capital loss (excluding coupon income) over the period 1926-87, or -0.34 percent per year. An investor who rebalances yearly, choosing bonds according to the method set forth above, fares better, earning the 0.2 percent per year capital gain recorded here.

EXHIBIT 9
INFLATION: RATES OF CHANGE
AND CUMULATIVE INDEXES

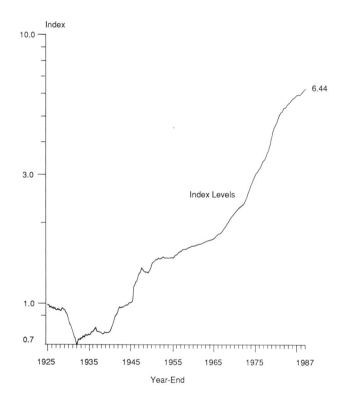

The reason for this performance relates to the way the intermediate-term bond series was constructed. For the period 1926-33, we use a constant maturity of five years, rebalancing monthly. For the period 1934-87, we use a one-bond portfolio, choosing, at the beginning of each year, the shortest bond not less than five years to maturity. We use callable and fully or partially tax-exempt bonds only when necessary to obtain a bond for that year. The maturities of the bonds selected range from five to eight years.

There are several possible reasons for the positive capital appreciation return; any or all of them could apply. First, intermediate-term government bonds were scarce in the 1930s and 1940s. As a consequence, we sometimes held bonds with maturities substantially longer than five years. Second, the 1930s and the first half of the 1940s were very bullish for the bond market. Longer bonds, used to construct this series, not only had higher yields but also had substantially higher capital gain returns than bonds with exactly five years to maturity would have had if any had existed. This upward bias is particularly noticeable in 1934, 1937, and 1938.

The conversion of the Treasury bond market from tax-exempt to taxable status produced a one-time upward jump in stated yields, but not a capital loss on any given bond. Thus, part of the increase in stated yield from 1926 to 1987 does not cause a capital loss on the intermediate-term bond index. Further, the use of callable bonds in the early part of the period may command a return premium for taking this extra risk.

4. Description of the Derived Series

Historical data suggest that investors are rewarded for taking risks and that returns are related to inflation rates. We can discern the risk-return and the real-nominal relations in the historical data by looking at the component parts of the basic asset series described in the previous chapter.

Geometric Subtraction Used to Calculate Derived Series

As noted in Chapter 1, the method of calculating series differences, or derived series (risk premiums and inflation-adjusted series) differs from the method used in some previous editions of this book. In this edition, derived series were calculated by division rather than by subtraction. In the division method that we use, returns on basic series A and B and derived series C are related as follows:

$$(1 + C) = (1 + A) / (1 + B), \qquad (4)$$

where

series A, B, and C are in decimal form (i.e., 5 percent is indicated by 0.05).

Thus, series C is given by:

$$C = (1 + A) / (1 + B) - 1. \tag{5}$$

This method is referred to as *geometric subtraction,* to distinguish it from arithmetic subtraction.

For example, suppose return A equals 15 percent, or 0.15; and return B is 5 percent, or 0.05. Then, C equals (1.15/1.05) - 1 = 0.0952, or 9.52 percent. This result is different from the simple arithmetic difference of 10 percent.

Definitions of the Derived (Component) Series

From the seven basic asset classes—common stocks, small stocks, long-term corporate bonds, long-term government bonds, intermediate-term government bonds, U.S. Treasury bills (T-bills), and consumer goods (inflation)—10 additional series are derived representing the component or elemental parts of the asset returns. These 10 derived series are

Series Title	Derivation
Risk Premium Series	
(1) Bond horizon premiums	(LT Govt bonds) - (T-Bills)
(2) Bond default premiums	(LT Corp bonds) - (LT Govt bonds)
(3) Equity risk premiums	(Common stocks) - (T-bills)
(4) Small stock premiums	(Small stocks) - (Common stocks)
Inflation-Adjusted Series	
(5) Inflation-adjusted T-bill returns (Real riskless rate of return)	(Treasury bills) - (Inflation)
(6) Inflation-adjusted common stock returns (Series 3 + 5)	(Common stocks) - (Inflation)

(7)	Inflation-adjusted small stock returns (Series 3 + 4 + 5)	(Small stocks) - (Inflation)
(8)	Inflation-adjusted corporate bond returns (Series 1 + 2 + 5)	(LT Corp bonds) - (Inflation)
(9)	Inflation-adjusted long-term government bond returns (Series 1 + 5)	(LT Govt bonds) - (Inflation)
(10)	Inflation-adjusted intermediate-term government bond returns	(IT Govt bonds) - (Inflation)

As noted, the 10 derived series are produced using geometric, not arithmetic, subtraction. The minus (–) sign is used for convenience in the above table, and in various places throughout this book, to express geometric subtraction. Also, the plus (+) sign at various points in the left column of the above table refers to geometric, not arithmetic, addition. The geometric sum of A and B, signified by C, is formed as follows:

$$C = [(1 + A) \times (1 + B)] - 1 \qquad (6)$$

In the more lengthy description of each series, given below, the full mathematical expression is shown.

Two Categories of Derived Series

The 10 derived series may be categorized as risk premiums, or payoffs for taking various types of risk, and inflation-adjusted asset returns. The risk premium series are the bond horizon and default premiums, the equity risk premium, and the small stock premium. The inflation-adjusted asset return series are the six series constructed by geometrically subtracting inflation from an asset total return series.

The construction and interpretation of the derived series is discussed in the following paragraphs.

EXHIBIT 10
U.S. TREASURY BILLS: REAL AND
NOMINAL RETURN INDEXES
(1925-1987)

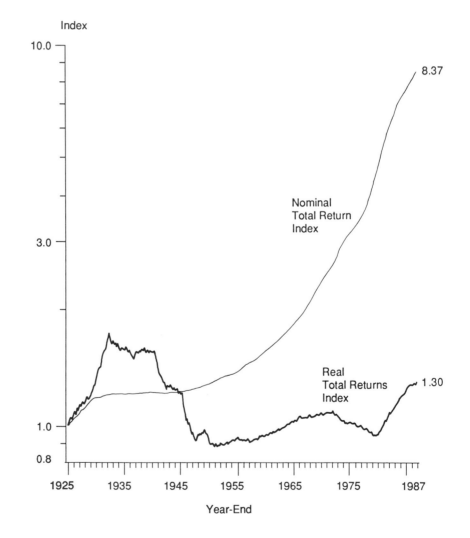

Inflation-Adjusted U.S. Treasury Bill Returns (Real Riskless Rates of Return)

In contemporary finance, the real riskless rate of interest is commonly estimated as the difference in returns between consumer goods (inflation) and U.S. Treasury bills, which are a short-term, virtually risk-free asset. Thus, we call the real return on risk-free bills the real riskless rate of interest, R_r. This is represented by:

$$R_r = R_{fr} = [(1 + R_f)/(1 + R_I)] - 1 \qquad (7)$$

where

R_f =   return on 30-day Treasury bills,

R_I =   rate of inflation, and

R_{fr} = R_f adjusted for inflation; the r in the expression signifies "real".

Results

Treasury bills returned 3.5 percent compounded annually over the 1926-87 period in nominal terms, but only 0.4 percent in real (inflation-adjusted) terms. (See Exhibit 10.) Thus, an investor in Treasury bills would have barely kept ahead of inflation over the 62-year period.

Bond Horizon Premiums

Long-term government bonds behave differently from short-term bills in that their prices (and hence returns) are more sensitive to interest-rate fluctuations. There is reason to believe that investors demand a premium for holding long-term bonds instead of short-term U.S. Treasury bills. This premium is called the bond horizon premium, R_h.

The bond horizon premium is given by:

$$R_h = [(1 + R_g)/(1 + R_f)] - 1 \qquad (8)$$

where

R_g =   return on long-term government bonds, and

R_f =   return on 30-day Treasury bills.

The bond horizon premium, R_h, has sometimes been referred to by the misnomer "liquidity premium." In fact, Treasury securities are almost always highly liquid (marketable), regardless of their term to maturity. The rationale behind the term "horizon premium" is discussed below.

We use long-term rather than intermediate-term government bonds to derive the bond horizon premium because they contain a "full unit" of price fluctuation risk. Intermediate-term government bonds may be expected to display a partial horizon premium, that is, one that is smaller than that observed as the difference between long-term bonds and short-term bills.

Does Maturity or Duration Determine the Bond Premium?

In the previous edition of this work, R_h was referred to as the "maturity premium," based on the observation that bonds with longer maturities commanded a return premium over shorter-maturity bonds. Term to maturity, however, is not the bond characteristic that determines this return premium. More likely, the duration of a given bond determines the amount of return premium arising from differences in bond life.

Duration is the present-value-weighted average time to receipt of cash flows (coupons and principal) from holding a bond, and may be calculated from the bond's yield, coupon rate, and term to maturity.

Why a "Horizon" Premium?

Investors often strive to match the duration of their bond holdings (cash inflows) with the estimated duration of their obligations, or cash outflows. As a consequence, investors with short time horizons regard long-duration bonds as risky (because of price fluctuation risk), and short-term bills as riskless. Conversely, investors with long time horizons regard short-term bills as risky (because of the uncertainty of the yield at which bills may be reinvested), and long-duration bonds as riskless or less risky.

Empirically, long-duration bonds have higher yields than short-term bills. That is, the yield curve slopes upward on average over time. Likewise, long-duration bond returns historically exceed bill returns. These observations indicate that more investors are averse to the price fluctuation risk of long bonds than to the reinvestment risk of bills. In other words, it appears that there are more investors with short time horizons than with long ones.

The conclusion, then, is that bond-duration risk is in the eye of the beholder, or bondholder. Therefore, rather than labeling R_h as a premium for long-bond risk (which implies a judgment that short-horizon investors are "correct" in their risk perceptions), it is better to go directly to the source of the return differential—the differing time horizons of investors—and label R_h a "horizon premium."

Bond Default Premiums

Investors in corporate bonds face the possibility of default. Thus, in addition to inflation, the real riskless rate, and the horizon premium, holders of corporate bonds expect to receive a premium which reflects this default possibility. This default premium is measured as the difference in returns between corporate bonds and government bonds of equal maturity. The monthly default premiums, R_d, are estimated according to:

$$R_d = [(1 + R_c)/(1 + R_g)] - 1 \qquad (9)$$

where

R_c =   return on long-term corporate bonds, and

R_g =   return on long-term government bonds.

Components of the Default Premium

Bonds susceptible to default have higher expected returns than default-free bonds. Default on a bond may range from a small loss—such as a late interest payment—to loss of principal. Thus, part of the *ex ante* default premium on a portfolio of bonds is lost if some bonds default.

The remainder of the default premium—in excess of the portion lost by defaults—is a realized risk premium, which takes into account actual loss experience. The true expected return on a corporate bond, or portfolio of corporate bonds, then, is less than the bond's yield. The portfolio's yield may be thought of as an upper bound on the expected return. The expected return on a corporate bond is equal to the expected return on a government bond of like maturity, plus some estimate of the realized risk premium.

Callability Risk is Captured in the Default Premium

Because the long-term U.S. government bond series and the long-term corporate bond series have approximately equal maturities, the net rate of return between the two series is primarily related to differences in the probability of coupon or principal default. It should be noted, however, that the bond default premium as measured here also inadvertently captures any premium that investors may demand or receive for callability risk.

Callability risk is the risk that a bond will be redeemed (at or near par) by its issuer before maturity, at a time when market interest rates are lower than the bond's coupon rate. The possibility of redemption causes risk because such a redemption would prevent the bondholder whose issue has been redeemed from reinvesting the proceeds at the original (higher) interest rate.

Inflation-Adjusted Long-Term Government Bond Returns

The monthly inflation-adjusted long-term government bond returns, R_{gr}, are estimated as:

$$R_{gr} = [(1 + R_g)/(1 + R_I)] - 1 \qquad (10)$$

where

R_g =   return on long-term government bonds, and

R_I =   rate of inflation.

The additional subscript r on the symbol, R_{gr}, reflects the fact that the series is real (inflation-adjusted).

Because government bond returns are composed of inflation, the real riskless rate (R_r), and the horizon premium (R_h), the inflation-adjusted government bond returns may also be expressed as:

$$R_{gr} = [(1 + R_r) \times (1 + R_h)] - 1 \qquad (11)$$

Results

Long-term government bonds returned 4.3 percent compounded annually in nominal terms, and 1.2 percent in real (inflation-adjusted) terms (see Exhibit 11) over the past 62 years. Thus, over this period, government bonds have outpaced inflation despite generally falling bond prices.

EXHIBIT 11
LONG-TERM GOVERNMENT BONDS: REAL AND NOMINAL RETURN INDEXES (1925-1987)

Inflation-Adjusted Intermediate-Term Government Bond Returns

The monthly inflation-adjusted intermediate-term government bond returns, R_{nr}, are estimated as:

$$R_{nr} = [(1 + R_n)/(1 + R_I)] - 1 \qquad (12)$$

where

R_n =   return on intermediate-term government bonds, and

R_I =   rate of inflation.

The additional subscript r on the symbol, R_{nr}, reflects the fact that the series is real (inflation-adjusted). The symbol n is used here to represent intermediate-term government bonds.

Inflation-Adjusted Corporate Bond Returns

Monthly inflation-adjusted corporate bond returns, R_{cr}, are estimated as:

$$R_{cr} = [(1 + R_c)/(1 + R_I)] - 1 \qquad (13)$$

where

R_c =   return on long-term corporate bonds, and

R_I =   rate of inflation.

The additional subscript r on the symbol, R_{cr}, signifies real returns.

Long-term corporate bond returns contain all of the components of long-term government bond returns, R_{gr} (i.e., government bonds adjusted for inflation) plus the default premium (R_d); hence

$$R_{cr} = [(1 + R_{gr}) \times (1 + R_d)] - 1 \qquad (14)$$

47

Equivalently,

$$R_{cr} = (1 + R_r) \times (1 + R_h) \times (1 + R_d) - 1 \qquad (15)$$

where the variables are defined as above.

Equity Risk Premiums

Because common stocks are not strictly comparable with bonds, horizon and default premiums are omitted in analysis of the components of equity returns. (Common stocks have characteristics which are analogous to horizon and default risk, but they are not the same thing.) Hence, the difference between common stock returns and U.S. Treasury bill returns is taken as a whole and entitled the "equity risk premium."

Common stock returns, then, are considered in this analysis to be composed of inflation, the real riskless rate, and the equity risk premium.

Estimation of the monthly risk premiums, R_p, is given by

$$R_p = [(1 + R_m)/(1 + R_f)] - 1 \qquad (16)$$

where

R_m = return on common stock, and

R_f = return on 30-day Treasury bill.

Inflation-Adjusted Common Stock Returns

Monthly inflation-adjusted common stock returns, R_{mr}, are estimated as:

$$R_{mr} = [(1 + R_m)/(1 + R_I)] - 1 \qquad (17)$$

where

R_m = return on common stock, and

R_I = rate of inflation.

EXHIBIT 12
COMMON STOCKS: REAL AND NOMINAL RETURN INDEXES
(1925-1987)

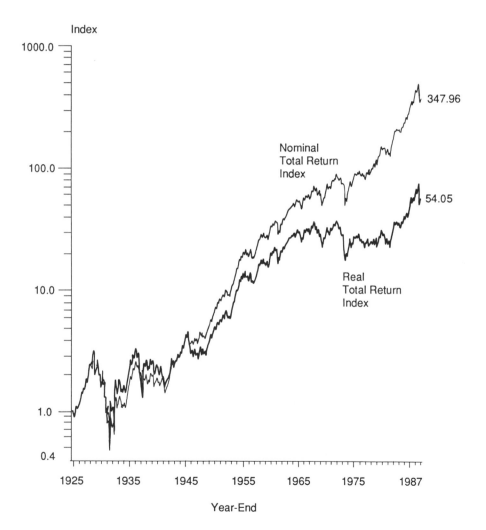

This may also be expressed as the sum of the real riskless rate (R_r) and the equity risk premium (R_p):

$$R_{mr} = [(1 + R_r) \times (1 + R_p)] - 1 \qquad (18)$$

Results

Common stock total returns were 9.9 percent compounded annually from 1926 to 1987 in nominal terms (see Exhibit 12). In real (inflation-adjusted) terms, stocks provided a 6.6 percent compound return, indicating that a common stock investor would have experienced a great increase in real wealth, or purchasing power, over the 62-year period.

Small-Stock Premiums

The small-stock premium, R_q, is defined as the excess of monthly small-stock returns (R_s) over monthly common stock (S&P) returns (R_m). (The letter q in R_q signifies the fifth "quintile.") Thus, R_q is given by

$$R_q = [(1 + R_s)/(1 + R_m)] - 1 \qquad (19)$$

Inflation-Adjusted Small-Stock Returns

Monthly inflation-adjusted small-stock returns, R_{sr}, are estimated as:

$$R_{sr} = [(1 + R_s)/(1 + R_I)] - 1 \qquad (20)$$

where

R_s = return on small-company stocks, and

R_I = rate of inflation.

This may also be expressed as the sum of the components of common stock real returns (R_{mr}) plus the small-stock premium (R_q), hence:

$$R_{sr} = [(1 + R_{mr}) \times (1 + R_q)] - 1 \qquad (21)$$

This is equivalent to

$$R_{sr} = [(1 + R_r) \times (1 + R_p) \times (1 + R_q)] - 1 \qquad (22)$$

where

R_r = real riskless rate,

R_p = equity risk premium, and

R_q = small-stock premium.

Component Returns: A Summary

As illustrated above, the returns on various types of securities may be broken into their component parts. Exhibit 13 presents a summary table of the basic and derived series component parts.

EXHIBIT 13
THE COMPONENT PARTS OF SECURITY RETURNS

Return Series	Components					
	Inflation (RI)	Real Riskless Returns (Rr)	Equity Risk Premiums (Rp)	Small-Stock Premiums (Rq)	Default Premiums (Rd)	Horizon Premiums (Rh)
Basic Series						
Common Stocks (R_m)	X	X	X			
Small-Company Stocks (R_s)	X	X	X	X		
Long-Term Corporate Bonds (R_c)	X	X			X	X
Long-Term Government Bonds (R_g)	X	X				X
Treasury Bills (R_f)	X	X				
Inflation (R_I)	X					
Inflation-Adjusted Series						
Inflation-Adjusted Common Stocks (R_{mr})		X	X			
Inflation-Adjusted Small-Company Stocks (R_{sr})		X	X	X		
Inflation-Adjusted Long-Term Corporate Bonds (R_{cr})		X			X	X
Inflation-Adjusted Long-Term Government Bonds (R_{gr})		X				X
Inflation-Adjusted Treasury Bills, or Real Riskless Rates of Return (R_{fr} or R_r)		X				

5. Presentation of the Data: Returns and Indexes

Annual and Monthly Returns

Returns on the Basic Asset Classes

Exhibit 14 displays annual total returns on each of the seven basic asset classes. Annual returns, R_T, are formed by compounding the 12 monthly returns. (This method applies to total return and capital appreciation series; income and yield series are annualized differently.) To compound, or link, monthly returns, one multiplies return relatives and subtracts one from the result. A return relative is simply the return, expressed as a decimal, plus one. A simple example for three hypothetical months illustrates the compounding method:

Month	Return (Percent)	Return (Decimal)	Return Relative
1	+ 10%	0.10	1.10
2	- 10%	-0.10	0.90
3	+ 15%	0.15	1.15

The return for this hypothetical quarter is given by:

$$(1.10) \times (.90) \times (1.15) - 1 = 1.1385 - 1 = 0.1385, \quad (23)$$

or a gain of 13.85 percent. Note that this is different from the simple addition result, (10 - 10 + 15) = 15 percent. The compound return reflects the growth of funds invested in

EXHIBIT 14
BASIC SERIES:
YEAR-BY-YEAR TOTAL RETURNS
(1926-1987)

Year	Common Stocks	Small-Company Stocks	Long-Term Corporate Bonds	Long-Term Government Bonds	Intermediate-Term Government Bonds	U.S. Treasury Bills	Consumer Price Index
1926	0.1162	0.0028	0.0737	0.0777	0.0538	0.0327	-0.0149
1927	0.3749	0.2210	0.0744	0.0893	0.0452	0.0312	-0.0208
1928	0.4361	0.3969	0.0284	0.0010	0.0092	0.0324	-0.0097
1929	-0.0842	-0.5136	0.0327	0.0342	0.0601	0.0475	0.0019
1930	-0.2490	-0.3815	0.0798	0.0466	0.0671	0.0241	-0.0603
1931	-0.4334	-0.4975	-0.0185	-0.0531	-0.0232	0.0107	-0.0952
1932	-0.0819	-0.0539	0.1082	0.1684	0.0881	0.0096	-0.1030
1933	0.5399	1.4287	0.1038	-0.0008	0.0182	0.0030	0.0051
1934	-0.0144	0.2422	0.1384	0.1002	0.0900	0.0016	0.0203
1935	0.4767	0.4019	0.0961	0.0498	0.0701	0.0017	0.0299
1936	0.3392	0.6480	0.0674	0.0751	0.0306	0.0018	0.0121
1937	-0.3503	-0.5801	0.0275	0.0023	0.0156	0.0031	0.0310
1938	0.3112	0.3280	0.0613	0.0553	0.0623	-0.0002	-0.0278
1939	-0.0041	0.0035	0.0397	0.0594	0.0452	0.0002	-0.0048
1940	-0.0978	-0.0516	0.0339	0.0609	0.0296	0.0000	0.0096
1941	-0.1159	-0.0900	0.0273	0.0093	0.0049	0.0006	0.0972
1942	0.2034	0.4451	0.0260	0.0322	0.0194	0.0027	0.0929
1943	0.2590	0.8837	0.0283	0.0208	0.0281	0.0035	0.0316
1944	0.1975	0.5372	0.0473	0.0281	0.0180	0.0033	0.0211
1945	0.3644	0.7361	0.0408	0.1073	0.0222	0.0033	0.0225
1946	-0.0807	-0.1163	0.0172	-0.0010	0.0100	0.0035	0.1817
1947	0.0571	0.0092	-0.0234	-0.0263	0.0091	0.0050	0.0901
1948	0.0550	-0.0211	0.0414	0.0340	0.0185	0.0081	0.0271
1949	0.1879	0.1975	0.0331	0.0645	0.0232	0.0110	-0.0180
1950	0.3171	0.3875	0.0212	0.0006	0.0070	0.0120	0.0579
1951	0.2402	0.0780	-0.0269	-0.0394	0.0036	0.0149	0.0587
1952	0.1837	0.0303	0.0352	0.0116	0.0163	0.0166	0.0088
1953	-0.0099	-0.0649	0.0341	0.0363	0.0323	0.0182	0.0063
1954	0.5262	0.6058	0.0539	0.0719	0.0268	0.0086	-0.0050

EXHIBIT 14 (Continued)

Year	Common Stocks	Small-Company Stocks	Long-Term Corporate Bonds	Long-Term Government Bonds	Intermediate-Term Government Bonds	U.S. Treasury Bills	Consumer Price Index
1955	0.3156	0.2044	0.0048	-0.0130	-0.0065	0.0157	0.0037
1956	0.0656	0.0428	-0.0681	-0.0559	-0.0042	0.0246	0.0286
1957	-0.1078	-0.1457	0.0871	0.0745	0.0784	0.0314	0.0302
1958	0.4336	0.6489	-0.0222	-0.0610	-0.0129	0.0154	0.0176
1959	0.1196	0.1640	-0.0097	-0.0226	-0.0039	0.0295	0.0150
1960	0.0047	-0.0329	0.0907	0.1378	0.1175	0.0266	0.0148
1961	0.2689	0.3209	0.0482	0.0097	0.0185	0.0213	0.0067
1962	-0.0873	-0.1190	0.0795	0.0689	0.0556	0.0273	0.0122
1963	0.2280	0.2357	0.0219	0.0121	0.0164	0.0312	0.0165
1964	0.1648	0.2352	0.0477	0.0351	0.0404	0.0354	0.0119
1965	0.1245	0.4175	-0.0046	0.0071	0.0102	0.0393	0.0192
1966	-0.1006	-0.0701	0.0020	0.0365	0.0468	0.0476	0.0335
1967	0.2398	0.8357	-0.0495	-0.0919	0.0101	0.0421	0.0304
1968	0.1106	0.3597	0.0257	-0.0026	0.0453	0.0521	0.0472
1969	-0.0850	-0.2505	-0.0809	-0.0508	-0.0074	0.0658	0.0611
1970	0.0401	-0.1743	0.1837	0.1210	0.1686	0.0653	0.0549
1971	0.1431	0.1650	0.1101	0.1323	0.0872	0.0439	0.0336
1972	0.1898	0.0443	0.0726	0.0568	0.0516	0.0384	0.0341
1973	-0.1466	-0.3090	0.0114	-0.0111	0.0460	0.0693	0.0880
1974	-0.2647	-0.1995	-0.0306	0.0435	0.0569	0.0800	0.1220
1975	0.3720	0.5282	0.1464	0.0919	0.0783	0.0580	0.0701
1976	0.2384	0.5738	0.1865	0.1675	0.1287	0.0508	0.0481
1977	-0.0718	0.2538	0.0171	-0.0067	0.0140	0.0512	0.0677
1978	0.0656	0.2346	-0.0007	-0.0116	0.0348	0.0718	0.0903
1979	0.1844	0.4346	-0.0418	-0.0122	0.0409	0.1038	0.1331
1980	0.3242	0.3988	-0.0262	-0.0395	0.0391	0.1124	0.1240
1981	-0.0491	0.1388	-0.0096	0.0185	0.0945	0.1471	0.0894
1982	0.2141	0.2801	0.4379	0.4035	0.2910	0.1054	0.0387
1983	0.2251	0.3967	0.0470	0.0068	0.0741	0.0880	0.0380
1984	0.0627	-0.0667	0.1639	0.1543	0.1402	0.0985	0.0395
1985	0.3216	0.2466	0.3090	0.3097	0.2033	0.0772	0.0377
1986	0.1847	0.0685	0.1985	0.2444	0.1514	0.0616	0.0113
1987	0.0523	-0.0930	-0.0027	-0.0269	0.0290	0.0547	0.0441

an asset. A dollar invested in this hypothetical asset at the beginning of the three-month period grows to slightly less than $1.14, not $1.15.

Equivalently, annual returns may be formed by dividing index values according to:

$$R_T = \frac{V_T}{V_{T-1}} - 1 \tag{24}$$

where

V_T = index value as of year-end T, and

V_{T-1} = index value for the previous year-end, T-1.

The construction of index values is discussed later in this chapter.

Annual Income Returns

Annual income returns are constructed unlike other annual returns. The dividend or coupon-income payments, in dollars, are summed over the 12 months in a year. (The dollar payments are scaled to an investment equal to the index level at the previous year-end, V_{T-1}.) This sum is then divided by V_{T-1} to form the annual income return. Mathematically,

$$R_T = \frac{\sum_{m=1}^{12} INC_m}{V_{T-1}} \tag{25}$$

where

INC_m = income payment in the mth month of the year from the previous year-end, T-1, to the present year-end, T, and

V_{T-1} = index value for the previous year end, T-1.

This method produces the true annual income return. For an investor who purchases a security at time T-1 and holds it to time T, it is the return before figuring any capital gain or loss. This method differs from that used in the 1982 edition of this book.

Capital Appreciation, Income, Reinvestment Returns, and Yields on Common Stocks and Government Bonds

Exhibit 15 provides further detail on the returns of common stocks, and on the returns and yields of long- and intermediate-term government bonds. Total annual returns are shown as the sum of three components: returns from capital appreciation, returns from the receipt of income, and returns from the reinvestment of income. (The capital appreciation and income components were previously explained in Chapter 3.) The third component, reinvestment return, reflects monthly income reinvested in the total return index in subsequent months in the year. Thus, for a single month the reinvestment return is zero, but over any longer period of time it is nonzero. Because the returns in Exhibit 15 are annual, reinvestment return is relevant. Such returns are generally positive when capital appreciation for the year is positive, because the income is being reinvested in a rising market; in a falling market, reinvestment returns are generally negative.

Because of this reinvestment return, the annual total return formed by compounding the monthly total returns does not equal the sum of the annual capital appreciation and income components; the difference is the return received from reinvesting the income component. A simple example illustrates this point. In 1985, an "up" year, the total annual return on common stocks was 32.16 percent. The annual capital appreciation was 26.34 percent and the annual

EXHIBIT 15
COMMON STOCKS, LONG-TERM GOVERNMENT BONDS, AND INTERMEDIATE-TERM GOVERNMENT BONDS:
YEAR-BY-YEAR INCOME, CAPITAL APPRECIATION, REINVESTMENT RETURNS, AND YIELDS
(1926-1987)

Year	Common Stocks				Long-Term Government Bonds					Intermediate-Term Government Bonds				
	Capital Apprec. Return	Income Return	Rein-vest-ment Return	Total Return	Capital Apprec. Return	Income Return	Rein-vest-ment Return	Total Return	Year-end Yield	Capital Apprec. Return	Income Return	Rein-vest-ment Return	Total Return	Year-end Yield
1926	.0572	.0541	.0050	.1162	.0391	.0373	.0014	.0777	.0361	.0150	.0378	.0010	.0538	.0361
1927	.3091	.0571	.0087	.3749	.0539	.0341	.0012	.0893	.0323	.0096	.0349	.0007	.0452	.0340
1928	.3788	.0481	.0091	.4361	-.0313	.0322	.0001	.0010	.0347	-.0274	.0364	.0002	.0092	.0401
1929	-.1191	.0398	-.0049	-.0842	-.0021	.0348	.0015	.0342	.0347	.0177	.0407	.0018	.0601	.0362
1930	-.2848	.0457	-.0098	-.2490	.0128	.0332	.0005	.0466	.0337	.0330	.0330	.0011	.0671	.0291
1931	-.4707	.0535	-.0162	-.4334	-.0847	.0333	-.0017	-.0531	.0385	-.0541	.0316	-.0008	-.0232	.0412
1932	-.1515	.0616	.0080	-.0819	.1292	.0369	.0023	.1684	.0321	.0502	.0363	.0016	.0881	.0304
1933	.4659	.0639	.0101	.5399	-.0314	.0312	-.0005	-.0008	.0353	-.0099	.0283	-.0002	.0182	.0325
1934	-.0594	.0446	.0004	-.0144	.0676	.0318	.0009	.1002	.0298	.0597	.0293	.0009	.0900	.0249
1935	.4137	.0495	.0135	.4767	.0214	.0281	.0003	.0498	.0293	.0494	.0202	.0005	.0701	.0163
1936	.2792	.0536	.0064	.3392	.0464	.0277	.0010	.0751	.0252	.0160	.0144	.0002	.0306	.0129
1937	-.3859	.0466	-.0109	-.3503	-.0248	.0266	.0005	.0023	.0279	.0005	.0148	.0003	.0156	.0114
1938	.2521	.0483	.0107	.3112	.0283	.0264	.0006	.0553	.0257	.0437	.0182	.0004	.0623	.0152
1939	-.0545	.0469	.0035	-.0041	.0348	.0240	.0006	.0594	.0238	.0318	.0131	.0003	.0452	.0098
1940	-.1529	.0536	.0014	-.0978	.0377	.0223	.0009	.0609	.0198	.0204	.0090	.0002	.0296	.0057
1941	-.1786	.0671	-.0044	-.1159	-.0102	.0194	.0000	.0093	.0254	-.0017	.0067	-.0000	.0049	.0082
1942	.1243	.0679	.0112	.2034	.0073	.0246	.0003	.0322	.0242	.0117	.0076	.0000	.0194	.0072
1943	.1945	.0624	.0021	.2590	-.0038	.0244	.0002	.0208	.0253	.0123	.0156	.0002	.0281	.0145
1944	.1380	.0548	.0047	.1975	.0032	.0246	.0003	.0281	.0259	.0034	.0144	.0001	.0180	.0140
1945	.3072	.0497	.0074	.3644	.0827	.0234	.0012	.1073	.0203	.0102	.0119	.0001	.0222	.0103
1946	-.1187	.0409	-.0029	-.0807	-.0215	.0204	.0001	-.0010	.0216	-.0008	.0108	.0000	.0100	.0112
1947	-.0000	.0549	.0022	.0571	-.0470	.0213	-.0006	-.0263	.0240	-.0031	.0121	.0000	.0091	.0134
1948	-.0065	.0608	.0008	.0550	.0096	.0240	-.0004	-.0340	.0241	.0027	.0156	.0001	.0185	.0151
1949	.1026	.0750	.0103	.1879	.0414	.0225	.0006	.0645	.0220	.0095	.0136	.0001	.0232	.0123
1950	.2178	.0877	.0116	.3171	-.0207	.0212	.0006	.0006	.0243	-.0070	.0139	.0001	.0070	.0162
1951	.1646	.0691	.0065	.2402	-.0627	.0238	-.0004	-.0394	.0274	-.0163	.0198	.0001	.0036	.0217
1952	.1178	.0593	.0066	.1837	-.0148	.0266	-.0002	.0116	.0275	-.0058	.0219	.0001	.0163	.0235
1953	-.0662	.0546	.0018	-.0099	.0067	.0284	.0012	.0363	.0278	.0061	.0255	.0007	.0323	.0218
1954	.4502	.0621	.0139	.5262	.0435	.0279	.0005	.0719	.0271	.0108	.0160	.0001	.0268	.0172

EXHIBIT 15 (Continued)

Year	Common Stocks				Long-Term Government Bonds					Intermediate-Term Government Bonds				
	Capital Apprec. Return	Income Return	Reinvestment Return	Total Return	Capital Apprec. Return	Income Return	Reinvestment Return	Total Return	Yearend Yield	Capital Apprec. Return	Income Return	Reinvestment Return	Total Return	Yearend Yield
1955	.2640	.0456	.0060	.3156	-.0407	.0275	.0003	-.0130	.0306	-.0311	.0245	.0000	-.0065	.0280
1956	.0262	.0383	.0011	.0656	-.0846	.0299	-.0012	-.0559	.0352	-.0346	.0305	-.0002	-.0042	.0363
1957	-.1431	.0384	-.0030	-.1078	.0381	.0344	-.0020	.0745	.0329	.0405	.0359	.0020	.0784	.0284
1958	.3806	.0438	.0093	.4336	-.0923	.0327	-.0013	-.0610	.0376	-.0418	.0293	-.0005	-.0129	.0381
1959	.0848	.0331	.0016	.1196	-.0620	.0401	-.0007	-.0226	.0426	-.0456	.0418	-.0001	-.0039	.0498
1960	-.0297	.0326	.0019	.0047	.0929	.0426	.0023	.1378	.0404	.0742	.0415	.0019	.1175	.0331
1961	.2313	.0348	.0028	.2689	-.0286	.0383	-.0000	.0097	.0447	-.0172	.0354	.0003	.0185	.0384
1962	-.1181	.0298	.0010	-.0873	-.0278	.0400	.0011	.0689	.0391	.0173	.0373	.0010	.0556	.0350
1963	.1889	.0361	.0030	.2280	-.0270	.0389	.0002	.0121	.0422	-.0210	.0371	.0003	.0164	.0404
1964	.1297	.0333	.0018	.1648	-.0072	.0415	.0008	.0351	.0402	-.0004	.0400	.0008	.0404	.0403
1965	.0906	.0321	.0018	.1245	-.0345	.0419	-.0003	.0071	.0457	-.0311	.0415	-.0003	.0102	.0490
1966	-.1309	.0311	-.0008	-.1006	-.0106	.0449	.0022	.0365	.0479	-.0042	.0493	.0018	.0468	.0479
1967	.2009	.0363	.0025	.2398	-.1355	.0459	-.0023	-.0919	.0604	-.0386	.0488	-.0001	.0101	.0577
1968	.0766	.0318	.0022	.1106	-.0551	.0550	-.0025	-.0026	.0609	-.0099	.0549	-.0004	.0453	.0596
1969	-.1142	.0304	-.0013	-.0850	-.1083	.0595	-.0019	-.0508	.0677	-.0728	.0665	-.0011	-.0074	.0829
1970	.0016	.0341	.0043	.0401	.0484	.0674	.0052	.1210	.0617	.0871	.0749	.0066	.1686	.0590
1971	.1079	.0333	.0019	.1431	.0660	.0632	.0031	.1323	.0608	.0272	.0575	.0026	.0872	.0525
1972	.1563	.0309	.0026	.1898	-.0035	.0587	.0017	.0568	.0651	-.0075	.0575	.0016	.0516	.0585
1973	-.1737	.0286	-.0016	-.1466	-.0773	.0651	.0010	-.0111	.0740	-.0219	.0658	.0022	.0460	.0679
1974	-.2972	.0369	-.0044	-.2647	-.0346	.0727	.0054	.0435	.0828	-.0200	.0724	.0044	.0569	.0712
1975	.3155	.0537	.0029	.3720	.0073	.0799	.0047	.0919	.0793	.0012	.0735	.0036	.0783	.0719
1976	.1915	.0438	.0031	.2384	.0807	.0789	.0080	.1675	.0764	.0525	.0710	.0051	.1287	.0600
1977	-.1150	.0431	.0001	-.0718	-.0795	.0724	.0004	-.0067	.0801	-.0515	.0649	.0006	.0140	.0751
1978	.0106	.0533	.0017	.0656	-.0908	.0795	-.0003	-.0116	.0899	-.0449	.0783	.0015	.0348	.0883
1979	.1231	.0571	.0042	.1844	-.0979	.0883	-.0026	-.0122	.0987	-.0507	.0904	.0012	.0409	.1033
1980	.2577	.0573	.0092	.3242	-.1377	.0974	.0008	-.0395	.1184	-.0681	.1055	.0017	.0391	.1245
1981	-.0972	.0489	-.0008	-.0491	-.1040	.1160	.0065	.0185	.1405	-.0455	.1297	.0103	.0945	.1396
1982	.1476	.0550	.0115	.2141	.2386	.1356	.0293	.4035	.1061	.1423	.1281	.0206	.2910	.0990
1983	.1727	.0500	.0024	.2251	-.0992	.1050	.0010	.0068	.1198	-.0330	.1035	.0035	.0741	.1141
1984	.0139	.0456	.0031	.0627	.0226	.1175	.0142	.1543	.1162	.0122	.1168	.0112	.1402	.1104
1985	.2634	.0509	.0072	.3216	.1779	.1128	.0190	.3097	.0946	.0901	.1029	.0104	.2033	.0855
1986	.1463	.0374	.0010	.1847	.1515	.0883	.0046	.2444	.0796	.0699	.0772	.0043	.1514	.0685
1987	.0203	.0364	-.0044	.0523	-.1065	.0789	.0006	-.0269	.0920	-.0473	.0749	.0014	.0290	.0832

income return was 5.09 percent. These two components sum to 31.43 percent; the remaining 0.72 percent of the total 1985 return came from the reinvestment of dividends in the appreciating market.

For the two government bond asset classes, we also give year-end yields. Unlike returns, which measure the behavior of an asset over time, the yield of a bond characterizes the bond at a point in time. The yield of a bond is approximately its expected return, on a per-year compound basis, if held to maturity. Bond yields are discussed in greater detail in Chapters 2 and 3.

Returns on the Derived Series

Annual returns for all 10 of the component or derived series are calculated from monthly returns in the same manner as the annual total return and capital appreciation series. Exhibit 16 presents annual returns for each of these series. As noted in Chapter 4, four of the derived series are risk premiums and six are inflation-adjusted total returns on asset classes.

Index Values

Index values represent the cumulative effect of returns on a dollar invested. For example, a dollar invested in common stocks (with dividends reinvested) as of December 31, 1925 grew to $1.12 by December 1926, reflecting the 12 percent return in 1926. Over the year 1927, the $1.12 grew to $1.54, reflecting the 37 percent return for that year.

Exhibit 17 presents indexes of total return for the seven basic asset classes, and indexes of capital appreciation for common stocks and long- and intermediate-term government bonds. Exhibit 18 gives indexes of the derived return series.

EXHIBIT 16
DERIVED SERIES:
YEAR-BY-YEAR TOTAL RETURNS
(1926-1987)

Year	Equity Risk Premiums	Small-Stock Premiums	Default Premiums	Horizon Premiums	Common Stocks	Small-Company Stocks	Inflation-Adjusted Long-Term Corporate Bonds	Inflation-Adjusted Long-Term Government Bonds	Intermed. Government Bonds	U.S. Treasury Bills
1926	0.0809	-0.1017	-0.0037	0.0436	0.1331	0.0179	0.0900	0.0940	0.0697	0.0483
1927	0.3332	-0.1119	-0.0136	0.0563	0.4041	0.2469	0.0973	0.1124	0.0674	0.0531
1928	0.3910	-0.0273	0.0274	-0.0304	0.4501	0.4106	0.0384	0.0108	0.0190	0.0425
1929	-0.1257	-0.4689	-0.0014	-0.0127	-0.0859	-0.5145	0.0307	0.0322	0.0581	0.0454
1930	-0.2666	-0.1764	0.0317	0.0219	-0.2008	-0.3418	0.1491	0.1137	0.1356	0.0898
1931	-0.4394	-0.1133	0.0366	-0.0632	-0.3737	-0.4446	0.0848	0.0465	0.0796	0.1171
1932	-0.0907	0.0305	-0.0515	0.1573	0.0235	0.0547	0.2354	0.3025	0.2130	0.1255
1933	0.5353	0.5772	0.1046	-0.0037	0.5321	1.4163	0.0982	-0.0058	0.0131	-0.0021
1934	-0.0160	0.2604	0.0347	0.0985	-0.0340	0.2175	0.1158	0.0784	0.0683	-0.0183
1935	0.4742	-0.0506	0.0441	0.0481	0.4339	0.3613	0.0644	0.0194	0.0390	-0.0273
1936	0.3368	-0.2306	-0.0072	0.0732	0.3232	0.6283	0.0547	0.0623	0.0183	-0.0102
1937	-0.3523	-0.3537	0.0251	-0.0008	-0.3698	-0.5927	-0.0035	-0.0279	-0.0150	-0.0271
1938	0.3114	0.0128	0.0057	0.0555	0.3487	0.3659	0.0917	0.0855	0.0926	0.0284
1939	-0.0043	0.0076	-0.0186	0.0592	0.0007	0.0083	0.0446	0.0645	0.0502	0.0050
1940	-0.0979	0.0513	-0.0254	0.0608	-0.1064	-0.0605	0.0241	0.0508	0.0198	-0.0094
1941	-0.1164	0.0293	0.0178	0.0087	-0.1942	-0.1706	-0.0637	-0.0801	-0.0841	-0.0880
1942	0.2002	0.2008	-0.0060	0.0294	0.1011	0.3223	-0.0612	-0.0555	-0.0673	-0.0825
1943	0.2546	0.4962	0.0073	0.0173	0.2204	0.8260	-0.0032	-0.0105	-0.0034	-0.0273
1944	0.1936	0.2837	0.0186	0.0248	0.1728	0.5055	0.0257	0.0069	-0.0031	-0.0174
1945	0.3599	0.2725	-0.0601	0.1037	0.3343	0.6979	0.0178	0.0830	-0.0003	-0.0188
1946	-0.0839	-0.0387	0.0183	-0.0046	-0.2220	-0.2521	-0.1391	-0.1546	-0.1452	-0.1507
1947	0.0518	-0.0453	0.0030	-0.0311	0.0303	-0.0742	-0.1041	-0.1067	-0.0743	-0.0780
1948	0.0465	-0.0722	0.0071	0.0257	0.0272	-0.0469	0.0139	0.0067	-0.0084	-0.0185
1949	0.1750	0.0080	-0.0295	0.0529	0.2097	0.2195	0.0521	0.0840	0.0420	0.0296
1950	0.3016	0.0534	0.0206	-0.0113	0.2450	0.3115	-0.0347	-0.0542	-0.0481	-0.0434
1951	0.2219	-0.1307	0.0130	-0.0535	0.1714	0.0182	-0.0809	-0.0927	-0.0521	-0.0414
1952	0.1644	-0.1296	0.0234	-0.0049	0.1733	0.0213	0.0262	0.0027	0.0074	0.0077
1953	-0.0276	-0.0555	-0.0021	0.0178	-0.0160	-0.0707	0.0277	0.0299	0.0259	0.0119
1954	0.5132	0.0521	-0.0168	0.0627	0.5339	0.6138	0.0591	0.0772	0.0319	0.0137
1955	0.2952	-0.0845	0.0180	-0.0282	0.3107	0.1999	0.0010	-0.0166	-0.0102	0.0119
1956	0.0400	-0.0213	-0.0130	-0.0785	0.0359	0.0138	-0.0941	-0.0821	-0.0319	-0.0039
1957	-0.1350	-0.0425	0.0117	0.0418	-0.1340	-0.1708	0.0552	0.0430	0.0467	0.0011
1958	0.4119	0.1501	0.0413	-0.0752	0.4088	0.6203	-0.0391	-0.0772	-0.0300	-0.0022
1959	0.0874	0.0397	0.0132	-0.0506	0.1030	0.1468	-0.0243	-0.0370	-0.0187	0.0143

EXHIBIT 16 (Continued)

Year	Equity Risk Premiums	Small-Stock Premiums	Default Premiums	Horizon Premiums	Common Stocks	Small-Company Stocks	Inflation-Adjusted Long-Term Corporate Bonds	Long-Term Government Bonds	Intermed. Government Bonds	U.S. Treasury Bills
1960	-0.0214	-0.0374	-0.0414	0.1082	-0.0099	-0.0470	0.0748	0.1212	0.1013	0.0117
1961	0.2425	0.0410	0.0381	-0.0113	0.2604	0.3121	0.0412	0.0030	0.0117	0.0144
1962	-0.1116	-0.0348	0.0099	0.0404	-0.0983	-0.1297	0.0664	0.0559	0.0429	0.0149
1963	0.1909	0.0062	0.0097	-0.0185	0.2081	0.2156	0.0054	-0.0043	-0.0001	0.0144
1964	0.1250	0.0604	0.0122	-0.0003	0.1511	0.2207	0.0354	0.0229	0.0282	0.0232
1965	0.0820	0.2606	-0.0116	-0.0310	0.1033	0.3908	-0.0234	-0.0119	-0.0089	0.0197
1966	-0.1415	0.0339	-0.0333	-0.0106	-0.1298	-0.1003	-0.0306	0.0029	0.0129	0.0136
1967	0.1897	0.4807	0.0466	-0.1285	0.2031	0.7815	-0.0776	-0.1187	-0.0198	0.0113
1968	0.0557	0.2243	0.0285	-0.0520	0.0605	0.2984	-0.0205	-0.0476	-0.0018	0.0046
1969	-0.1416	-0.1809	-0.0318	-0.1094	-0.1377	-0.2937	-0.1338	-0.1054	-0.0645	0.0045
1970	-0.0236	-0.2061	0.0559	0.0524	-0.0141	-0.2173	0.1221	0.0627	0.1078	0.0098
1971	0.0951	0.0191	-0.0196	0.0847	0.1060	0.1271	0.0741	0.0955	0.0519	0.0099
1972	0.1458	-0.1222	0.0149	0.0177	0.1505	0.0099	0.0372	0.0220	0.0169	0.0041
1973	-0.2019	-0.1903	0.0227	-0.0752	-0.2156	-0.3649	-0.0704	-0.0911	-0.0385	-0.0172
1974	-0.3192	0.0887	-0.0710	-0.0338	-0.3446	-0.2865	-0.1360	-0.0700	-0.0581	-0.0374
1975	0.2968	0.1138	0.0499	0.0320	0.2821	0.4280	0.0713	0.0204	0.0076	-0.0113
1976	0.1785	0.2708	0.0162	0.1111	0.1816	0.5015	0.1320	0.1140	0.0769	0.0026
1977	-0.1171	0.3508	0.0240	-0.0551	-0.1307	0.1743	-0.0474	-0.0697	-0.0503	-0.0155
1978	-0.0058	0.1586	0.0110	-0.0778	-0.0226	0.1324	-0.0834	-0.0934	-0.0508	-0.0169
1979	0.0731	0.2113	-0.0300	-0.1050	0.0453	0.2662	-0.1543	-0.1282	-0.0813	-0.0259
1980	0.1904	0.0563	0.0139	-0.1366	0.1781	0.2445	-0.1336	-0.1455	-0.0756	-0.0103
1981	-0.1710	0.1976	-0.0276	-0.1121	-0.1271	0.0453	-0.0909	-0.0651	0.0047	0.0530
1982	0.0983	0.0543	0.0245	0.2696	0.1688	0.2323	0.3843	0.3512	0.2428	0.0642
1983	0.1261	0.1400	0.0399	-0.0746	0.1803	0.3456	0.0087	-0.0300	0.0348	0.0482
1984	-0.0326	-0.1217	0.0083	0.0508	0.0222	-0.1022	0.1196	0.1104	0.0968	0.0567
1985	0.2268	-0.0567	-0.0005	0.2158	0.2736	0.2013	0.2615	0.2621	0.1596	0.0381
1986	0.1159	-0.0981	-0.0369	0.1722	0.1715	0.0566	0.1851	0.2305	0.1385	0.0498
1987	-0.0022	-0.1381	0.0249	-0.0774	0.0079	-0.1313	-0.0448	-0.0680	-0.0144	0.0101

EXHIBIT 17
BASIC SERIES:
INDEXES OF YEAR-END CUMULATIVE WEALTH (1926-1987)
(DECEMBER 1925 = 1.00)

Year	Common Stocks Total Returns	Common Stocks Capital Appreciation	Small Stocks Total Returns	Long-Term Corp. Bonds Total Returns	Long-Term Government Bonds Total Returns	Long-Term Government Bonds Capital Appreciation	Intermediate-Term Government Bonds Total Returns	Intermediate-Term Government Bonds Capital Appreciation	U.S. T-Bills Total Returns	Consumer Price Index
1925	1.0000	1.0000	1.0000	1.0000	1.0000	1.0000	1.0000	1.0000	1.0000	1.0000
1926	1.1162	1.0572	1.0028	1.0737	1.0777	1.0391	1.0538	1.0150	1.0327	0.9851
1927	1.5347	1.3840	1.2243	1.1537	1.1739	1.0951	1.1014	1.0248	1.0649	0.9646
1928	2.2040	1.9083	1.7103	1.1864	1.1751	1.0609	1.1116	0.9968	1.0995	0.9553
1929	2.0185	1.6810	0.8319	1.2253	1.2153	1.0587	1.1784	1.0144	1.1517	0.9572
1930	1.5159	1.2022	0.5146	1.3230	1.2719	1.0722	1.2575	1.0478	1.1794	0.8994
1931	0.8590	0.6364	0.2586	1.2985	1.2043	0.9814	1.2283	0.9912	1.1921	0.8138
1932	0.7886	0.5400	0.2446	1.4390	1.4071	1.1082	1.3365	1.0410	1.2035	0.7300
1933	1.2144	0.7915	0.5941	1.5883	1.4060	1.0734	1.3609	1.0307	1.2071	0.7337
1934	1.1969	0.7445	0.7380	1.8082	1.5470	1.1459	1.4833	1.0922	1.2091	0.7486
1935	1.7674	1.0525	1.0346	1.9821	1.6241	1.1705	1.5872	1.1461	1.2111	0.7709
1936	2.3669	1.3464	1.7051	2.1157	1.7461	1.2248	1.6357	1.1644	1.2133	0.7803
1937	1.5379	0.8268	0.7160	2.1738	1.7501	1.1944	1.6611	1.1649	1.2170	0.8045
1938	2.0165	1.0353	0.9508	2.3072	1.8469	1.2282	1.7646	1.2158	1.2168	0.7821
1939	2.0082	0.9788	0.9541	2.3987	1.9566	1.2710	1.8444	1.2545	1.2171	0.7784
1940	1.8117	0.8292	0.9049	2.4801	2.0757	1.3188	1.8990	1.2801	1.2171	0.7858
1941	1.6017	0.6810	0.8235	2.5478	2.0950	1.3054	1.9084	1.2779	1.2179	0.8622
1942	1.9275	0.7657	1.1900	2.6140	2.1624	1.3150	1.9453	1.2928	1.2211	0.9423
1943	2.4267	0.9146	2.2417	2.6881	2.2075	1.3101	2.0000	1.3088	1.2254	0.9721
1944	2.9060	1.0408	3.4459	2.8153	2.2696	1.3143	2.0359	1.3133	1.2294	0.9925
1945	3.9649	1.3605	5.9825	2.9300	2.5132	1.4230	2.0811	1.3267	1.2335	1.0149
1946	3.6448	1.1991	5.2871	2.9805	2.5106	1.3924	2.1019	1.3256	1.2378	1.1993
1947	3.8529	1.1991	5.3354	2.9109	2.4447	1.3270	2.1211	1.3215	1.2441	1.3073
1948	4.0649	1.1912	5.2227	3.0312	2.5277	1.3396	2.1602	1.3251	1.2541	1.3426
1949	4.8287	1.3135	6.2541	3.1315	2.6907	1.3951	2.2104	1.3377	1.2680	1.3184
1950	6.3601	1.5995	8.6774	3.1978	2.6923	1.3663	2.2258	1.3283	1.2831	1.3948
1951	7.8875	1.8629	9.3546	3.1118	2.5863	1.2806	2.2338	1.3067	1.3023	1.4767
1952	9.3363	2.0823	9.6378	3.2213	2.6162	1.2616	2.2703	1.2991	1.3238	1.4898
1953	9.2440	1.9444	9.0125	3.3312	2.7113	1.2701	2.3437	1.3071	1.3480	1.4991
1954	14.1085	2.8198	14.4726	3.5106	2.9061	1.3253	2.4065	1.3212	1.3596	1.4916
1955	18.5615	3.5643	17.4309	3.5275	2.8685	1.2714	2.3908	1.2801	1.3810	1.4972
1956	19.7784	3.6575	18.1774	3.2871	2.7081	1.1638	2.3806	1.2359	1.4150	1.5400
1957	17.6458	3.1340	15.5290	3.5735	2.9100	1.2082	2.5672	1.2859	1.4594	1.5866
1958	25.2976	4.3268	25.6052	3.4943	2.7326	1.0966	2.5341	1.2322	1.4819	1.6145
1959	28.3220	4.6936	29.8040	3.4605	2.6708	1.0286	2.5241	1.1760	1.5257	1.6387

EXHIBIT 17 (Continued)

Year	Common Stocks Total Returns	Common Stocks Capital Appreciation	Small Stocks Total Returns	Long-Term Corp. Bonds Total Returns	Long-Term Government Bonds Total Returns	Long-Term Government Bonds Capital Appreciation	Intermediate-Term Government Bonds Total Returns	Intermediate-Term Government Bonds Capital Appreciation	U.S. T-Bills Total Returns	Consumer Price Index
1960	28.4549	4.5541	28.8231	3.7742	3.0388	1.1242	2.8208	1.2632	1.5663	1.6629
1961	36.1060	5.6074	38.0718	3.9561	3.0682	1.0920	2.8729	1.2415	1.5996	1.6741
1962	32.9546	4.9451	33.5402	4.2704	3.2795	1.1224	3.0328	1.2630	1.6433	1.6946
1963	40.4685	5.8793	41.4441	4.3641	3.3192	1.0920	3.0825	1.2364	1.6945	1.7225
1964	47.1389	6.6419	51.1928	4.5724	3.4356	1.0842	3.2071	1.2359	1.7544	1.7430
1965	53.0082	7.2437	72.5676	4.5515	3.4599	1.0468	3.2398	1.1975	1.8233	1.7765
1966	47.6738	6.2955	67.4793	4.5604	3.5862	1.0357	3.3915	1.1925	1.9101	1.8361
1967	59.1039	7.5603	123.8708	4.3346	3.2568	0.8953	3.4257	1.1465	1.9905	1.8920
1968	65.6415	8.1395	168.4290	4.4462	3.2482	0.8460	3.5809	1.1352	2.0942	1.9814
1969	60.0589	7.2100	126.2336	4.0865	3.0833	0.7543	3.5545	1.0526	2.2320	2.1024
1970	62.4652	7.2218	104.2263	4.8372	3.4565	0.7908	4.1537	1.1442	2.3777	2.2179
1971	71.4056	8.0008	121.4232	5.3699	3.9137	0.8431	4.5159	1.1753	2.4820	2.2924
1972	84.9556	9.2516	126.8073	5.7598	4.1361	0.8401	4.7489	1.1665	2.5773	2.3706
1973	72.5000	7.6450	87.6183	5.8254	4.0902	0.7752	4.9675	1.1409	2.7559	2.5791
1974	53.3107	5.3730	70.1427	5.6470	4.2682	0.7484	5.2501	1.1181	2.9764	2.8939
1975	73.1439	7.0682	107.1891	6.4740	4.6606	0.7539	5.6611	1.1194	3.1492	3.0968
1976	90.5837	8.4216	168.6916	7.6812	5.4414	0.8147	6.3897	1.1782	3.3092	3.2458
1977	84.0760	7.4530	215.5006	7.8126	5.4050	0.7499	6.4794	1.1175	3.4787	3.4655
1978	89.5916	7.5321	261.1212	7.8071	5.3424	0.6818	6.7052	1.0673	3.7285	3.7784
1979	106.1118	8.4591	374.6157	7.4807	5.2774	0.6151	6.9796	1.0132	4.1153	4.2812
1980	140.5126	10.6387	523.9944	7.2850	5.0687	0.5304	7.2522	0.9441	4.5777	4.8119
1981	133.6151	9.6049	596.7196	7.2150	5.1624	0.4752	7.9377	0.9012	5.2510	5.2421
1982	162.2213	11.0227	763.8327	10.3741	7.2453	0.5886	10.2472	1.0294	5.8046	5.4450
1983	198.7435	12.9264	1066.8340	10.8616	7.2945	0.5302	11.0060	0.9954	6.3154	5.6517
1984	211.1974	13.1061	995.6855	12.6418	8.4200	0.5422	12.5488	1.0075	6.9374	5.8752
1985	279.1142	16.5582	1241.2400	16.5485	11.0272	0.6386	15.0999	1.0983	7.4732	6.0967
1986	330.6680	18.9805	1326.2810	19.8330	13.7222	0.7354	17.3857	1.1751	7.9337	6.1656
1987	347.9646	19.3659	1202.9720	19.7799	13.3525	0.6571	17.8902	1.1195	8.3673	6.4375

EXHIBIT 18
DERIVED SERIES
INDEXES OF YEAR-END CUMULATIVE WEALTH (1926-1987)
(DECEMBER 1925 = 1.00)

| Year | Equity Risk Premiums | Small-Stock Premiums | Default Premiums | Horizon Premiums | Common Stocks | Small-Company Stocks | Inflation-Adjusted | | | |
							Long-Term Corporate Bonds	Long-Term Government Bonds	Intermed. Government Bonds	U.S. Treasury Bills
1925	1.0000	1.0000	1.0000	1.0000	1.0000	1.0000	1.0000	1.0000	1.0000	1.0000
1926	1.0809	0.8983	0.9963	1.0436	1.1331	1.0179	1.0900	1.0940	1.0697	1.0483
1927	1.4411	0.7978	0.9828	1.1023	1.5910	1.2693	1.1960	1.2170	1.1418	1.1040
1928	2.0046	0.7760	1.0097	1.0688	2.3071	1.7904	1.2420	1.2301	1.1636	1.1509
1929	1.7527	0.4122	1.0082	1.0552	2.1088	0.8692	1.2801	1.2697	1.2311	1.2032
1930	1.2853	0.3394	1.0402	1.0784	1.6854	0.5721	1.4709	1.4141	1.3981	1.3113
1931	0.7206	0.3010	1.0782	1.0103	1.0555	0.3177	1.5957	1.4799	1.5094	1.4649
1932	0.6552	0.3102	1.0227	1.1691	1.0803	0.3351	1.9713	1.9276	1.8309	1.6487
1933	1.0060	0.4892	1.1296	1.1648	1.6551	0.8097	2.1648	1.9164	1.8548	1.6452
1934	0.9899	0.6166	1.1688	1.2795	1.5988	0.9858	2.4154	2.0665	1.9814	1.6151
1935	1.4593	0.5854	1.2204	1.3410	2.2925	1.3420	2.5709	2.1066	2.0587	1.5710
1936	1.9508	0.7204	1.2117	1.4392	3.0335	2.1853	2.7116	2.2379	2.0963	1.5550
1937	1.2636	0.4656	1.2421	1.4381	1.9117	0.8900	2.7022	2.1755	2.0649	1.5128
1938	1.6572	0.4715	1.2492	1.5178	2.5782	1.2157	2.9499	2.3614	2.2562	1.5558
1939	1.6500	0.4751	1.2259	1.6076	2.5799	1.2258	3.0815	2.5136	2.3695	1.5636
1940	1.4885	0.4995	1.1948	1.7054	2.3054	1.1515	3.1559	2.6413	2.4165	1.5488
1941	1.3152	0.5141	1.2161	1.7203	1.8577	0.9551	2.9550	2.4299	2.2134	1.4125
1942	1.5785	0.6174	1.2088	1.7709	2.0456	1.2629	2.7742	2.2949	2.0645	1.2959
1943	1.9804	0.9238	1.2177	1.8015	2.4964	2.3061	2.7653	2.2709	2.0575	1.2606
1944	2.3638	1.1858	1.2404	1.8461	2.9278	3.4718	2.8364	2.2866	2.0512	1.2386
1945	3.2144	1.5089	1.1658	2.0376	3.9067	5.8947	2.8870	2.4763	2.0505	1.2154
1946	2.9446	1.4505	1.1872	2.0283	3.0393	4.4086	2.4853	2.0935	1.7527	1.0322
1947	3.0971	1.3848	1.1907	1.9651	2.9473	4.0814	2.2267	1.8701	1.6225	0.9516
1948	3.2412	1.2848	1.1992	2.0155	3.0275	3.8899	2.2577	1.8827	1.6089	0.9341
1949	3.8083	1.2952	1.1638	2.1221	3.6625	4.7436	2.3752	2.0408	1.6765	0.9617
1950	4.9567	1.3644	1.1878	2.0982	4.5599	6.2213	2.2927	1.9302	1.5958	0.9199
1951	6.0567	1.1860	1.2032	1.9860	5.3412	6.3347	2.1072	1.7514	1.5127	0.8819
1952	7.0524	1.0323	1.2313	1.9762	6.2670	6.4693	2.1623	1.7561	1.5239	0.8886
1953	6.8576	0.9750	1.2286	2.0114	6.1665	6.0121	2.2222	1.8086	1.5634	0.8992
1954	10.3766	1.0258	1.2080	2.1374	9.4585	9.7026	2.3536	1.9483	1.6133	0.9115

EXHIBIT 18 (Continued)

Year	Equity Risk Premiums	Small-Stock Premiums	Default Premiums	Horizon Premiums	Common Stocks	Small-Company Stocks	Inflation-Adjusted Long-Term Corporate Bonds	Inflation-Adjusted Long-Term Government Bonds	Inflation-Adjusted Intermed. Government Bonds	U.S. Treasury Bills
1955	13.4403	0.9391	1.2297	2.0770	12.3974	11.6423	2.3560	1.9159	1.5968	0.9224
1956	13.9777	0.9191	1.2138	1.9139	12.8428	11.8032	2.1344	1.7585	1.5458	0.9188
1957	12.0910	0.8800	1.2280	1.9940	11.1218	9.7876	2.2523	1.8341	1.6181	0.9198
1958	17.0710	1.0122	1.2787	1.8440	15.6688	15.8592	2.1643	1.6925	1.5696	0.9179
1959	18.5638	1.0523	1.2957	1.7506	17.2828	18.1872	2.1117	1.6298	1.5403	0.9310
1960	18.1672	1.0129	1.2420	1.9401	17.1112	17.3325	2.2696	1.8273	1.6963	0.9419
1961	22.5721	1.0544	1.2894	1.9182	21.5672	22.7414	2.3631	1.8328	1.7161	0.9555
1962	20.0538	1.0178	1.3022	1.9957	19.4468	19.7924	2.5200	1.9353	1.7897	0.9697
1963	23.3820	1.0241	1.3148	1.9588	23.4936	24.0599	2.5336	1.9269	1.7895	0.9837
1964	26.8684	1.0860	1.3309	1.9582	27.0444	29.3702	2.6233	1.9711	1.8400	1.0065
1965	29.0721	1.3690	1.3155	1.8976	29.8379	40.8477	2.5620	1.9476	1.8236	1.0263
1966	24.9586	1.4154	1.2717	1.8775	25.9643	36.7509	2.4837	1.9531	1.8471	1.0403
1967	29.6925	2.0958	1.3310	1.6361	31.2389	65.4710	2.2910	1.7214	1.8106	1.0521
1968	31.3451	2.5659	1.3688	1.5511	33.1291	85.0059	2.2440	1.6394	1.8073	1.0569
1969	26.9078	2.1018	1.3254	1.3814	28.5665	60.0420	1.9437	1.4666	1.6907	1.0616
1970	26.2715	1.6685	1.3995	1.4537	28.1643	46.9936	2.1810	1.5585	1.8728	1.0720
1971	28.7699	1.7005	1.3721	1.5769	31.1493	52.9685	2.3425	1.7073	1.9700	1.0827
1972	32.9635	1.4926	1.3926	1.6048	35.8375	53.4921	2.4297	1.7448	2.0033	1.0872
1973	26.3074	1.2085	1.4242	1.4842	28.1101	33.9718	2.2587	1.5859	1.9260	1.0685
1974	17.9109	1.3157	1.3231	1.4340	18.4220	24.2385	1.9514	1.4749	1.8142	1.0285
1975	23.2264	1.4654	1.3891	1.4799	23.6189	34.6125	2.0905	1.5050	1.8280	1.0169
1976	27.3731	1.8623	1.4116	1.6443	27.9079	51.9721	2.3665	1.6765	1.9686	1.0195
1977	24.1691	2.5156	1.4454	1.5538	24.2605	61.0294	2.2543	1.5596	1.8697	1.0038
1978	24.0291	2.9145	1.4613	1.4329	23.7115	69.1088	2.0662	1.4139	1.7746	0.9868
1979	25.7845	3.5304	1.4175	1.2824	24.7856	87.5026	1.7473	1.2327	1.6303	0.9613
1980	30.6950	3.7291	1.4373	1.1073	29.2009	108.8950	1.5140	1.0534	1.5071	0.9513
1981	25.4455	4.4659	1.3976	0.9831	25.4889	113.8323	1.3764	0.9848	1.5142	1.0017
1982	27.9468	4.7086	1.4318	1.2482	29.7924	140.2800	1.9052	1.3306	1.8819	1.0660
1983	31.4699	5.3679	1.4890	1.1550	35.1649	188.7612	1.9218	1.2907	1.9474	1.1174
1984	30.4434	4.7144	1.5014	1.2137	35.9472	169.4718	2.1517	1.4331	2.1359	1.1808
1985	37.3488	4.4470	1.5007	1.4756	45.7809	203.5904	2.7143	1.8087	2.4767	1.2258
1986	41.6789	4.0109	1.4453	1.7296	53.6309	215.1083	3.2167	2.2256	2.8198	1.2868
1987	41.5861	3.4571	1.4814	1.5958	54.0527	186.8687	3.0726	2.0742	2.7791	1.2998

The inflation-adjusted indexes in Exhibit 18 show the growth of each asset class in constant dollars or real terms. Thus, an investment in common stock, with dividends reinvested, multiplied real wealth by a factor of 54.05 between the end of 1925 and the end of 1987.

By using some mathematical notation, it is possible to describe the nature of the indexes in Exhibits 17 and 18 precisely. At the end of each month n, a cumulative wealth index (V_n) for each of the monthly return series (basic and derived) is formed. This index is initialized as of December 1925 at 1.00 (represented by $V_{12/25} = 1.00$). This index is formed for month n in the following manner:

$$V_n = V_{12/25} \times (1 + R_{1/26}) \times (1 + R_{2/26}) \times \ldots \times (1 + R_n) \qquad (26)$$

where

$V_{12/25}$ = initial index value as of December 1925 = 1.00,

$R_{1/26}$ = return for January 1926, and

$R_{2/26}$ = return for February 1926.

In general then, R_n = return for month n.

Using product notation, the cumulative index may be abbreviated as:

$$V_n = \prod_n (1 + R_n) \qquad (27)$$

6. Statistics of the Stocks, Bonds, Bills, and Inflation Returns

Arithmetic Mean Returns

The arithmetic mean of a series is the simple average of the elements of the series. Stated mathematically, the arithmetic mean from time T_1 to time T_2 is given by

$$R_A(T_1,T_2) = \frac{1}{n} \sum_{t=T_1}^{T_2} R_t \tag{28}$$

where

n is the number of periods from T_1 to T_2; that is, $(T_2 - T_1 + 1)$.

Geometric Mean Returns

The geometric mean (compound) annual return is the rate of return per annum compounded annually. It is given by

$$R_G(T_1,T_2) = \prod_{t=T_1}^{T_2} (1+R_t)^{(1/n)} - 1 \tag{29}$$

Using index values simplifies the above formula to

$$R_G(T_1,T_2) = \left[\frac{V_{T2}}{V_{T1}}\right]^{(1/n)} - 1 \tag{30}$$

where again

n is the number of periods from T_1 to T_2.

Standard Deviations

The standard deviation of a series is a measure of the extent to which observations in the series differ from the arithmetic mean of the series. For a series of asset returns, the standard deviation is a measure of the volatility, or risk, of the asset.

In a normally distributed series, about two-thirds of the observations lie within plus or minus one standard deviation of the arithmetic mean; about 95 percent of the observations, within two standard deviations; and more than 99 percent, within three standard deviations.

Mathematically, the standard deviation is given by

$$\sigma_r = \sqrt{\frac{1}{n-1} \sum_{t=1}^{n} (r_t - \bar{r})^2} \tag{31}$$

where

r_t =   is the return in period t,

$\bar{r}$ =   is the arithmetic mean of the returns designated by r, and

n   =   is the number of periods.

First-Order Autocorrelations

The first-order autocorrelation of a return series describes the extent to which the return in one period relates to the return in the next period. A return series with a high (near 1) first-order autocorrelation is very predictable from one period to the next, whereas one with a low (near zero) first-order autocorrelation is random and unpredictable. A more thorough treatment of autocorrelation, and of correlation in general, appears in Chapter 7.

Presentation of the Summary Statistics for Basic and Derived Series

For each asset class, summary statistics of annual total returns, and, where applicable, income and capital appreciation, are given in Exhibit 19. The summary statistics presented here are arithmetic mean, geometric mean, standard deviation, and first-order autocorrelation. Exhibits 20 and 21 present summary statistics for the four risk-premium series and for the six inflation-adjusted total return series, respectively.

Highlights of the Summary Statistics

Exhibit 19 shows that small stocks are the riskiest asset class and provide the greatest rewards to long-term investors, with an arithmetic mean annual return of 17.7 percent and a standard deviation of annual returns of 35.9 percent over the period 1926-87. The geometric mean of the small stock series is 12.1 percent. Common stocks, long-term corporate bonds, long-term government bonds, and intermediate-term government bonds are progressively less risky, and with correspondingly lower average returns. The only exception to this pattern is intermediate-term government bonds, which outperformed long-term bonds as a result of the general decline in the bond market over the period. Treasury bills were nearly riskless and had the lowest return. In general, then, risk is rewarded over the long term by higher returns.

In Exhibit 20, the equity risk premium exhibits the highest return and greatest variability. The mean horizon premium was 1.1 percent, which is small given its standard deviation.

Inflation-adjusted basic series summary statistics are presented in Exhibit 21. Note that the real rate of interest is close to zero (0.5 percent) on average. Both negative and

EXHIBIT 19
BASIC ASSET CLASSES:
TOTAL RETURNS, INCOME, AND CAPITAL APPRECIATION:
SUMMARY STATISTICS OF ANNUAL RETURNS
(1926-1987)

Series	Geometric Mean	Arithmetic Mean	Standard Deviation	First-Order Auto-Correlation
Common Stocks:				
Total Returns	9.9 %	12.0%	21.1%	0.01
Income	4.8	4.8	1.3	0.79
Capital Appreciation	4.9	6.9	20.2	0.00
Small Company Stocks:				
Total Returns	12.1	17.7	35.9	0.10
Long-Term Corporate Bonds:				
Total Returns	4.9	5.2	8.5	0.17
Long-Term Government Bonds:				
Total Returns	4.3	4.6	8.5	0.10
Income	4.8	4.8	2.9	0.96
Capital Appreciation	−0.7	−0.4	7.4	−0.02
Intermediate-Term Government Bonds:				
Total Returns	4.8	4.9	5.5	0.28
Income	4.4	4.5	3.2	0.95
Capital Appreciation	0.2	0.3	4.1	−0.07
U.S. Treasury Bills:				
Total Returns	3.5	3.5	3.4	0.92
Inflation Rates	3.0	3.2	4.8	0.64

EXHIBIT 20
RISK PREMIUM SERIES:
SUMMARY STATISTICS OF ANNUAL RETURNS
(1926-1987)

Series	Geometric Mean	Arithmetic Mean	Standard Deviation	First-Order Auto-Correlation
Equity Risk Premiums (stocks–bills)	6.2 %	8.3 %	21.1 %	0.02
Small-Stock Premiums (small stocks–stocks)	2.0	3.7	19.0	0.38
Default Premiums (LT corps–LT govts)	0.6	0.7	3.0	−0.30
Horizon Premiums (LT govts–bills)	0.8	1.1	8.0	0.07

EXHIBIT 21
INFLATION-ADJUSTED SERIES:
SUMMARY STATISTICS OF ANNUAL RETURNS
(1926-1987)

Series	Geometric Mean	Arithmetic Mean	Standard Deviation	First-Order Auto-Correlation
Inflation-Adjusted Common Stocks	6.6 %	8.8 %	21.2 %	0.00
Inflation-Adjusted Small Stocks	8.8	14.2	35.2	0.07
Inflation-Adjusted Long-Term Corporate Bonds	1.8	2.3	10.0	0.29
Inflation-Adjusted Long-Term Government Bonds	1.2	1.7	10.2	0.18
Inflation-Adjusted Intermediate-Term Government Bonds	1.7	1.9	7.1	0.34
Inflation-Adjusted U.S. Treasury Bills (Real Interest Rates)	0.4	0.5	4.4	0.66

positive real interest rates occur historically. The geometric and arithmetic means of inflation-adjusted series are lower than the nominal series by approximately the amount of inflation.

The standard deviations of common-stock and small-company-stock returns remain approximately the same after adjusting for inflation, while bonds and bills are more volatile (i.e., have higher standard deviations) after adjusting for inflation.

Volatility of the Markets

The bar graph of monthly returns in Exhibit 22 gives a picture of the changing volatility of stocks and long-term bonds, in isolation and compared with each other. The stock market was unusually volatile in the early years reflecting the 1920s boom, the crash of 1929-32, and the volatile markets of the Great Depression. The market was much more stable between World War II and the 1970s. Since then, stock market volatility increased, but not to the extreme levels of the early years except for October 1987.

Bonds present a different picture. The nominal returns on long-term government bonds were stable in the 1920s and 1930s. Starting in the late 1960s, bond volatility soared; in the 1973-74 stock market decline, bonds did not provide the shelter they once offered. Bond yields peaked in 1981 and returns since then have been high, but the volatility of the bond market continues.

Additional Series Differences

Because the reader may wish to make other comparisons among stock, bond, and bill returns, summary statistics of several additional series differences are given in Exhibit 23.

EXHIBIT 22
MONTH-BY-MONTH RETURNS
ON STOCKS AND BONDS
(1926-1987)

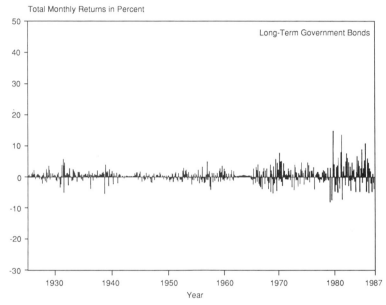

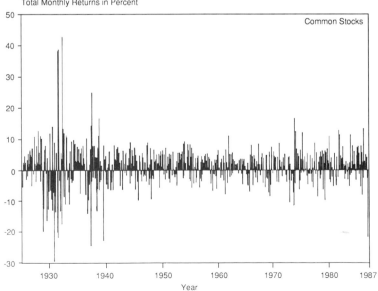

EXHIBIT 23
SERIES DIFFERENCES:
SUMMARY STATISTICS OF DIFFERENCES BETWEEN ANNUAL RETURNS ON COMMON STOCKS, LONG- AND INTERMEDIATE-TERM BONDS, AND BILLS (1926-1987)

Series	Geometric Mean	Arithmetic Mean	Standard Deviation	First-Order Auto-Correlation
Stocks Minus Bonds and Bills:				
Common stock total returns minus long-term government bond total returns	5.4%	7.6%	21.5%	−0.02
Common stock total returns minus intermediate-term government bond total returns	4.9	7.0	21.0	0.01
Equity risk premiums: Common stock total returns minus Treasury bill total returns	6.2	8.3	21.1	0.02
Long-horizon equity risk premiums: Common stock total returns minus long-term government bond yield (income) returns	4.7	6.8	20.5	0.03
Intermediate-horizon equity risk premiums: Common stock total returns minus intermediate-term government bond yield (income) returns	5.2	7.3	20.6	0.03

EXHIBIT 23 (Continued)

Series	Geometric Mean	Arithmetic Mean	Standard Deviation	First-Order Auto-Correlation
Bonds and Bills				
Long-term government bond total returns minus intermediate-term government bond total returns	–0.5	–0.4	4.0	0.09
Horizon premiums: Long-term government bond total returns minus Treasury bill total returns	0.8	1.1	8.0	0.07
Intermediate-term government bond total returns minus Treasury bill total returns	1.2	1.3	4.5	0.05

Geometric Mean Rates of Return for Different Holding Periods

Compound (geometric mean) annual returns for the seven basic series for all calendar year holding periods from 1926 to 1987 are presented in matrix form in the appendix, Exhibits A-1 through A-7. The year-by-year annual returns are on the diagonals of each matrix. To find the compound annual return for any holding period, look in the beginning year column and the ending year row. For example, in Exhibit A-1, the compound annual return for common stocks for the period 1960-79 is 6.8 percent (column 1960, row 1979).

Matrices for two component series, equity risk premiums and real riskless rates of interest, are presented in Exhibits A-8 and A-9, respectively. Finally, Exhibit A-10 provides the long-horizon equity risk premium, which is calculated as total returns for stocks in excess of the yield return, or income return, on long-term government bonds. This series is useful in determining the equity cost of capital over a long future period (see Chapter 9). The long-horizon equity risk premium, R_{lh}, is calculated as:

$$R_{lh} = [(1 + R_m) / (1 + R_y)] - 1 \qquad (32)$$

where

R_m is the return on common stock, and

R_y is the income return on long-term government bonds.

Rolling Period Compound Mean Returns

Because of the interest in returns across certain holding periods, compound annual returns for 5-, 10-, and 20-year periods are presented for the basic series (Exhibits 24-A, 24-B, and 24-C), and for the equity risk premium, the real

79

EXHIBIT 24-A
BASIC SERIES:
COMPOUND ANNUAL RETURNS FOR
FIVE-YEAR HOLDING PERIODS
(Percent per Annum)
(1926-1987)

Period	Common Stocks	Small Company Stocks	Long-Term Corp. Bonds	Long-Term Govt. Bonds	Interm. Govt. Bonds	U.S. Treasury Bills	Inflation
1926-1930	8.68	−12.44	5.76	4.93	4.69	3.36	−2.10
1927-1931	−5.10	−23.74	3.87	2.25	3.11	2.91	−3.75
1928-1932	−12.47	−27.54	4.52	3.69	3.94	2.48	−5.42
1929-1933	−11.24	−19.06	6.01	3.65	4.13	1.89	−5.14
1930-1934	−9.93	−2.37	8.09	4.95	4.71	0.98	−4.80
1931-1935	3.12	14.99	8.42	5.01	4.77	0.53	−3.04
1932-1936	22.47	45.83	10.26	7.71	5.90	0.35	−0.84
1933-1937	14.29	23.96	8.60	4.46	4.45	0.22	1.96
1934-1938	10.67	9.86	7.75	5.61	5.33	0.16	1.29
1935-1939	10.91	5.27	5.81	4.81	4.45	0.13	0.78
1936-1940	0.50	−2.64	4.59	5.03	3.65	0.10	0.38
1937-1941	−7.51	−13.55	3.79	3.71	3.13	0.08	2.02
1938-1942	4.62	10.70	3.76	4.32	3.21	0.07	3.21
1939-1943	3.77	18.71	3.10	3.63	2.54	0.14	4.44
1940-1944	7.67	29.28	3.25	3.01	2.00	0.20	4.98
1941-1945	16.96	45.90	3.39	3.90	1.85	0.27	5.25
1942-1946	17.87	45.05	3.19	3.69	1.95	0.33	6.82
1943-1947	14.86	35.00	2.17	2.48	1.74	0.37	6.77
1944-1948	10.87	18.43	2.43	2.75	1.55	0.47	6.67
1945-1949	10.69	12.66	2.15	3.46	1.66	0.62	5.84
1946-1950	9.91	7.72	1.76	1.39	1.35	0.79	6.57
1947-1951	16.70	12.09	0.87	0.60	1.22	1.02	4.25
1948-1952	19.37	12.55	2.05	1.37	1.37	1.25	2.65
1949-1953	17.86	11.53	1.91	1.41	1.64	1.45	2.23
1950-1954	23.92	18.27	2.31	1.55	1.71	1.41	2.50
1951-1955	23.89	14.97	1.98	1.28	1.44	1.48	1.43
1952-1956	20.18	14.21	1.10	0.92	1.28	1.67	0.84
1953-1957	13.58	10.01	2.10	2.15	2.49	1.97	1.27
1954-1958	22.31	23.22	0.96	0.16	1.57	1.91	1.50
1955-1959	14.96	15.54	−0.29	−1.67	0.96	2.33	1.90

EXHIBIT 24-A (Continued)

Period	Common Stocks	Small-Company Stocks	Long-Term Corp. Bonds	Long-Term Govt. Bonds	Interm. Govt. Bonds	U.S. Treasury Bills	Inflation
1956-1960	8.92	10.58	1.36	1.16	3.36	2.55	2.12
1957-1961	12.79	15.93	3.77	2.53	3.83	2.48	1.68
1958-1962	13.31	16.65	3.63	2.42	3.39	2.40	1.33
1959-1963	9.85	10.11	4.55	3.97	4.00	2.72	1.30
1960-1964	10.73	11.43	5.73	5.16	4.91	2.83	1.24
1961-1965	13.25	20.28	3.82	2.63	2.81	3.09	1.33
1962-1966	5.72	12.13	2.88	3.17	3.37	3.61	1.86
1963-1967	12.39	29.86	0.30	−0.14	2.47	3.91	2.23
1964-1968	10.16	32.37	0.37	−0.43	3.04	4.33	2.84
1965-1969	4.96	19.78	−2.22	−2.14	2.08	4.93	3.82
1966-1970	3.34	7.51	1.23	−0.02	5.10	5.45	4.54
1967-1971	8.42	12.47	3.32	1.76	5.89	5.38	4.54
1968-1972	7.53	0.47	5.85	4.90	6.75	5.30	4.61
1969-1973	2.01	−12.25	5.55	4.72	6.76	5.65	5.41
1970-1974	−2.36	−11.09	6.68	6.72	8.11	5.93	6.60
1971-1975	3.21	0.56	6.00	6.16	6.39	5.78	6.90
1972-1976	4.87	6.80	7.42	6.81	7.19	5.92	7.20
1973-1977	−0.21	10.77	6.29	5.50	6.41	6.18	7.89
1974-1978	4.32	24.41	6.03	5.49	6.18	6.23	7.94
1975-1979	14.76	39.80	5.78	4.34	5.86	6.69	8.15
1976-1980	13.95	37.35	2.39	1.69	5.08	7.77	9.21
1977-1981	8.08	28.75	−1.24	−1.05	4.43	9.67	10.06
1978-1982	14.05	29.28	5.84	6.04	9.60	10.78	9.46
1979-1983	17.27	32.51	6.83	6.43	10.42	11.12	8.39
1980-1984	14.76	21.59	11.06	9.79	12.45	11.01	6.53
1981-1985	14.71	18.82	17.83	16.82	15.80	10.30	4.85
1982-1986	19.87	17.32	22.41	21.59	16.98	8.60	3.30
1983-1987	16.49	9.51	13.78	13.01	11.79	7.59	3.41

EXHIBIT 24-B
BASIC SERIES:
COMPOUND ANNUAL RETURNS FOR
10-YEAR HOLDING PERIODS
(Percent per Annum)
(1926-1987)

Period	Common Stocks	Small-Company Stocks	Long-Term Corp. Bonds	Long-Term Govt. Bonds	Interm. Govt. Bonds	U.S. Treasury Bills	Inflation
1926-1935	5.86	0.34	7.08	4.97	4.73	1.93	−2.57
1927-1936	7.81	5.45	7.02	4.94	4.50	1.62	−2.30
1928-1937	0.02	−5.22	6.54	4.07	4.19	1.34	−1.80
1929-1938	−0.89	−5.70	6.88	4.63	4.73	1.02	−1.98
1930-1939	−0.05	1.38	6.95	4.88	4.58	0.55	−2.05
1931-1940	1.80	5.81	6.49	5.02	4.21	0.32	−1.34
1932-1941	6.43	12.28	6.97	5.69	4.50	0.21	0.58
1933-1942	9.35	17.14	6.15	4.39	3.83	0.15	2.59
1934-1943	7.17	14.20	5.40	4.61	3.93	0.15	2.85
1935-1944	9.28	16.66	4.53	3.91	3.22	0.17	2.86
1936-1945	8.42	19.18	3.99	4.46	2.75	0.18	2.79
1937-1946	4.41	11.98	3.49	3.70	2.54	0.20	4.39
1938-1947	9.62	22.24	2.96	3.40	2.47	0.22	4.97
1939-1948	7.26	18.57	2.77	3.19	2.04	0.30	5.55
1940-1949	9.17	20.69	2.70	3.24	1.83	0.41	5.41
1941-1950	13.38	25.37	2.57	2.64	1.60	0.53	5.91
1942-1951	17.28	27.51	2.02	2.13	1.59	0.67	5.53
1943-1952	17.09	23.27	2.11	1.92	1.56	0.81	4.69
1944-1953	14.31	14.93	2.17	2.08	1.60	0.96	4.43
1945-1954	17.12	15.43	2.23	2.50	1.69	1.01	4.16
1946-1955	16.69	11.29	1.87	1.33	1.40	1.14	3.96
1947-1956	18.43	13.14	0.98	0.76	1.25	1.35	2.53
1948-1957	16.44	11.27	2.07	1.76	1.93	1.61	1.96
1949-1958	20.06	17.23	1.43	0.78	1.61	1.68	1.86
1950-1959	19.35	16.90	1.00	−0.07	1.34	1.87	2.20
1951-1960	16.16	12.75	1.67	1.22	2.40	2.01	1.77
1952-1961	16.43	15.07	2.43	1.72	2.55	2.08	1.26
1953-1962	13.44	13.28	2.86	2.29	2.94	2.19	1.30
1954-1963	15.91	16.48	2.74	2.04	2.78	2.31	1.40
1955-1964	12.82	13.47	2.68	1.69	2.91	2.58	1.57

EXHIBIT 24-B (Continued)

Period	Common Stocks	Small-Company Stocks	Long-Term Corp. Bonds	Govt. Bonds	Interm. Govt. Bonds	U.S. Treasury Bills	Inflation
1956-1965	11.06	15.33	2.58	1.89	3.09	2.82	1.73
1957-1966	9.20	14.02	3.33	2.85	3.60	3.05	1.77
1958-1967	12.85	23.08	1.95	1.13	2.93	3.15	1.78
1959-1968	10.00	20.73	2.44	1.74	3.52	3.52	2.07
1960-1969	7.81	15.53	1.68	1.45	3.48	3.88	2.52
1961-1970	8.18	13.72	2.51	1.30	3.95	4.26	2.92
1962-1971	7.06	12.30	3.10	2.46	4.63	4.49	3.19
1963-1972	9.93	14.22	3.04	2.35	4.59	4.60	3.41
1964-1973	6.00	7.77	2.93	2.11	4.89	4.98	4.12
1965-1974	1.24	3.20	2.13	2.19	5.05	5.43	5.20
1966-1975	3.27	3.98	3.59	3.02	5.74	5.62	5.71
1967-1976	6.63	9.60	5.35	4.26	6.54	5.65	5.86
1968-1977	3.59	5.50	6.07	5.20	6.58	5.74	6.24
1969-1978	3.16	4.48	5.79	5.10	6.47	5.94	6.67
1970-1979	5.86	11.49	6.23	5.52	6.98	6.31	7.37
1971-1980	8.44	17.53	4.18	3.90	5.73	6.77	8.05
1972-1981	6.47	17.26	3.00	2.81	5.80	7.78	8.62
1973-1982	6.68	19.67	6.06	5.77	7.99	8.46	8.67
1974-1983	10.61	28.40	6.43	5.96	8.28	8.65	8.16
1975-1984	14.76	30.38	8.39	7.03	9.10	8.83	7.34
1976-1985	14.33	27.75	9.84	8.99	10.31	9.03	7.01
1977-1986	13.82	22.90	9.95	9.69	10.53	9.14	6.63
1978-1987	15.26	18.99	9.73	9.47	10.69	9.17	6.39

EXHIBIT 24-C
BASIC SERIES:
COMPOUND ANNUAL RETURNS FOR
20-YEAR HOLDING PERIODS
(Percent per Annum)
(1926-1987)

Period	Common Stocks	Small-Company Stocks	Long-Term Corp. Bonds	Long-Term Govt. Bonds	Interm. Govt. Bonds	U.S. Treasury Bills	Inflation
1926-1945	7.13	9.36	5.52	4.72	3.73	1.05	0.07
1927-1946	6.10	8.67	5.24	4.32	3.51	0.91	0.99
1928-1947	4.71	7.64	4.74	3.74	3.33	0.78	1.53
1929-1948	3.11	5.74	4.80	3.90	3.38	0.66	1.72
1930-1949	4.46	10.61	4.80	4.05	3.20	0.48	1.61
1931-1950	7.43	15.17	4.51	3.82	2.90	0.42	2.22
1932-1951	11.72	19.65	4.47	3.90	3.04	0.44	3.02
1933-1952	13.15	20.16	4.11	3.15	2.68	0.48	3.63
1934-1953	10.68	14.56	3.77	3.34	2.76	0.55	3.64
1935-1954	13.13	16.04	3.37	3.20	2.45	0.59	3.51
1936-1955	12.48	15.17	2.92	2.88	2.07	0.66	3.37
1937-1956	11.20	12.56	2.23	2.22	1.89	0.77	3.46
1938-1957	12.98	16.63	2.52	2.57	2.20	0.91	3.45
1939-1958	13.48	17.90	2.10	1.98	1.83	0.99	3.69
1940-1959	14.15	18.78	1.85	1.57	1.58	1.14	3.79
1941-1960	14.76	18.89	2.12	1.92	2.00	1.27	3.82
1942-1961	16.86	21.13	2.22	1.93	2.07	1.37	3.37
1943-1962	15.25	18.17	2.48	2.10	2.25	1.50	2.98
1944-1963	15.11	15.70	2.45	2.06	2.19	1.63	2.90
1945-1964	14.95	14.44	2.45	2.09	2.30	1.79	2.86
1946-1965	13.84	13.29	2.23	1.61	2.24	1.97	2.84
1947-1966	13.72	13.58	2.15	1.80	2.42	2.19	2.15
1948-1967	14.63	17.03	2.01	1.44	2.43	2.38	1.87
1949-1968	14.92	18.97	1.93	1.26	2.56	2.60	1.96
1950-1969	13.43	16.21	1.34	0.68	2.40	2.87	2.36
1951-1970	12.10	13.23	2.09	1.26	3.17	3.13	2.35
1952-1971	11.65	13.67	2.77	2.09	3.58	3.28	2.22
1953-1972	11.67	13.75	2.95	2.32	3.76	3.39	2.35
1954-1973	10.85	12.04	2.83	2.08	3.83	3.64	2.75
1955-1974	6.87	8.21	2.41	1.94	3.98	4.00	3.37

EXHIBIT 24-C (Continued)

Period	Common Stocks	Small-Company Stocks	Long-Term Corp. Bonds	Long-Term Govt. Bonds	Interm. Govt. Bonds	U.S. Treasury Bills	Inflation
1956-1975	7.10	9.51	3.08	2.46	4.40	4.21	3.70
1957-1976	7.91	11.78	4.34	3.55	5.06	4.34	3.80
1958-1977	8.12	13.95	3.99	3.14	4.74	4.44	3.98
1959-1978	6.53	12.31	4.10	3.41	4.99	4.72	4.34
1960-1979	6.83	13.49	3.93	3.46	5.22	5.09	4.92
1961-1980	8.31	15.61	3.34	2.59	4.83	5.51	5.46
1962-1981	6.76	14.75	3.05	2.64	5.21	6.12	5.87
1963-1982	8.30	16.92	4.54	4.04	6.28	6.51	6.01
1964-1983	8.28	17.63	4.66	4.02	6.57	6.80	6.12
1965-1984	7.79	16.00	5.22	4.58	7.06	7.12	6.26
1966-1985	8.66	15.25	6.67	5.97	8.00	7.31	6.36
1967-1986	10.17	16.06	7.63	6.94	8.52	7.38	6.24
1968-1987	9.27	12.04	7.89	7.31	8.62	7.44	6.31

riskless rates of interest, and the excess of total returns on stocks over yield returns on long-term government bonds (Exhibit 25).

The maximum and minimum values of rolling period returns are given in Exhibits 26-A and 26-B. These extreme values show the limits of the historical experience. For example, five-year holding period returns for common stocks range from a high of 23.9 percent compounded annually in the period 1950-54 to a low of -12.5 percent compounded annually in the period 1928-32.

Geometric Mean versus Arithmetic Mean

The arithmetic and geometric means formed by equations (28) and (29), respectively, are of course different. Each has a specific meaning in the interpretation of returns; and they should not be confused with each other.

In general, the geometric mean for any time period is less than or equal to the arithmetic mean, as illustrated below:

$$R_G(T_1,T_2) \leq R_A(T_1,T_2) \qquad (33)$$

The two means are equal only when returns are constant across the time period; the difference between the two is positively related to the variability or standard deviation of the returns. For example, in Exhibit 19, the difference between the arithmetic and geometric mean is much larger for risky common stocks than it is for nearly riskless Treasury bills. The mathematical relation between the two means is detailed in Chapter 9.

Change in Wealth Over Time versus Performance in One Period

A simple example illustrates the difference between geometric and arithmetic means. Suppose $1.00 is invested in a common stock portfolio that experiences successive annual returns of +50 percent and -50 percent. At the end

EXHIBIT 25
EQUITY RISK PREMIUMS, LONG-HORIZON EQUITY PREMIUMS, AND REAL RISKLESS RETURNS:
COMPOUND ANNUAL RETURNS FOR DIFFERENT HOLDING PERIODS
(Percent Per Annum)
(1926-1987)

Five-Year Holding Period Returns

Period	Equity Risk Premiums	Long-Horizon Equity Risk Premiums	Real Riskless Returns
1926-1930	5.15	5.07	5.57
1927-1931	-7.79	-8.29	6.92
1928-1932	-14.58	-15.41	8.35
1929-1933	-12.88	-14.23	7.41
1930-1934	-10.80	-12.88	6.07
1931-1935	2.57	-0.18	3.68
1932-1936	22.04	18.87	1.20
1933-1937	14.04	11.02	-1.71
1934-1938	10.50	7.70	-1.11
1935-1939	10.76	8.06	-0.65
1936-1940	0.40	-1.90	-0.28
1937-1941	-7.58	-9.73	-1.90
1938-1942	4.55	2.19	-3.05
1939-1943	3.63	1.37	-4.12
1940-1944	7.45	5.13	-4.55
1941-1945	16.65	14.19	-4.73
1942-1946	17.49	15.17	-6.08
1943-1947	14.43	12.23	-5.99
1944-1948	10.35	8.35	-5.82
1945-1949	10.01	8.26	-4.93
1946-1950	9.05	7.42	-5.42
1947-1951	15.52	13.92	-3.10
1948-1952	17.89	16.45	-1.36
1949-1953	16.17	14.90	-0.76
1950-1954	22.20	20.68	-1.07
1951-1955	22.08	20.50	0.05
1952-1956	18.21	16.72	0.82
1953-1957	11.38	10.19	0.69
1954-1958	20.01	18.43	0.41
1955-1959	12.34	10.98	0.42

Ten-Year Holding Period Returns

Period	Equity Risk Premiums	Long-Horizon Equity Risk Premiums	Real Riskless Returns
1926-1935	3.85	2.42	4.62
1927-1936	6.08	4.41	4.02
1928-1937	-1.31	-3.09	3.20
1929-1938	-1.89	-3.88	3.06
1930-1939	-0.60	-2.97	2.65
1931-1940	1.48	-1.04	1.68
1932-1941	6.20	3.59	-0.36
1933-1942	9.19	6.51	-2.38
1934-1943	7.01	4.49	-2.63
1935-1944	9.09	6.59	-2.62
1936-1945	8.22	5.84	-2.53
1937-1946	4.20	1.97	-4.02
1938-1947	9.38	7.09	-4.53
1939-1948	6.94	4.80	-4.97
1940-1949	8.72	6.69	-4.74
1941-1950	12.78	10.75	-5.08
1942-1951	16.50	14.54	-4.60
1943-1952	16.15	14.32	-3.70
1944-1953	13.22	11.58	-3.32
1945-1954	15.94	14.30	-3.02
1946-1955	15.38	13.77	-2.72
1947-1956	16.85	15.31	-1.16
1948-1957	14.59	13.28	-0.34
1949-1958	18.07	16.65	-0.18
1950-1959	17.16	15.73	-0.32
1951-1960	13.87	12.46	0.24
1952-1961	14.06	12.53	0.80
1953-1962	11.02	9.52	0.88
1954-1963	13.29	11.75	0.90
1955-1964	9.98	8.63	1.00

Twenty-Year Holding Period Returns

Period	Equity Risk Premiums	Long-Horizon Equity Risk Premiums	Real Riskless Returns
1926-1945	6.01	4.11	0.98
1927-1946	5.14	3.18	-0.08
1928-1947	3.90	1.87	-0.74
1929-1948	2.43	0.37	-1.04
1930-1949	3.96	1.74	-1.11
1931-1950	6.98	4.69	-1.76
1932-1951	11.23	8.93	-2.51
1933-1952	12.62	10.35	-3.04
1934-1953	10.07	7.98	-2.98
1935-1954	12.47	10.38	-2.82
1936-1955	11.74	9.73	-2.63
1937-1956	10.35	8.43	-2.60
1938-1957	11.95	10.14	-2.46
1939-1958	12.37	10.57	-2.60
1940-1959	12.86	11.12	-2.56
1941-1960	13.33	11.60	-2.46
1942-1961	15.27	13.53	-1.94
1943-1962	13.55	11.89	-1.44
1944-1963	13.26	11.66	-1.23
1945-1964	12.92	11.43	-1.03
1946-1965	11.64	10.22	-0.84
1947-1966	11.28	9.96	0.04
1948-1967	11.97	10.65	0.50
1949-1968	12.01	10.74	0.62
1950-1969	10.27	9.06	0.50
1951-1970	8.70	7.59	0.77
1952-1971	8.10	6.98	1.03
1953-1972	8.02	6.82	1.01
1954-1973	6.95	5.79	0.87
1955-1974	2.77	1.73	0.61

EXHIBIT 25 (Continued)

Five-Year Holding Period Returns

Period	Equity Risk Premiums	Long-Horizon Equity Risk Premiums	Real Riskless Returns
1956-1960	6.21	4.96	0.42
1957-1961	10.06	8.49	0.79
1958-1962	10.65	8.85	1.06
1959-1963	6.95	5.44	1.40
1960-1964	7.67	6.33	1.57
1961-1965	9.86	8.65	1.73
1962-1966	2.03	1.36	1.72
1963-1967	8.17	7.32	1.64
1964-1968	5.59	4.81	1.45
1965-1969	0.03	-0.65	1.07
1966-1970	-2.01	-2.49	0.88
1967-1971	2.88	2.06	0.80
1968-1972	2.11	1.13	0.66
1969-1973	-3.44	-4.30	0.22
1970-1974	-7.82	-8.65	-0.63
1971-1975	-2.43	-3.76	-1.05
1972-1976	-0.99	-2.49	-1.20
1973-1977	-6.02	-7.47	-1.58
1974-1978	-1.80	-3.55	-1.58
1975-1979	7.56	5.78	-1.34
1976-1980	5.73	4.29	-1.32
1977-1981	-1.45	-2.21	-0.35
1978-1982	2.95	2.69	1.21
1979-1983	5.54	5.03	2.52
1980-1984	3.38	2.45	4.20
1981-1985	4.00	2.85	5.20
1982-1986	10.37	8.66	5.14
1983-1987	8.27	5.87	4.04

Ten-Year Holding Period Returns

Period	Equity Risk Premiums	Long-Horizon Equity Risk Premiums	Real Riskless Returns
1956-1965	8.02	6.79	1.07
1957-1966	5.97	4.86	1.25
1958-1967	9.40	8.09	1.35
1959-1968	6.27	5.13	1.42
1960-1969	3.78	2.78	1.32
1961-1970	3.76	2.93	1.30
1962-1971	2.46	1.71	1.26
1963-1972	5.10	4.18	1.15
1964-1973	0.97	0.15	0.83
1965-1974	-3.97	-4.73	0.22
1966-1975	-2.22	-3.12	-0.09
1967-1976	0.93	-0.24	-0.20
1968-1977	-2.04	-3.27	-0.47
1969-1978	-2.62	-3.93	-0.68
1970-1979	-0.43	-1.69	-0.99
1971-1980	1.57	0.19	-1.19
1972-1981	-1.22	-2.35	-0.77
1973-1982	-1.64	-2.52	-0.20
1974-1983	1.81	0.65	0.45
1975-1984	5.45	4.10	1.39
1976-1985	4.86	3.57	1.89
1977-1986	4.29	3.08	2.36
1978-1987	5.58	4.27	2.62

Twenty-Year Holding Period Returns

Period	Equity Risk Premiums	Long-Horizon Equity Risk Premiums	Real Riskless Returns
1956-1975	2.77	1.71	0.49
1957-1976	3.42	2.28	0.52
1958-1977	3.52	2.25	0.44
1959-1978	1.72	0.50	0.36
1960-1979	1.66	0.52	0.16
1961-1980	2.66	1.55	0.05
1962-1981	0.60	-0.34	0.24
1963-1982	1.67	0.77	0.47
1964-1983	1.39	0.40	0.64
1965-1984	0.63	-0.41	0.80
1966-1985	1.26	0.17	0.89
1967-1986	2.60	1.40	1.07
1968-1987	1.70	0.43	1.06

EXHIBIT 26-A
MINIMUM AND MAXIMUM VALUES OF ANNUAL AND FIVE-YEAR ROLLING PERIOD RETURNS
(Compound Annual Rates of Return in Percent)

Series	Maximum Value		Minimum Value		Times Positive (out of 62 years)
	Return	Year(s)	Return	Year(s)	
Annual Returns					
Basic Series					
Common Stocks	53.99 %	1933	−43.34 %	1931	43
Small-Company Stocks	142.87	1933	−58.01	1937	42
Long-Term Corporate Bonds	43.79	1982	−8.09	1969	47
Long-Term Government Bonds	40.35	1982	−9.19	1967	44
Intermediate Government Bonds	29.10	1982	−2.32	1931	56
U.S. Treasury Bills	14.71	1981	−0.02	1938	61
Inflation	18.17	1946	−10.30	1932	52
Selected Derived Series					
Equity Risk Premiums	53.53	1933	−43.94	1931	38
Long-Horizon Equity Risk Premiums	49.34	1933	−45.16	1931	38
Inflation-Adjusted Common Stocks	53.39	1954	−37.37	1931	41
Inflation-Adjusted LT Govt Bonds	35.12	1982	−15.46	1946	35
Real Riskless Rates	12.55	1932	−15.07	1946	36
Five-Year Rolling Period Returns					
Basic Series					
Common Stocks	23.92 %	1950-54	−12.47 %	1928-32	
Small-Company Stocks	45.90	1941-45	−27.54	1928-32	
Long-Term Corporate Bonds	22.41	1982-86	−2.22	1965-69	
Long-Term Government Bonds	21.59	1982-86	−2.14	1965-69	
Intermediate Government Bonds	16.98	1982-86	0.96	1955-59	
U.S. Treasury Bills	11.12	1979-83	0.07	1938-42	
Inflation	10.06	1977-81	−5.42	1928-32	
Selected Derived Series					
Equity Risk Premiums	22.20	1950-54	−14.58	1928-32	
Long-Horizon Equity Risk Premiums	20.68	1950-54	−15.41	1928-32	
Inflation-Adjusted Common Stocks	23.51	1932-36	−9.34	1937-41	
Inflation-Adjusted LT Govt Bonds	17.71	1982-86	−10.09	1977-81	
Real Riskless Rates	8.35	1928-32	−6.08	1942-46	

EXHIBIT 26-B
MINIMUM AND MAXIMUM VALUES OF 10- AND 20-YEAR
ROLLING PERIOD RETURNS
(Compound Annual Rates of Return in Percent)

Series	Maximum Value Return	Year(s)	Minimum Value Return	Year(s)
10-Year Rolling Period Returns				
Basic Series				
Common Stocks	20.06 %	1949-58	−0.89 %	1929-38
Small-Company Stocks	30.38	1975-84	−0.57	1929-38
Long-Term Corporate Bonds	9.95	1977-86	0.98	1947-56
Long-Term Government Bonds	9.69	1977-86	−0.07	1950-59
Intermediate Government Bonds	10.69	1978-87	1.25	1947-56
U.S. Treasury Bills	9.17	1978-87	0.15	1933-42
Inflation	8.67	1973-82	−2.57	1926-35
Selected Derived Series				
Equity Risk Premiums	18.07	1949-58	−3.97	1965-74
Long-Horizon Equity Risk Premiums	16.65	1949-58	−4.73	1965-74
Inflation-Adjusted Common Stocks	17.87	1949-58	−3.77	1965-74
Inflation-Adjusted LT Govt Bonds	7.74	1926-35	−5.35	1972-81
Real Riskless Rates	4.62	1926-35	−5.08	1941-50
20-Year Rolling Period Returns				
Basic Series				
Common Stocks	16.86 %	1942-61	3.11 %	1929-48
Small-Company Stocks	21.13	1942-61	5.74	1929-48
Long-Term Corporate Bonds	7.89	1968-87	1.34	1950-69
Long-Term Government Bonds	7.31	1968-87	0.68	1950-69
Intermediate Government Bonds	8.62	1968-87	1.58	1940-59
U.S. Treasury Bills	7.44	1968-87	0.42	1931-50
Inflation	6.36	1966-85	0.07	1926-45
Selected Derived Series				
Equity Risk Premiums	15.27	1942-61	0.60	1962-81
Long-Horizon Equity Risk Premiums	13.53	1942-61	-0.41	1965-84
Inflation-Adjusted Common Stocks	13.04	1942-61	0.84	1962-81
Inflation-Adjusted LT Govt Bonds	4.64	1926-45	−3.06	1962-81
Real Riskless Rates	1.07	1967-86	−3.04	1933-52

of the first year, the portfolio is worth $1.50. At the end of the second year, the portfolio is worth $0.75. The annual arithmetic mean is zero percent, whereas the annual geometric mean is -13.4 percent. The geometric mean is backward-looking, measuring the change in wealth over more than one period. On the other hand, the arithmetic mean is a better representation of typical performance over single periods, and is the correct rate for cost of capital estimation, forecasting, and discounting (see Chapters 9 and 10).

7. Time Series Behavior of the Returns

Correlation Coefficients: Serial and Cross-Correlations

This chapter focuses on the behavior of the return series over time. Time series behavior is interesting because it reveals the predictability of an asset or component return. For example, a series may be revealed to be random, or unpredictable; or it may be subject to trends, cycles, or other patterns, making the series predictable to a greater or lesser degree. The first-order autocorrelation, or serial correlation, of a series determines its predictability given knowledge of the latest observation. The cross-correlation (correlation) between two series determines the predictability of one series, conditional on knowledge of the other.

Mathematically, the correlation between two return series A and B is given by:

$$\rho_{A,B} = [\text{cov}(A,B)]/[\sigma_A \sigma_B] \qquad (34)$$

where

σ_A and σ_B are the standard deviations of series A and B respectively (see Chapter 5), and

$\text{cov}(A,B)$ is the covariance of series A and B and is given as follows:

$$\text{cov}(A,B) = \frac{1}{n-1} \sum_{t=1}^{n} (A_t - \overline{A})(B_t - \overline{B})$$

(35)

where

A_t and B_t are the returns on series A and B, respectively, in period t,

$\overline{A}$ and $\overline{B}$ are the arithmetic means of series A and B, respectively, and

n is the number of periods.

The serial correlation of a single series is calculated in the same manner as the correlation between two series. For the serial correlation, the correlation is calculated between the series itself and the "lagged" series. The lagged series is the series of one-period-old returns, as in the following example (for an annual series starting in year 1):

Year	Return	Lagged Return
1	0.10	undefined
2	-0.10	0.10
3	0.15	-0.10
4	0.00	0.15
etc.		

Correlations of the Basic Series

Exhibit 27 presents the yearly cross-correlations and serial correlations for the seven basic series. Long- and intermediate-term government and long-term corporate bond returns are highly correlated with each other but negatively correlated with inflation. Because the inflation was largely unanticipated, it had a negative effect on fixed-income securities. In addition, U.S. Treasury bills and inflation are reasonably highly correlated, a result of the

EXHIBIT 27
BASIC ASSET CLASSES:
SAMPLE SERIAL AND CROSS-CORRELATIONS
OF HISTORICAL YEARLY RETURNS*
(1926-1987)

	Common Stocks	Small Stocks	Long-Term Corporate Bonds	Long-Term Government Bonds	Intermed. Government Bonds	U.S. Treasury Bills	Inflation
Common Stocks	1.00						
Small Stocks	0.82	1.00					
Long-Term Corp. Bonds	0.19	0.08	1.00				
Long-Term Govt. Bonds	0.11	−0.01	0.93	1.00			
Intermediate Govt. Bonds	0.03	−0.07	0.89	0.89	1.00		
U.S. Treasury Bills	−0.07	−0.09	0.18	0.21	0.50	1.00	
Inflation	−0.02	0.06	−0.17	−0.17	0.01	0.41	1.00
Serial Correlations	0.01	0.10	0.17	0.10	0.28	0.92	0.64

*The standard error for all estimates is 0.13.

post-1951 "tracking" described earlier in Chapter 2. Finally, both the U.S. Treasury bills and inflation series display high serial correlations.

Correlations of the Component Series

The yearly cross-correlations and serial correlations for the four risk premium series and inflation are presented in Exhibit 28. These correlations reveal that the small stock premiums and perhaps bond default premiums are significantly correlated with equity risk premiums. With one exception, the remaining series are independent of one another, having cross-correlations which do not differ from zero at the 5 percent statistical significance level. The exception is that inflation is negatively correlated with the horizon premium, because unexpected increases in inflation cause long-term bond yields to rise and prices to fall; unexpected decreases have the opposite effect.

Exhibit 29 presents yearly cross-correlations and serial correlations for the inflation-adjusted asset return series. It is interesting to observe how the asset return relations differ substantially when they are expressed in inflation-adjusted form (compared to Exhibit 27). In general, the cross-correlations between asset classes are *higher* when one accounts for inflation (i.e., subtracts inflation out of the nominal returns).

The Meaning of Serial Correlation

A direct way to test for patterns in the series is to examine the one-year serial-correlation coefficients. As noted above, the coefficients measure the degree of correlation between returns from each year and the previous year for the same series. Highly positive (near 1) serial correlations indicate trends, while highly negative (near -1) serial correlations indicate cycles. Serial correlations near zero suggest no patterns (i.e., random walks).

EXHIBIT 28
RISK PREMIUMS AND INFLATION:
SERIAL AND CROSS-CORRELATIONS
OF HISTORICAL YEARLY RETURNS*
(1926-1987)

	Equity Risk Premiums	Small-Stock Premiums	Default Premiums	Horizon Premiums	Inflation Rates
Equity Risk Premiums	1.00				
Small-Stock Premiums	0.39	1.00			
Default Premiums	0.23	0.13	1.00		
Horizon Premiums	0.16	−0.07	−0.21	1.00	
Inflation Rates	−0.08	0.15	−0.01	−0.34	1.00
Serial Correlations	0.02	0.38	−0.30	0.11	0.64

*The standard error for all estimates is 0.13

EXHIBIT 29
INFLATION-ADJUSTED BASIC SERIES:
SERIAL AND CROSS-CORRELATIONS OF
HISTORICAL YEARLY RETURNS*
(1926-1987)

	Common Stocks	Small Stocks	Inflation-Adjusted Total Returns				
			Long-Term Corp Bonds	Long-Term Govt Bonds	Inter-mediate Govt Bonds	T-Bills (Real Interest Rates)	Inflation Rates
Inflation-Adjusted:							
Common Stocks	1.00						
Small Stocks	0.82	1.00					
LT Corporate Bonds	0.27	0.11	1.00				
LT Government Bonds	0.20	0.03	0.95	1.00			
Intermed. Govt. Bonds	0.15	−0.02	0.94	0.94	1.00		
Treasury Bills (Real Interest Rates)	0.09	−0.06	0.61	0.62	0.77	1.00	
Inflation Rates	−0.22	−0.07	−0.61	−0.60	−0.66	−0.76	1.00
Serial Correlations	0.00	0.07	0.28	0.18	0.34	0.66	0.64

*The standard error for all estimates is 0.13.

Serial Correlation in the Component Series: Trends or Random Walks?

The risk-return relations in the historical data are represented in the equity risk premiums, the small-stock premiums, the bond horizon premiums, and the bond default premiums. The real/nominal historical relations are represented in the inflation rates and the real interest rates. (See Exhibits 20 and 21.) The objective is to uncover whether each series is random or whether it is subject to any trends or cycles.

Each of the component series' serial correlations can be interpreted as following a random walk, trend, or uncertain path. Equity risk premiums and bond horizon premiums appear to follow random walks. Conversely, there is strong evidence that both inflation rates and real riskless rates follow trends. Small-stock premiums and bond default premiums fall into a middle range; it cannot be determined with certainty that they follow either a trend or a random walk, although the serial correlation of small-stock premiums suggests some kind of pattern. The interpretation of each of the component series' correlations is in Exhibit 30.

The term "random walk" is used somewhat loosely here. In a random walk, the best estimate of the next index level is the last index level. The cumulative index values formed by linking the returns on random variables follow a random walk, in the formal sense. The randomly distributed returns themselves are more precisely described as a stationary process with no serial correlation. In such a process, the best estimate of the next return is the arithmetic mean of historical returns.

The terminology used here has the advantage of being intuitively sensible. A random variable is said to follow a

EXHIBIT 30
INTERPRETATION OF THE YEARLY
FIRST-ORDER SERIAL
CORRELATIONS FOR COMPONENT SERIES

Series	Serial Correlation	Interpretation*
Equity Risk Premiums	0.02	Random Walk
Small-Stock Premiums	0.38	Likely Trend
Bond Default Premiums	0.30	Uncertain
Bond Horizon Premiums	0.11	Random Walk
Inflation Rates	0.64	Trend
Real Interest Rates	0.66	Trend

*The standard error for all estimates is 0.13. To be statistically different from zero at the 5 percent significance level, serial correlations must have an absolute value greater than 0.26.

random walk. One should be aware, however, of the formal definitions set forth above.

Changes in the Risk of Assets over Time

If a time series is stable, its risk (volatility) will not change much over time. A simple test of stability is to examine standard deviations of the series over different subperiods.

Exhibit 31 displays the annualized standard deviation of monthly returns on each of the basic and derived series for every year from 1926 to 1987. The standard deviation of a series for a particular year is the standard deviation of the 12 monthly returns for that year (around that year's arithmetic mean). This monthly estimate is then annualized, i.e., converted to annual-equivalent form, by multiplying by the square root of 12.

Earlier, in Exhibits 2 and 15 through 18, we reported the 62-year standard deviation of annual returns (around the 62-year annual arithmetic mean). It is important to remember that the estimates in Exhibit 31 are not strictly comparable to the annual 62-year results because the arithmetic mean drifts for a series which does not follow a random walk. A series with a drifting mean will have much higher deviations around its long-term mean than it has around the mean during a particular calendar year.

Exhibit 31 is revealing. Common stocks and equity risk premiums have virtually the same monthly standard deviations because there is very little deviation in the U.S. Treasury bill series. These two series also have much higher variability in the pre-World War II period than in the postwar period. On the other hand, the various bond series (long- and intermediate-term government bonds, long-term corporate bonds, horizon premiums, and default premiums) have been quite volatile in the Great Depression and even more so recently.

EXHIBIT 31
BASIC AND DERIVED SERIES:
ANNUALIZED MONTHLY STANDARD
DEVIATIONS FOR EACH YEAR (1926-1987)
(Standard Deviations in Percent)

Year	Basic Series							Derived Series				
	Common Stocks	Small Stocks	Long-Term Corp. Bonds	Long-Term Govt. Bonds	Interm. Govt. Bonds	U.S. Treas. Bills	Consumer Price Index	Equity Risk Premiums	Small-Stock Premiums	Bond Default Premiums	Bond Horizon Premiums	Inflation-Adjusted T-Bills
1926	11.74	16.54	0.90	1.76	0.97	0.31	2.05	11.75	10.67	1.64	1.61	1.98
1927	13.22	17.32	1.39	2.66	1.01	0.11	2.83	13.18	12.29	2.94	2.62	2.89
1928	17.35	20.56	1.82	3.21	1.26	0.59	1.73	17.17	14.64	2.68	3.20	1.78
1929	31.02	32.72	2.35	6.52	2.67	0.20	1.62	30.89	13.67	7.01	6.43	1.56
1930	26.26	36.19	2.21	2.25	2.29	0.29	2.15	26.17	13.78	2.38	2.07	2.13
1931	43.94	63.85	6.00	5.49	3.80	0.16	1.48	43.90	29.00	5.08	5.49	1.58
1932	68.02	94.36	7.00	10.31	2.72	0.29	1.93	68.05	37.41	14.95	10.27	2.15
1933	56.07	86.73	10.65	5.11	3.64	0.10	4.21	55.95	42.90	6.98	5.07	4.15
1934	22.22	51.58	2.75	4.12	3.76	0.04	1.99	22.20	31.96	2.44	4.09	1.97
1935	16.33	25.43	2.32	2.76	2.61	0.01	2.12	16.33	15.57	1.31	2.76	2.10
1936	14.40	38.39	1.11	2.10	1.23	0.02	1.54	14.39	29.57	1.79	2.11	1.52
1937	23.36	42.33	1.94	5.02	2.41	0.05	1.69	23.35	23.62	3.84	5.01	1.67
1938	41.19	66.48	2.26	2.23	2.34	0.07	1.83	41.17	28.96	1.88	2.20	1.84
1939	29.51	70.55	5.16	8.11	4.85	0.02	2.27	29.50	39.35	8.51	8.12	2.23
1940	26.70	42.81	1.96	4.92	3.16	0.02	1.08	26.69	23.62	4.01	4.91	1.08
1941	14.30	29.98	1.63	3.67	1.49	0.03	2.11	14.28	19.72	3.53	3.67	2.07
1942	14.71	25.75	0.71	1.38	0.78	0.03	1.28	14.68	21.20	1.16	1.38	1.27
1943	15.62	36.95	0.88	0.64	0.49	0.01	2.29	15.62	22.73	0.58	0.64	2.27
1944	7.86	18.97	1.28	0.36	0.28	0.01	0.95	7.86	11.93	1.10	0.36	0.95
1945	13.13	21.96	1.37	2.70	0.49	0.01	1.29	13.13	13.42	2.03	2.71	1.28
1946	18.70	28.89	2.12	2.74	0.93	0.00	5.70	18.69	12.52	1.71	2.73	5.40
1947	9.59	17.72	2.18	2.93	0.52	0.07	3.09	9.58	10.95	3.25	2.98	3.01
1948	19.94	23.70	2.12	1.90	0.58	0.07	2.83	19.92	6.88	1.90	1.91	2.77
1949	10.19	15.65	2.10	1.72	0.46	0.02	1.66	10.19	6.65	2.51	1.72	1.66
1950	10.79	15.03	1.05	1.45	0.33	0.03	1.72	10.78	8.37	1.32	1.45	1.69
1951	12.23	14.74	4.02	3.14	1.91	0.05	1.70	12.20	6.93	2.63	3.11	1.69
1952	11.32	9.35	2.76	3.20	1.30	0.07	1.14	11.31	4.29	3.74	3.24	1.13
1953	9.35	11.49	5.35	4.99	3.16	0.10	1.00	9.39	9.16	3.50	4.98	0.94
1954	12.95	12.84	2.24	3.25	1.88	0.06	0.74	12.92	9.57	2.36	3.24	0.76

EXHIBIT 31 (Continued)

Year	Basic Series							Derived Series				
	Common Stocks	Small Stocks	Long-Term Corp. Bonds	Long-Term Govt. Bonds	Interm. Govt. Bonds	U.S. Treas. Bills	Consumer Price Index	Equity Risk Premiums	Small-Stock Premiums	Bond Default Premiums	Bond Horizon Premiums	Inflation-Adjusted T-Bills
1955	12.41	6.48	2.16	3.64	1.66	0.13	0.67	12.43	9.52	2.32	3.56	0.70
1956	14.76	8.04	3.20	4.50	2.65	0.10	1.05	14.75	7.99	2.63	4.47	1.00
1957	12.62	11.92	8.66	7.71	5.19	0.07	0.65	12.58	10.31	5.41	7.67	0.65
1958	6.27	9.70	4.65	6.64	4.55	0.26	0.88	6.16	7.01	3.59	6.60	0.88
1959	8.00	8.95	3.94	3.31	2.73	0.17	0.64	8.00	7.03	3.30	3.33	0.59
1960	13.42	13.62	3.63	5.72	4.50	0.26	0.70	13.46	7.30	4.00	5.65	0.79
1961	8.92	14.54	3.47	3.51	1.55	0.07	0.51	8.92	7.41	3.79	3.54	0.50
1962	20.09	23.39	2.12	3.48	2.05	0.08	0.66	20.04	8.61	2.15	3.49	0.69
1963	9.81	11.01	1.23	0.71	0.59	0.08	0.54	9.77	7.20	1.27	0.74	0.55
1964	4.02	5.80	1.40	0.88	0.75	0.06	0.40	4.01	3.58	1.82	0.87	0.38
1965	8.54	14.72	1.96	1.50	1.81	0.08	0.65	8.57	9.00	1.10	1.51	0.63
1966	10.89	18.60	4.79	7.78	3.96	0.11	0.69	10.84	13.20	5.55	7.71	0.72
1967	12.11	20.66	7.65	7.16	3.77	0.15	0.43	12.04	11.97	4.92	7.09	0.53
1968	13.02	20.79	7.20	7.92	3.36	0.09	0.40	12.95	13.47	3.48	7.86	0.40
1969	12.98	23.47	7.46	10.36	5.57	0.20	0.59	12.91	11.58	7.59	10.32	0.62
1970	20.29	30.93	9.61	13.42	6.10	0.21	0.42	20.23	16.02	8.73	13.31	0.47
1971	13.67	24.87	10.04	9.47	6.45	0.18	0.55	13.62	14.18	6.21	9.37	0.63
1972	6.63	15.70	3.01	5.55	1.88	0.16	0.40	6.61	12.70	3.91	5.51	0.41
1973	13.87	29.05	7.46	8.19	4.78	0.34	1.42	13.68	16.92	3.21	8.05	1.36
1974	23.93	23.82	11.68	8.28	5.43	0.34	0.82	23.99	19.88	6.15	8.27	0.92
1975	17.89	29.82	10.07	8.38	5.29	0.20	0.73	17.77	17.75	4.23	8.27	0.77
1976	13.72	31.67	4.44	4.71	3.80	0.13	0.46	13.60	21.49	1.53	4.67	0.45
1977	9.55	13.70	4.50	5.55	2.70	0.19	0.72	9.46	10.06	1.27	5.52	0.87
1978	16.61	32.63	4.45	4.49	2.01	0.33	0.62	16.54	22.44	1.61	4.53	0.79
1979	13.36	24.05	10.77	10.90	7.02	0.26	0.47	13.24	12.98	2.24	10.79	0.61
1980	18.31	27.83	20.80	21.33	15.93	0.89	1.31	18.55	13.66	4.40	20.69	1.19
1981	12.89	18.56	20.73	22.16	10.82	0.45	1.07	12.74	13.44	5.18	21.87	0.95
1982	19.14	17.21	12.47	10.51	7.03	0.71	1.59	19.33	7.44	4.37	10.70	1.34
1983	9.92	15.82	11.16	11.33	5.35	0.17	0.71	9.92	12.58	3.63	11.27	0.65
1984	14.01	15.29	12.90	11.54	6.35	0.31	0.59	13.88	4.92	2.85	11.30	0.58
1985	12.17	14.59	10.76	12.22	5.64	0.16	0.32	12.05	6.76	2.84	12.07	0.33
1986	17.94	14.38	8.19	17.30	5.73	0.19	1.02	17.83	7.24	9.80	17.16	1.12
1987	30.50	34.53	9.64	10.28	4.80	0.22	0.66	30.45	12.71	2.96	10.15	0.64

The series with drifting means (U.S. Treasury bills, inflation rates, and inflation-adjusted U.S. Treasury bills) all tend to have very low annualized monthly standard deviations, reflecting the fact that these series are quite predictable from month to month. Over the long term, however, these series are much less predictable because it is difficult to predict the direction and magnitude of the drift in the long-term mean.

8.   Firm Size and Return

Introduction

One of the most remarkable discoveries of modern finance is Rolf Banz's finding of a relation between firm size and return (Banz 1981). On average, small companies have higher returns than large ones. Earlier chapters document this phenomenon for the smallest stocks on the NYSE. In this chapter, we examine the returns of the entire spectrum of firm sizes. Firm size is defined throughout as equity market capitalization—that is, price per share times the number of shares outstanding. We rank all stocks listed on the NYSE according to their size, and sort them into 10 size groups (each containing one-tenth of the stocks). The group containing the largest stocks is the first decile, and that containing the smallest stocks, the tenth.

Each portfolio is market-capitalization weighted. All returns are total returns. We rerank stocks annually to determine the group boundaries, in contrast to the five-year rerankings used to generate the small-company return series described in earlier chapters.

The relation between firm size and return cuts across the entire size spectrum. It is not restricted to just the smallest stocks.

The firm size phenomenon is remarkable in several ways. First, the greater risk of small stocks does not, in the context of the capital asset pricing model (CAPM), account for their higher returns. In the CAPM, only systematic, or beta, risk is rewarded; small stocks have abnormal returns—that is, returns in excess of those implied by the betas of small stocks. This is Banz's key finding.

Several corollary findings about firm size and return are as unexpected as the finding of higher returns on small stocks. The calendar annual return differences between small and large companies are serially correlated. This suggests that past annual returns may be of some value in predicting future annual returns. Such serial correlation, or autocorrelation, is practically unknown in the market for large stocks and in most other capital markets. In addition, the firm-size effect is seasonal. For example, small stocks outperformed large stocks in the month of January in a great many years. Again, such predictability is surprising and suspicious in light of modern capital market theory. These three aspects of the firm-size effect will be analyzed after the data are presented.

Presentation of the Data

Summary statistics of annual returns on the 10 deciles, over the period 1926-87, are presented in Exhibit 32. The average return tends to increase from the largest decile to the smallest. Because securities are ranked annually, returns on the ninth and tenth deciles are higher than those suggested by the small-company stock index presented in earlier chapters.

The total risk, or standard deviation of annual returns, also increases as firm size decreases. The serial correlation point estimates are near zero for all but the smallest two or three deciles.

Exhibit 33 provides a year-by-year history of the returns for the different size categories. Exhibit 34 shows the

EXHIBIT 32
CAPITALIZATION DECILES OF THE NYSE:
SUMMARY STATISTICS OF ANNUAL RETURNS
(1926-1987)

Decile	Geometric Mean	Arithmetic Mean	Standard Deviation	First-Order Auto-Correlation
1 (largest)	9.13 %	10.96 %	19.43 %	0.042
2	10.58	13.05	22.75	0.058
3	10.08	12.91	24.50	0.035
4	11.74	15.19	28.26	−0.009
5	11.65	15.47	29.33	0.025
6	11.56	15.36	28.97	0.037
7	12.11	16.80	32.70	0.066
8	11.71	16.81	33.69	0.087
9	13.23	19.04	36.74	0.133
10 (smallest)	14.98	22.87	46.03	0.133
NYSE Value-Weighted Index	9.56	11.66	20.93	0.034

EXHIBIT 33
YEAR-BY-YEAR RETURNS ON DECILE PORTFOLIOS OF THE NYSE
SORTED BY MARKET CAPITALIZATION
(1926-1987)
(Returns in decimal form)

Year	Decile 1	Decile 2	Decile 3	Decile 4	Decile 5	Decile 6	Decile 7	Decile 8	Decile 9	Decile 10
1926	0.1431	0.0831	0.0468	0.0315	-0.0549	0.0432	-0.0477	-0.0811	-0.0284	0.0717
1927	0.3440	0.2998	0.2951	0.4103	0.3359	0.2338	0.3474	0.3079	0.2042	0.3656
1928	0.3714	0.4339	0.3642	0.4028	0.5019	0.3367	0.3650	0.3885	0.6698	0.8024
1929	-0.0893	-0.0741	-0.2269	-0.2349	-0.2330	-0.3119	-0.3739	-0.4295	-0.4620	-0.4904
1930	-0.2488	-0.3185	-0.3855	-0.3395	-0.3396	-0.3541	-0.3943	-0.4436	-0.4752	-0.4041
1931	-0.4269	-0.4934	-0.5007	-0.4455	-0.4714	-0.4546	-0.4738	-0.4936	-0.4689	-0.5345
1932	-0.0883	-0.0360	-0.0110	-0.0835	-0.2013	-0.0577	-0.1824	-0.1044	-0.0598	-0.0035
1933	0.4852	0.7104	0.8499	1.1860	1.0863	1.1049	1.0998	1.1857	1.3090	2.1455
1934	0.0213	0.0669	0.0864	0.1383	0.1575	0.1553	0.1818	0.1840	0.2448	0.3955
1935	0.4229	0.5088	0.3848	0.3800	0.6274	0.5066	0.7360	0.5221	0.7495	0.5753
1936	0.3146	0.3035	0.2707	0.4497	0.4975	0.4627	0.5762	0.6332	0.6104	0.6641
1937	-0.3126	-0.3696	-0.3888	-0.4344	-0.4688	-0.4970	-0.4817	-0.5324	-0.5144	-0.5772
1938	0.2482	0.3325	0.3466	0.3766	0.4137	0.4128	0.3677	0.3588	0.3342	0.0558
1939	0.0413	-0.0591	-0.0330	-0.0028	-0.0134	0.0203	0.0417	-0.1020	-0.1050	0.0180
1940	-0.0767	-0.1000	-0.0766	-0.0638	-0.0158	-0.0556	-0.0724	-0.0264	-0.0744	-0.2956
1941	-0.1045	-0.0662	-0.0531	-0.0879	-0.1331	-0.0664	-0.1016	-0.1115	-0.0777	-0.0691
1942	0.1329	0.2405	0.1954	0.2330	0.2412	0.2726	0.2653	0.3475	0.4722	0.7106
1943	0.2310	0.3389	0.3427	0.4150	0.4876	0.4309	0.7023	0.6868	0.9447	1.1796
1944	0.1701	0.2595	0.2322	0.3340	0.3999	0.4027	0.3996	0.5102	0.5636	0.6771
1945	0.2989	0.4895	0.4975	0.6252	0.5911	0.5639	0.6412	0.6782	0.7384	0.9591
1946	-0.0525	-0.0336	-0.0912	-0.0942	-0.1103	-0.0480	-0.1637	-0.1091	-0.0810	-0.1757
1947	0.0528	0.0005	-0.0001	0.0297	0.0296	-0.0097	-0.0253	0.0031	-0.0385	0.0199
1948	0.0380	0.0188	0.0017	-0.0073	-0.0262	-0.0256	-0.0463	-0.0677	-0.0853	0.0006
1949	0.1855	0.2677	0.2213	0.2128	0.1998	0.2261	0.1832	0.2109	0.1922	0.2348
1950	0.2858	0.3249	0.2500	0.3297	0.4093	0.3206	0.3959	0.4138	0.4090	0.6024
1951	0.2166	0.2353	0.1985	0.1866	0.1389	0.1680	0.1541	0.1677	0.1009	0.0303
1952	0.1398	0.1376	0.1221	0.1128	0.1120	0.0925	0.1172	0.0864	0.0801	0.0526
1953	0.0059	0.0199	0.0011	-0.0215	-0.0268	-0.0085	-0.0219	-0.0490	-0.0505	-0.0525
1954	0.4885	0.4758	0.5863	0.5628	0.5679	0.6099	0.6034	0.5369	0.6105	0.6660

EXHIBIT 33 (Continued)

Year	Decile 1	Decile 2	Decile 3	Decile 4	Decile 5	Decile 6	Decile 7	Decile 8	Decile 9	Decile 10
1955	0.2829	0.2132	0.1645	0.1758	0.2084	0.2158	0.1909	0.2014	0.2070	0.2489
1956	0.0849	0.1155	0.0678	0.0934	0.0739	0.0961	0.0610	0.0936	0.0766	-0.0186
1957	-0.1043	-0.0822	-0.1241	-0.1088	-0.1166	-0.1655	-0.1363	-0.1597	-0.1490	-0.1297
1958	0.4024	0.4784	0.5388	0.5795	0.5782	0.5760	0.6794	0.6870	0.6640	0.7907
1959	0.1290	0.0832	0.1396	0.1674	0.1674	0.1925	0.1763	0.1980	0.2203	0.1488
1960	-0.0077	0.0731	0.0374	0.0218	-0.0323	-0.0009	-0.0841	0.0031	-0.0541	-0.0765
1961	0.2628	0.2892	0.2948	0.2893	0.2947	0.2550	0.3710	0.2968	0.3402	0.2772
1962	-0.0823	-0.0920	-0.1105	-0.1353	-0.1368	-0.1909	-0.1254	-0.1158	-0.1467	-0.0827
1963	0.2286	0.1955	0.1793	0.1721	0.1602	0.1802	0.1779	0.2347	0.2391	0.1671
1964	0.1627	0.1464	0.1865	0.1868	0.1683	0.1451	0.1893	0.1578	0.2133	0.2595
1965	0.0878	0.2118	0.2436	0.2573	0.2778	0.3770	0.3591	0.3781	0.3647	0.4564
1966	-0.1025	-0.0471	-0.0680	-0.0577	-0.0614	-0.1106	-0.0612	-0.0695	-0.0402	-0.1375
1967	0.2147	0.2288	0.3306	0.4367	0.5235	0.5046	0.7584	0.7082	0.7422	0.9640
1968	0.0742	0.1752	0.1863	0.1963	0.2780	0.3057	0.3289	0.3364	0.4258	0.6347
1969	-0.0560	-0.1442	-0.1013	-0.1692	-0.1764	-0.2215	-0.2087	-0.2748	-0.2896	-0.2666
1970	0.0299	0.0046	0.0236	-0.0221	-0.0333	-0.0403	-0.0540	-0.0607	-0.0703	-0.0749
1971	0.1444	0.1456	0.2041	0.2239	0.1746	0.2912	0.1666	0.1886	0.1504	0.1954
1972	0.2289	0.1197	0.1061	0.1029	0.0528	0.0360	0.0829	0.0602	0.0596	0.0353
1973	-0.1296	-0.2088	-0.2501	-0.2492	-0.2882	-0.2723	-0.3175	-0.3225	-0.3318	-0.3126
1974	-0.2765	-0.2367	-0.2418	-0.2709	-0.2476	-0.2641	-0.2377	-0.2730	-0.2768	-0.2351
1975	0.3117	0.4562	0.5406	0.6768	0.5580	0.5758	0.6434	0.6821	0.6999	0.7609
1976	0.2117	0.2977	0.3714	0.3878	0.4493	0.4770	0.4897	0.5845	0.5698	0.5786
1977	-0.0843	-0.0372	-0.0142	0.0415	0.0970	0.1502	0.1717	0.1897	0.2399	0.2022
1978	0.0720	0.0524	0.0911	0.0973	0.0916	0.1608	0.1514	0.1394	0.1917	0.1954
1979	0.1491	0.2814	0.3605	0.3281	0.3436	0.3607	0.4517	0.4150	0.4978	0.4348
1980	0.3371	0.3177	0.3015	0.3224	0.2792	0.3199	0.3480	0.3023	0.3014	0.2357
1981	-0.0916	0.0310	0.0427	0.0168	0.0891	0.0677	0.0428	0.1091	0.1401	0.1613
1982	0.1838	0.1883	0.2376	0.2726	0.3673	0.3318	0.3809	0.4094	0.3734	0.3863
1983	0.2197	0.1929	0.2492	0.2859	0.2720	0.3264	0.3397	0.3949	0.4053	0.5111
1984	0.0725	0.0683	-0.0020	-0.0117	0.0021	0.0160	-0.0057	-0.0150	0.0269	-0.0866
1985	0.3050	0.3852	0.3082	0.3223	0.2995	0.2583	0.2376	0.2653	0.2711	0.3604
1986	0.2076	0.2000	0.1482	0.1462	0.1856	0.1212	0.1304	0.0799	0.0947	0.0550
1987	0.0871	-0.0093	0.0372	0.0386	-0.0086	-0.0246	-0.0757	-0.0708	-0.0635	-0.0811

EXHIBIT 34
YEAR-END INDEX VALUES OF RETURNS ON DECILE PORTFOLIOS OF THE NYSE
SORTED BY MARKET CAPITALIZATION
(1925-1987)
(Year-end 1925 = 1.000)

Year	Decile 1	Decile 2	Decile 3	Decile 4	Decile 5	Decile 6	Decile 7	Decile 8	Decile 9	Decile 10
1925	1.000	1.000	1.000	1.000	1.000	1.000	1.000	1.000	1.000	1.000
1926	1.143	1.083	1.047	1.031	0.945	1.043	0.952	0.919	0.972	1.072
1927	1.536	1.408	1.356	1.455	1.263	1.287	1.283	1.202	1.170	1.463
1928	2.107	2.019	1.849	2.041	1.896	1.720	1.751	1.669	1.954	2.638
1929	1.919	1.869	1.430	1.561	1.454	1.184	1.097	0.952	1.051	1.344
1930	1.441	1.274	0.879	1.031	0.961	0.765	0.664	0.530	0.552	0.801
1931	0.826	0.645	0.439	0.572	0.508	0.417	0.349	0.268	0.293	0.373
1932	0.753	0.622	0.434	0.524	0.406	0.393	0.286	0.240	0.275	0.372
1933	1.118	1.064	0.803	1.146	0.846	0.827	0.600	0.525	0.636	1.169
1934	1.142	1.135	0.872	1.304	0.979	0.956	0.709	0.622	0.792	1.631
1935	1.625	1.713	1.207	1.800	1.594	1.440	1.231	0.946	1.385	2.569
1936	2.137	2.233	1.534	2.609	2.387	2.106	1.940	1.546	2.230	4.276
1937	1.469	1.408	0.938	1.476	1.268	1.059	1.006	0.723	1.083	1.808
1938	1.833	1.876	1.263	2.031	1.792	1.496	1.375	0.982	1.445	1.909
1939	1.909	1.765	1.221	2.026	1.768	1.527	1.433	0.882	1.293	1.943
1940	1.763	1.588	1.127	1.896	1.741	1.442	1.329	0.859	1.197	1.369
1941	1.578	1.483	1.068	1.730	1.509	1.346	1.194	0.763	1.104	1.274
1942	1.788	1.840	1.276	2.133	1.873	1.713	1.511	1.028	1.625	2.179
1943	2.201	2.464	1.713	3.018	2.786	2.452	2.572	1.734	3.161	4.750
1944	2.576	3.103	2.111	4.026	3.900	3.439	3.599	2.619	4.943	7.966
1945	3.346	4.622	3.162	6.543	6.206	5.378	5.907	4.395	8.592	15.606
1946	3.170	4.466	2.873	5.926	5.521	5.120	4.940	3.915	7.897	12.863
1947	3.337	4.469	2.873	6.102	5.685	5.070	4.816	3.927	7.593	13.119
1948	3.464	4.553	2.878	6.058	5.536	4.940	4.592	3.661	6.945	13.127
1949	4.107	5.771	3.515	7.347	6.642	6.057	5.434	4.434	8.280	16.209
1950	5.281	7.647	4.394	9.769	9.361	7.999	7.585	6.268	11.666	25.972
1951	6.425	9.446	5.266	11.592	10.661	9.343	8.754	7.319	12.843	26.761
1952	7.323	10.746	5.909	12.899	11.855	10.207	9.780	7.951	13.873	28.167
1953	7.366	10.959	5.915	12.622	11.537	10.120	9.566	7.562	13.172	26.689
1954	10.965	16.173	9.383	19.724	18.090	16.291	15.337	11.621	21.214	44.465

EXHIBIT 34 (Continued)

Year	Decile 1	Decile 2	Decile 3	Decile 4	Decile 5	Decile 6	Decile 7	Decile 8	Decile 9	Decile 10
1955	14.067	19.622	10.927	23.192	21.859	19.807	18.266	13.962	25.606	55.534
1956	15.262	21.888	11.667	25.359	23.475	21.710	19.380	15.269	27.568	54.500
1957	13.670	20.088	10.220	22.600	20.738	18.116	16.738	12.830	23.462	47.433
1958	19.171	29.697	15.725	35.697	32.728	28.552	28.111	21.644	39.041	84.939
1959	21.644	32.169	17.921	41.672	38.207	34.047	33.068	25.929	47.643	97.577
1960	21.478	34.521	18.590	42.581	36.974	34.017	30.287	26.009	45.068	90.116
1961	27.123	44.506	24.071	54.902	47.872	42.691	41.522	33.727	60.398	115.095
1962	24.891	40.413	21.410	47.474	41.324	34.542	36.313	29.822	51.535	105.580
1963	30.582	48.314	25.249	55.645	47.943	40.767	42.774	36.822	63.858	123.221
1964	35.559	55.386	29.957	66.038	56.013	46.683	50.872	42.632	77.476	155.198
1965	38.680	67.119	37.256	83.028	71.571	64.283	69.142	58.750	105.730	226.027
1966	34.716	63.957	34.721	78.237	67.180	57.171	64.911	54.667	101.481	194.938
1967	42.170	78.591	46.199	112.401	102.348	86.017	114.140	93.379	176.804	382.851
1968	45.300	92.360	54.806	134.470	130.805	112.310	151.682	124.789	252.091	625.858
1969	42.763	79.042	49.254	111.716	107.735	87.432	120.026	90.492	179.089	459.028
1970	44.040	79.407	50.417	109.246	104.092	83.911	113.539	84.996	166.499	424.639
1971	50.397	90.967	60.708	133.705	122.267	108.344	132.456	101.029	191.533	507.612
1972	61.935	101.853	67.147	147.469	128.720	112.246	143.434	107.114	202.950	525.549
1973	53.907	80.585	50.351	110.721	91.627	81.677	97.894	72.574	135.612	361.241
1974	39.002	61.507	38.178	80.722	68.941	60.104	74.620	52.762	98.076	276.324
1975	51.159	89.568	58.815	135.357	107.409	94.712	122.632	88.752	166.723	486.581
1976	61.991	116.232	80.656	187.853	155.671	139.887	182.685	140.625	261.721	768.130
1977	56.765	111.902	79.513	195.647	170.765	160.891	214.057	167.304	324.498	923.447
1978	60.851	117.767	86.757	214.681	186.415	186.761	246.463	190.622	386.714	1103.904
1979	69.926	150.912	118.037	285.123	250.467	254.126	357.781	269.731	579.225	1583.915
1980	93.497	198.851	153.621	377.036	320.402	335.425	482.281	351.283	753.777	1957.298
1981	84.935	205.015	160.184	383.356	348.949	358.127	502.941	389.623	859.390	2273.062
1982	100.547	243.612	198.251	487.873	477.132	476.941	694.536	549.141	1180.284	3151.129
1983	122.636	290.593	247.653	627.345	606.919	632.620	930.452	766.012	1658.675	4761.614
1984	131.525	310.437	247.150	620.006	608.171	642.766	925.146	754.534	1703.315	4349.399
1985	171.641	430.028	323.317	819.819	790.322	808.780	1144.917	954.726	2165.166	5916.709
1986	207.279	516.031	371.246	939.637	937.028	906.793	1294.264	1030.961	2370.112	6241.886
1987	225.326	511.210	385.072	975.870	928.982	884.490	1196.280	958.001	2219.541	5735.424

growth of a $1.00 invested at year-end 1925 in each of the categories.

The magnitude of the firm-size effect in some years is noteworthy. Although the largest stocks actually declined in 1977, the smallest stocks rose more than 20 percent. A more extreme case occurred in the depression-recovery year of 1933, when the difference between first and tenth decile returns was over 170 percent. This near independence of the smallest and largest firms is common. It is as if there is not one single stock market, but several markets, each one moving differently according to the size of its firms.

Size of the Deciles

Exhibit 35 reveals that most of the market value of the stocks listed on the NYSE is represented by the top three deciles. Two-thirds of the value is represented by the first decile, which currently consists of about 150 stocks. The smallest decile represents only 0.25 percent of the market value of the NYSE. The data in Exhibit 35 are averages across all years; of course, the proportions represented by the various deciles vary from year to year.

It is important to note that these proportions do not represent the AMEX or OTC markets. Small firms, as defined by NYSE rankings, make up far higher proportions of value in the AMEX and OTC markets. The aggregate market value of small firms in the AMEX and OTC markets is at least twice as large as the corresponding value on the NYSE. Thus, we cannot assume that findings which hold for NYSE firms will hold for firms elsewhere.

Serial Correlation in Small-Stock Returns

The serial correlation, or first-order autocorrelation, of returns on large capitalization stocks is near zero (see

Exhibit 32). If stock returns were autocorrelated, then one would gain some information from past returns. On the other hand, the first-order autocorrelation for the smallest deciles is above 0.1. This observation bears further examination.

To remove the randomizing effect of the market as a whole, we subtract [geometrically as in equation (5) in Chapter 4] the returns on the first decile from the returns on the other nine deciles. These series differences exhibit greater serial correlation than the decile series themselves. Autocorrelations of the excess returns of deciles two through ten are presented in Exhibit 36. These autocorrelations suggest some predictability of smaller-company excess returns. Caution is necessary, however. The autocorrelation of small-company excess returns for noncalendar years (February-through-January years, and so forth) do not always confirm the results shown for calendar years (January through December). The results for the noncalendar years, not shown in this book, mean that predicting small-company excess returns may not be easy.

Seasonality

Unlike returns on large stocks, the returns on small-company stocks appear to be seasonal. Small-company stocks outperform larger stocks more often and by larger amounts than in any other month. This "January effect" was first documented by Donald Keim (1983).

Exhibit 37 shows the returns of capitalization deciles two through ten in excess of the return on decile one. This exhibit segregates excess returns into months. For each decile, for each month, the exhibit shows both the average excess return and the number of times the excess return is positive. These two statistics measure the seasonality of the excess return in slightly different ways. The average excess

EXHIBIT 35
MARKET VALUE OF THE 10 CAPITALIZATION DECILES AS A PERCENTAGE OF THE TOTAL NYSE MARKET VALUE
(Average over 1926-1987)

Average Decile	Percent of Total Capitalization
1 (largest)	65.29
2	14.49
3	7.55
4	4.54
5	2.97
6	2.02
7	1.38
8	0.92
9	0.58
10 (smallest)	0.27

EXHIBIT 36
FIRST-ORDER AUTOCORRELATIONS OF
ANNUAL DECILE RETURNS IN EXCESS OF
THE FIRST (LARGEST) DECILE
(1926-1987)

Decile	First-Order Autocorrelation of Decile Return in Excess of Decile One Return
2	0.159
3	0.303
4	0.186
5	0.194
6	0.273
7	0.312
8	0.322
9	0.374
10 (smallest)	0.310

EXHIBIT 37
RETURNS ON CAPITALIZATION DECILES OF NYSE STOCKS, IN EXCESS OF THE FIRST (LARGEST) DECILE
(1926-1987)

Decile	Jan	Feb	Mar	Apr	May	Jun	Jul	Aug	Sep	Oct	Nov	Dec	Total (Jan-Dec)
2	1.16% 51	0.16% 34	-0.05% 27	-0.40% 24	0.05% 35	0.08% 32	0.00% 30	0.09% 30	-0.04% 29	-0.06% 33	0.32% 41	0.20% 38	1.52%
3	1.46 48	0.09 38	0.02 29	-0.34 24	-0.21 25	-0.13 28	0.12 30	-0.08 32	0.16 32	-0.29 30	0.33 41	0.03 37	1.15
4	1.85 49	0.36 37	-0.11 32	-0.09 27	-0.05 30	-0.13 29	0.21 31	0.22 37	0.38 34	-0.47 27	0.56 39	0.06 29	2.80
5	2.89 49	0.33 36	-0.22 28	-0.42 26	-0.16 26	-0.16 28	0.25 29	0.30 34	0.13 28	-0.60 28	0.39 33	0.16 31	2.89
6	3.43 53	0.29 36	-0.36 31	-0.36 25	0.09 25	-0.47 24	0.16 32	0.36 34	0.22 37	-0.98 28	0.58 35	-0.04 30	2.94
7	4.11 52	0.60 40	-0.23 34	-0.23 26	0.28 28	-0.46 23	0.27 31	-0.04 32	0.15 33	-0.65 27	0.30 31	-0.44 25	3.66
8	5.42 51	0.69 40	-0.47 29	-0.46 24	0.21 25	-0.69 24	0.35 32	-0.05 26	-0.23 32	-0.83 29	0.39 32	-0.65 28	3.69
9	7.06 56	0.87 36	-0.08 34	-0.40 25	0.20 27	-0.71 24	0.45 33	0.13 29	-0.08 29	-0.91 27	0.22 30	-1.07 24	5.67
10	10.27 57	0.94 32	-0.94 26	-0.30 23	0.37 29	-0.64 24	0.69 32	-0.07 26	0.83 30	-1.23 24	-0.27 23	-1.26 24	8.40

First row: average excess return in percent
Second row: number of times excess return was positive (in 62 years)

return shows the size of the effect, and the number of times positive shows the reliability of the effect.

Virtually all of the small-stock effect occurs in January. The other months are, on net, negative for small stocks. Excess returns in January relate to size in a precisely rank-ordered fashion. This January phenomenon seems to pervade all size groups.

9.   Estimating The Cost Of Capital Or Discount Rate

The data in this book may be used to forecast future returns on assets and portfolios. Such forecasts may take the form of probability distributions of future returns, so that risk as well as expected return is accounted for in the forecast. The means of these probabilistic forecasts have a useful application in the estimation of the cost of capital or discount rate.

In this chapter, we answer frequently asked questions about the estimation and use of cost of capital. We cover the debt and equity costs of capital, and the weighted-average cost of capital for a firm, project, or division. Chapter 10 addresses the more general issue of using historical data to make probabilistic forecasts of asset returns.

The cost of capital has three conceptual meanings. On the asset side of a firm's balance sheet, it is the discount rate which should be used to reduce future values (dividends or cash flows, for example) to a present value. On the liability side, it is the economic cost to the firm of attracting and retaining capital in a competitive environment where investors (capital providers) carefully analyze and compare all return-generating opportunities. To the investor, the cost of capital is the expected return.

The cost of capital is an opportunity cost. In fact, some people consider the phrase "opportunity cost of capital" to be the correct term, "cost of capital" being an abbreviation. The opportunity cost of an investment is the expected return that would be earned on the next-best investment. In a competitive world with many investment choices, a given investment and the next-best investment have practically identical expected returns.

Thus, cost of capital estimation is a forecasting problem—a special case of the more general forecasting issue treated in Chapter 10. A cost of capital estimate is a forecast because it seeks to discern the expected return, or forecast mean, of an investment.

Example of Cost-of-Capital Estimation

1.   Q.   Please provide an example of the method used to estimate cost of capital for the equity (stock) of a firm.

A.   This answer addresses the cost of equity capital over the short run. The long-run estimate has some additional subtleties which will be discussed later in this chapter.

The equity cost of capital equals the expected rate of return, or forecast mean, for the firm's equity. (This is the market-required cost of capital, before any flotation costs or other market inefficiency costs which might be imputed.) For a stock having an amount of economy risk similar to that of the market as a whole, the short-term equity cost of capital is equal to the riskless (Treasury bill) rate plus the arithmetic mean of the equity risk premium. This calculation may be done in either nominal or real terms.

2. Q. How would you estimate the cost of debt capital for the firm?

    A. In the SBBI component-return framework, the debt cost of capital equals the riskless rate plus the arithmetic means of the horizon and default premiums, assuming the debt in question has a maturity of 20 years and default risk similar to that of the long-term, high-grade index used to generate the corporate bond series. A simpler way to estimate the debt cost of capital, however, is to observe the yield to maturity on the debt, because that yield is the market-observable cost of capital for the debt.

    To be precise, because the yield to maturity includes a market compensation for expected loss from defaults (in the probabilistic sense), the cost of debt capital is equal to the yield to maturity on the debt, minus this expected loss.

3. Q. How do you calculate the cost of capital for the entire firm (debt and equity)?

    A. The cost of capital for the firm is the weighted-average cost of capital. This is simply the weighted average of the debt and equity costs of capital, where the weights are determined by some reasonable method. Market-value weights are theoretically the best to use, but that is not always practical.

The Capital Asset Pricing Model (CAPM)

There are several widely used approaches to estimating the cost of capital. Of these, one—the CAPM—relates directly to the information in this book. One of the key variables in the CAPM is the market risk premium. We posit that one reasonable estimate of the future market risk premium is the long-run historical market risk premium.

Other approaches, including arbitrage pricing theory (APT) and the discounted cash flow (DCF) models, also contribute a great deal to the understanding of the cost of capital. We treat these approaches briefly at the end of the chapter.

4. Q. Is there a simple method of estimating the cost of capital for a stock that has risks different from those of the market?

A. Yes. The CAPM, or beta model, produces a simple and useful result. (Other models will be discussed later.) The CAPM may be expressed, in its simplest form, as:

$$ECOC = R_f + B(R_p), \tag{36}$$

where

ECOC = the equity cost of capital,

R_f = the riskless rate,

B = the beta of the stock, and

R_p = the equity risk premium.

There are other risks and nonrisk costs of capital inherent in stocks, but measuring them requires more complex methods.

The CAPM For Different Time Horizons

5. Q. Should the CAPM be used to estimate the short-term or the long-term cost of capital?

A. The CAPM was originally formulated to measure the short-term cost of capital, but it may be adapted to measure the long-term cost of capital by using the expected return on a long-term government bond, instead of the risk-free rate of return, as the riskless rate.

6. Q. In what sense is the expected return on a long-term government bond riskless?

A. In nominal terms, a long-term government bond is riskless if held to maturity, because the coupon and principal payments are known in advance. Of course, the price of the bond fluctuates during the holding period, so this question merits a more complete answer.

Certain investors seek to minimize risk in nominal terms over a long time horizon. For these investors, a long-term government bond is practically riskless. (Coupon reinvestment risk cannot be eliminated for coupon-paying bonds, although it can be reduced by the technique known as immunization. The yield on a hypothetical zero–coupon bond issued directly by the Treasury would be a better measure of the riskless long-term rate, because such a bond has no coupon reinvestment risk.) If long-term government bonds were actually held only by investors who perceived them as riskless, they would yield the riskless long-term rate.

7. Q. How would you estimate the long-term cost of capital?

A. For debt, one uses the yield to maturity. For equity, the most satisfactory way is to take the long-term government bond yield (income return) as the long-term riskless rate—as described above—and the arithmetic mean excess of equity total returns over long-term government bond yield returns as the long-horizon equity risk premium. (We explain the construction of the long-horizon equity risk premium in Chapter 6.) Summary statistics of the long-horizon equity risk premium are shown in Exhibit 23, and more detailed data are shown in Appendix A (Exhibit A-10).

8. Q. In estimating the market risk premium, it is more traditional to subtract bill or bond total returns from equity total returns. Why do you subtract bond yield returns (the income component of bond total returns)?

    A. The object is to determine what the market expects. When such an expectancy is directly observable, as with bond yields, one should use that measure. Historical bond total returns are biased downward as a measure of expectancy, because bondholders suffered an unanticipated capital loss over the period 1926-87. Bond yields, by contrast, are an almost unbiased measure of expectancy.

    Total returns on equities are used to estimate the market risk premium because equities have no market-observable expected return, i.e., no counterpart to the yield to maturity on bonds. Therefore, the best measure available, realized total return, is used.

9. Q. Is your long-term formulation of the CAPM the only such formulation used?

    A. No. A variety of methods are available to estimate the long-term cost of capital, each with its own advantages and disadvantages.

10. Q. When is it appropriate to use the long-term cost of capital?

    A. It is necessary to use a long-term cost of capital when discounting cash flows projected over a long period. Also, regulated ratesetting processes often specify or suggest that the rate of return should allow the firm to attract and retain debt and equity capital over the long term. Thus, the long-term cost of capital is typically the appropriate cost of capital to use in regulated ratesetting.

Estimation of the CAPM Beta

11. Q. How would you estimate the beta?

A. The beta of a stock is typically estimated by regressing the stock's return on the overall equity market's return. The traditional or Sharpe-Lintner beta is obtained by subtracting the return on short-term Treasury bills from both the stock and market returns before performing the regression. Many other variants are used in practice.

CAPM betas are published widely. In addition, anyone with a software package that performs regressions, and has data on stock returns, the stock market, and the market for riskless securities, may calculate their own betas.

Arithmetic versus Geometric Mean

12. Q. In your initial example, you use the arithmetic mean historical risk premium as the forecast of the future risk premium. Why do you use the arithmetic mean, instead of the geometric mean (compound annual return)?

A. The arithmetic mean is the rate of return which, when compounded over multiple periods, gives the mean of the probability distribution of ending wealth values. Thus, the arithmetic mean return is appropriate for calculation of a discount rate, because expected cash flows (i.e., the means of distributions of future values) are discounted to arrive at a present value. Similarly, it is appropriate for the cost of capital or market-required rate of return.

Definitionally, the discount rate that equates expected (mean) future values with the present value of an investment is that investment's cost of capital (Van Horne 1977). The logic is that investors will discount their expected (mean) ending wealth values using the arithmetic mean. They will, therefore, require such an expected (mean) return prospectively.

13. Q. Please provide a mathematical example that illustrates why the arithmetic mean is the rate of return that gives the probability distribution of ending wealth values.

A. Assume that a dollar invested has two possible outcomes each year: it rises 30 percent or falls 10 percent. These outcomes occur with equal probability, that is, each with a probability of 0.5. After one year, the possible outcomes are:

Ending wealth value	Probability
$ 1.30	0.50
0.90	0.50

If the example is extended one more year, the investment could start at $1.30 and rise 30 percent or fall 10 percent, i.e., rise to $1.69 or fall to $1.17, each with a probability of 0.25. Alternatively, the investment could start at $0.90 and rise 30 percent or fall 10 percent, i.e., rise to $1.17 or fall to $0.81, again each with a probability of 0.25. After two years, the possible outcomes are

Ending wealth value	Probability	Value x Probability
$ 1.69	0.25	0.4225
1.17	0.50	0.5850
0.81	0.25	0.2025
		Summation: $1.2100

Note the extra column, value times probability. The summation ($1.21) represents the statistical expectancy of wealth after two years.

The return required for an investment to grow from $1.00 to (an expected) $1.21 in two years may now be calculated as follows: $(1.21/1.00)^{(1/2)} - 1$, and is 0.10 or 10 percent. Remarkably, 10 percent is also the arithmetic mean of the two returns, +30 and -10 percent. The geometric mean of the two returns is $(1.3 \times 0.9)^{(1/2)} - 1 = 8.2$ percent. Clearly, the arithmetic mean equates the expected future value of an investment with its present value. This property makes the arithmetic mean the correct return to use as the discount rate or cost of capital.

14. Q. What use, if any, does the geometric mean have in forecasting the future?

A. The geometric mean return is the best estimate of the future rate of growth of a continuously compounded investment.

15. Q. You say that the arithmetic mean, compounded over the holding period, provides the best estimate of an investment's terminal wealth. Yet, you also state that the geometric mean is the best estimate of the future growth rate of an investment. How do you reconcile these apparently contradictory statements?

A. The reason these statements are not contradictory is that an investment with uncertain returns will have a higher expected ending wealth value than an investment which simply earns (with certainty) its compound or geometric rate of return every year. In the above example, compounding at the geometric rate of return (8.2 percent) for two years yields a terminal wealth of $1.17. But holding the uncertain investment, with a possibility of high returns (two +30 percent years in a row) as well as low returns (two -10 percent years in a row), yields a higher expected terminal wealth, $1.21. In other words, higher-than-expected returns more than offset lower-than-expected returns.

If returns are subject to a probability distribution, the arithmetic mean is the measure of prospective return that accounts for uncertainty.

Applications of the Cost of Capital

As noted earlier, the cost of capital applies to investment management, corporate finance, regulatory and tax issues, valuation, and other settings. The following are three of the most commonly asked questions about applications.

The Cost of Capital as a Discount Rate

16. Q. You have stated that the cost of capital may be used as a discount rate. How would you use the cost of capital for reducing future values (for example, dividends, wages, or cash flows) to a present value in the customary valuation formulas?

A. The cost of capital, using the arithmetic mean and the riskless rate for the appropriate time horizon (short, intermediate, or long), is the discount rate for valuation. The numerator (the future value) should be the statistical expectancy of the future value. A common error is to use the "realistic best case" or some other measure which is not the expectancy. Possible applications include security valuations, valuation of businesses or real estate for planning, transaction, or tax purposes, and many other uses.

Regulatory Ratesetting

17. Q. Can the cost of capital methodology you have described be used directly in regulatory ratesetting, or do adjustments have to be made?

   A. Adjustments are often necessary. One widely held view is that the cost of capital should be adjusted for flotation costs, because these costs must be paid by the issuer to attract and retain capital. In addition, certain regulatory environments impose a ceiling return. If the shareholder earns more, future returns might be reduced by the regulating body. Under this asymmetrical condition, the allowed rate of return must be higher than the cost of capital for the regulated business to attract and maintain capital. There are other regulatory conditions which may require the allowed rate of return to be different from the cost of capital.

Project Selection in the Corporate Financial Setting

18. Q. How would you use the cost of capital for project selection?

   A. In a situation where there is no significant budget constraint, one should accept all projects whose internal rate of return exceeds the project-specific cost of capital. The internal rate of return on a project, business unit, or acquisition is the discount rate (found by iteration or trial and error) which equates the present value of all cash inflows, including the investment, with the present value of all cash outflows. If this discount rate, or internal rate of return, exceeds the project-specific cost of capital, then the project has a positive net present value and should be accepted because it would create value for the company.

The project-specific cost of capital is usually estimated using the CAPM or APT (see below), in which one seeks to find a set of publicly-traded companies which are comparable to the project under consideration in business type, size, and risk. The average beta of the comparable companies is then used as a proxy for the beta of the project. If such comparable companies cannot be found, it may be necessary to use accounting-based models of a project's beta.

Other Methods of Cost of Capital Estimation

This section focuses on methods of cost-of-capital estimation other than the CAPM. Of the methods discussed here, APT is the leading-edge model. The data and empirical research needed to put APT to practical use have not been available until recently. The discounted cash flow model is the most venerable approach, having been known since the 1930s and used very widely since the 1950s. Finally, a possible future approach based on investor costs is discussed.

Arbitrage Pricing Theory

19. Q. What is APT?

A. APT is a model of the expected return on a security. Stephen A. Ross originated APT, and

Richard Roll elaborated it. APT treats the expected return on a security (i.e., its cost of capital) as the sum of the payoffs for an indeterminate number of risk factors, where the amount of each risk factor inherent in a given security is estimated. Like the CAPM, APT is an equilibrium model that does not attempt to outguess the market. One may visualize APT as an extended CAPM with multiple "betas" and multiple risk premiums.

20. Q. Has any research been done indicating which risk factors are important?

A. Nai-Fu Chen, with Roll and Ross, conducted an empirical investigation of the APT, relating stock returns to macroeconomic factors. They found five factors to be important: (1) changes in industrial production, (2) changes in anticipated inflation, (3) unanticipated inflation, (4) the return differential between low-grade corporate bonds and government bonds (both with long maturities), and (5) the return differential between long-term government bonds and short-term Treasury bills.

21. Q. How would you apply APT to estimate the cost of capital for a stock, bond, or company?

A. One estimates the size of the payoffs for each risk factor and the amount of each risk factor in the given security.

22. Q. APT sounds complicated. Is it practical enough for cost of capital estimation?

A. Yes. There are software/data packages to form the estimates, and printed (hard copy) APT estimates which make the model usable. Because of the extraordinary flexibility of APT, it is reasonable to expect that this model will become more prominent in the future, as more is learned about its explanatory and predictive power.

The Discounted Cash Flow Model

23. Q. What is the DCF model?

    A. The DCF model, originated by John Burr Williams and elaborated by Myron J. Gordon and Eli Shapiro, is best described in terms of estimating the cost of equity capital for a dividend-paying stock. It specifies that the cost of equity capital is equal to $(d/V) + g$, where d is the expected dividend amount in the next period, V is the value of the stock (hence d/V is the dividend yield in percent), and g is the expected growth rate of dividends.

24. Q. How may the DCF model be applied to estimate the cost of capital or discount rate?

    A. The DCF is very simple to use. The next period dividend is forecasted easily because it is closely related to the most recent dividend payment. The value of a stock is directly observable in the market. The difficult part is obtaining an accurate dividend growth forecast. One way of obtaining such a forecast is to use a consensus of security analysts' estimates.

Future Directions for Cost of Capital Estimation

25. Q. Are there any other theories relevant to the problem of estimating the cost of capital?

    A. Yes. One such theory was sketched out in a 1984 paper by Roger G. Ibbotson, Jeffrey J. Diermeier, and Laurence B. Siegel. They call for a "new equilibrium theory" (NET) in which the cost of capital for a security is literally the sum of all of capital costs. Such costs include both nonrisk costs and risk costs. Nonrisk costs include marketability costs, taxes, maintenance, insurance and storage costs, nonpecuniary costs and benefits (negative costs), and diversification costs. Risk costs are the costs an investor bears for taking on market risk, inflation risk, and so forth. The cost of taking on a given risk may be thought of as the amount an investor would pay to eliminate the risk.

It is difficult to quantify these costs. The cost of a given attribute is different for each person. But NET may induce researchers to think of the cost of capital in terms of all of the attributes of a security, not just its risks. Moreover, NET allows one to think of all assets, including human capital as well as stocks, bonds, bills, real estate, and other conventional and unconventional investment assets, in a single, unified framework.

10. Using Historical Data to Forecast the Future

Forecasts based on historical data have numerous applications: multiperiod investment planning, funding of liabilities, and other asset allocation-related uses. Most of the commonly used asset allocation software programs use a probabilistic forecast method similar to that explained here. This chapter answers questions regarding use of the data to form probabilistic forecasts of future real and nominal returns on the asset classes.

The forecasts delineated here are *probabilistic* forecasts. These are forecasts of the entire return distribution of an investment. Common stocks may have a 5 percent probability of returning 51.9 percent or more (for example) over one year, a 50 percent probability of returning 12.6 percent or more, and a 95 percent probability of returning -16.6 percent or more. These forecasts are an attempt to discern what the market will do and are based on statistical time-series properties of historical data and on current yields in the market. Thus, the forecasts are not an attempt to outguess, or beat, the market.

General and Philosophical Issues

Before discussing the method of producing probabilistic forecasts, we answer several general questions about forecasting and the method described here.

Lognormal and Simulation Models

We used a simulation, or random drawing, method to produce asset return forecasts in the 1977 edition of *Stocks, Bonds, Bills, and Inflation.* The simulation method, known as Monte Carlo simulation, relies on drawings from the actual historical data sets. Later, other researchers showed that the results of the forecasts could be closely replicated, and made easier to use, by a purely mathematical method that uses summary statistics of the historical data. We used this latter method, the lognormal model, in the 1982 edition of this book. There are no specific numerical forecasts in this book: Only the principles of forecasting are discussed.

1.   Q.   Do you still recommend the lognormal model of forecast returns presented in the 1982 volume?

A. It depends. Both equity risk premiums and small-stock premiums have distributions that differ substantially from a normal or lognormal distribution. It is conceptually better to use a "bootstrapping" technique—one which uses the actual past distributions of these component returns without attempting to characterize the distribution as normal or lognormal.

The simulation model presented in the Ibbotson and Sinquefield *Journal of Business* article (July 1976) and the 1977 edition of this book is one of the simplest and best-known bootstrapping models, and we have used it periodically to supplement the results of the lognormal model.

Philosophy of Forecasting

2.   Q.   Before getting into specifics, what is the philosophy underlying your method of forecasting asset returns?

A. Our approach is to infer the market's forecast of asset returns as contained in two sources of market data. One source is the historical data on security and component returns, and the other source is the estimates of future interest rates as revealed in a U.S. government bond yield curve.

The key assumptions are that the component historical returns which have followed a random walk will continue to do so, and those that have followed a trend will also continue to do so. The bond yields reflect consensus forecasts of nominal interest rates, inflation rates, and real interest rates.

3. Q. Do your forecasts assume that markets are efficient?

A. Our approach to forecasting is consistent with efficient capital market theory. This theory suggests that the market price of an asset reflects all the information currently available. Stated another way, securities are fairly priced.

One does not, of course, have to believe in the literal truth of the efficient market hypothesis to put the forecasts to practical use. One must believe, however, that markets are inefficient to use more traditional forecasts that attempt to outguess the market. Thus, these forecasts have a wider set of applications than do traditional forecasts.

4. Q. In what ways are your forecasts consistent with efficient capital market theory?

A. Our forecasts employ the market efficiency assumption in two principal ways. First, the yield curve is used to forecast future expected interest and inflation rates. Because the prices of the bonds that comprise the yield curve are market-determined, the interest- and inflation-rate forecasts are market-determined. Second, the forecasts of the four risk premiums are based on the assumption of random walk behavior, discussed in detail later. Neither of the above procedures represents an attempt to outguess the market.

5.   Q. Why do you make probabilistic forecasts, as opposed to specific predictions?

A. We believe that it is better to look at forecasts in terms of the expected probability distributions, rather than as specific predictions. For example, a specific prediction might be that common stock returns will be 12.6 percent in 1989. Although this would reflect the market's expected return on that category of asset, it is more valuable to know that, in 1989, common stocks have a 5 percent probability of returning as little as -16.6 percent or worse, and a 5 percent probability of returning 51.9 percent or better.

6.   Q. Why do you believe such wide forecasts have any practical value?

A. Knowing the risk contained in different asset categories over various future periods of time may be just as important and useful as knowing the expected returns for those assets. Wide forecasts simply reflect the large risks inherent in some of the assets, particularly stocks. In other words, wide forecasts give a sense of the volatility or risk of the market, but "point estimates," or specific predictions, do not. Forecasts that understate risks are not only useless, but may lead to harmful investment decisions.

7. Q. Can your forecasting techniques be used to make any money in the market?

A. Because they are market consensus forecasts, or readings of what the market itself is forecasting, they cannot be used to beat the market. Our forecasts are useful, however, in evaluating the risks involved in various investment strategies and in determining the expected rewards from taking these risks. A long-run investor who takes these asset allocation issues into account is likely to make more money (all other things being equal) than one who ignores them.

The Stocks, Bonds, Bills, and Inflation Forecast Model

In this section, the forecast model is described in general terms, using examples to promote intuitive understanding of the issues.

Forecasting the One-Year Stock Return: An Example

8. Q. Please provide an example of the SBBI forecasting method.

A. The forecast of common stock total returns, for example, is the sum of the expected equity risk premium, the expected real riskless interest rate, and the expected inflation rate. The equity risk premium has historically followed a random walk centered on an arithmetic mean of 8.3 percent, or 6.2 percent compounded annually. The real riskless rate and the inflation rate both follow trends; that is, these two series have high serial correlations, and this year's rate is statistically related to last year's rate. Recent real riskless rates have been above their historical average, but they are likely to follow their historical pattern of gradually reverting toward their long-term mean of 0.5 percent. (This type of behavior for a return series is called an autoregressive process.) Therefore, we expect real riskless rates to decline slightly, but remain positive, in the future.

The inflation rate, which also follows a trend, varies a great deal from year to year. To forecast future inflation on the basis of past trends would give only a very approximate forecast. Fortunately, the market expresses its own forecasts of the inflation rate in the yield curve. If there were no inflation, the yield curve would reflect (1) the real riskless rate, which historically has averaged 0.5 percent; (2) the horizon premium, which may be estimated for each time to maturity; and (3) the default premium for the class of bonds under examination. Bond prices compensate investors for expected inflation as well as for these three factors. By looking at the difference between the observed yield curve and what the yield curve would be if inflation were not a factor, it is possible to observe the market's assessment of future inflation. Because the yield curve changes daily, a specific inflation forecast is not presented here.

The median forecast of total common stock annual returns for one year, then, is the sum of the expected equity risk premium (8.3 percent), the expected real riskless rate over that year as given by the autoregressive process, and the expected rate of inflation for that year as given by the present yield curve.

The distribution of returns around the mean, which was described earlier as the probabilistic forecast, is provided by the lognormal distribution model described below.

The Lognormal Distribution Model

9. Q. What is the method used to obtain the distributions around the forecast median or mean?

A. We use the lognormal model. In the lognormal model, the natural logarithms of asset return relatives are assumed to be normally distributed. (A return relative is one plus the return. That is, if an asset has a return of 15 percent in a given period, its return relative in that period is 1.15.)

The Normal Distribution

10. Q. Because the description of the lognormal model refers to the normal distribution, please describe the normal distribution.

A. The exact description of a normal distribution is too technical to include here, but we can provide some intuition. A normal distribution of returns, when graphed, is a bell-shaped curve. If the mean of the normal distribution is zero percent, with a standard deviation of 20 percent, the bell curve is centered on the zero percent line. About two-thirds of the observations fall within 20 percent, or one standard deviation, either way, of the mean. About 95 percent of the observations fall within two standard deviations of the mean. Under this scenario, returns of -50 percent and +50 percent are equally probable.

Problems with the Normal Distribution as a Model of the Market

11. Q. Does the normal distribution describe the returns on capital market assets?

A. Superficially, the normal distribution seems to characterize the stock market fairly well, except that one would raise all the numbers by 10 percent because the historical stock market mean return is roughly 10 percent per year, not zero.

On closer examination, however, there are some problems with the normal distribution as a model of the stock market. First, stocks cannot have a return below -100 percent. Second, an investor must gain more in percent, on average, than he or she loses, just to break even. Successive returns of -50 percent and +50 percent would result in a two-period loss of 25 percent; to break even, an investor with a one-period return of -50 percent would have to earn +100 percent in the next period. This observation is corroborated by the actual historical data: the distribution of stock returns is somewhat "right-tailed," meaning that there are more observations on the high-return end of the distribution than one would expect if stock returns had a normal distribution.

The Lognormal Distribution

12. Q. How are the problems with the normal distribution best resolved?

A. The lognormal model characterizes the behavior of the equity risk premium (the major component of stock returns) much better than does the normal distribution. With a lognormal distribution, returns are distributed so that a doubling or halving of the stock market's level are equally probable, assuming a mean of zero. On average, the equity risk premium is positive (that is, the stock market beats Treasury bills), so the correct mean is above zero. Lognormally distributed returns cannot ever be lower than or equal to -100 percent.

The returns at various probability rankings—for example, 95th percentile or 5th percentile—are easily estimated. One calculates, or looks up in a table, the number of standard deviations above or below the mean that correspond to the desired percentile ranking. For example, the 95th percentile return (that is, the return which is exceeded only 5 percent of the time), is 1.65 standard deviations above the mean. With a little more mathematics, multiperiod probability rankings of returns can be estimated also. These form the probabilistic forecasts.

It should be remembered that the lognormal model applies only to the randomly distributed components of asset returns. Trendlike series, such as real interest rates and inflation, are forecasted using a nonrandom process such as the autoregressive process mentioned earlier.

Random versus Nonrandom Variables
Only a subset of the component series are modeled using the lognormal distribution. That model is suitable for series which follow a random walk. For these, the best estimate of the next observation is the historical average of the series.

13. Q. You have stated that you expect the equity risk premium to remain at its historical mean because it follows what is known in statistics as a random walk.

Is there also a fundamental reason why you expect this?

A. There is no compelling evidence that either (1) the equilibrium price (market compensation) for a given amount of risk, or (2) the amount of risk in common stocks, has changed over time. For modeling purposes, we thus assume that these quantities will remain stable in the future. Models that allow for changing levels of risk or changing risk aversion are also reasonable. One cannot prove that either approach is exclusively correct.

14. Q. Much academic work suggests that the returns on common stocks follow a random walk, while you assume that instead, equity risk premiums follow a random walk. Is it possible that they both follow a random walk?

A. We have broken down the returns on common stocks into two components: the returns from holding a riskless security (Treasury bills) and the returns from the equity risk premium. The returns from holding Treasury bills do not follow a random walk. Thus, equity risk premiums and common stock returns cannot both follow a random walk. Evidence suggests the expected return from taking risk (the equity risk premium) is constant through time, i.e., it is the risk premium that behaves randomly. Because most of the variability from common stock returns arises from the risk premium, some researchers have mistakenly concluded that the whole of the common stock return follows a random walk. The research presented in this book indicates that only the risk premium component follows a random walk.

15. Q. Do you expect any of the other component returns to follow a random walk and remain at the same levels on average as in the past?

A. Yes. Although small-stock and bond default premiums historically show statistical evidence of trendlike behavior, the evidence is not sufficiently compelling to abandon the random walk hypothesis for these variables. Bond horizon premiums have followed a random walk in the past. For forecasting purposes, we assume that these three variables will follow random walks in the future.

Forecast Summary

16. Q. To recapitulate, you have said that the equity risk, small-company stock, default, and maturity premiums may be predicted using the assumption of a random walk around historical levels; the real riskless rate may be predicted using the historical trend; and the inflation rate may be forecasted using present bond yield information. Is this all the information that you need to make your forecasts?

A. Yes. Because all of the total asset return series are made up of these components, one can add the appropriate ones together to forecast the return on each category of asset.

Validity of the Forecasts

17. Q. Most forecasts incorporate estimates of macro-economic variables such as GNP, employment, and productivity. You seem to ignore them completely. Why?

A. The various macro- and microeconomic variables determine the prices of securities. In fact, the prices of securities are themselves forecasts of what occurs in the economy. Because our method uses the prices of securities as the inputs to our forecasts, these economic variables are implicitly contained in the forecasts.

18. Q. Many forecasts are produced by economists, financial analysts, or long-range planners. Are your forecasts in any way superior to theirs, and if so, how?

A. If capital markets are efficient, then at the very least our forecasts are not inferior to theirs. In fact, the forecasts of economists, financial analysts, long-range planners, and others help to determine the prices in the market, because investors incorporate these forecasts into their decision making. Because these prices are used to generate our forecasts, other forecasters' predictions are, once again, incorporated into these forecasts.

Issues Related to the 1926-87 Historical Period

19. Q. You treat all years in the historical period equally. Would it not be better to emphasize recent events by weighting recent returns more heavily than distant returns?

A. In the absence of any particular reason to weight particular years more heavily than others, it is appropriate to weight all of the years equally. In general, we attempt to maintain a spirit of neutrality or objectivity in the forecasts. Any particular weighting scheme runs the risk of imparting subjectivity and biases into the historical data.

20. Q. During the past 62 years, there were a severe depression, three wars, a period of pegged interest

rates, several periods of wage and price controls, periods of inflation and deflation, and, recently, a stock price crash. Are you suggesting that these events will happen in the future with the same frequency as they have in the past?

A. It is impossible to forecast which specific events will occur because no one knows the future. It is reasonable to believe, however, that historical events are not unrepresentative of the types of events that will occur in the future. Thus, the rate-of-return effects of these event-types should be expected to recur.

The Changing Variability of Returns

21. Q. The variability of stock market returns does not seem to be constant over the historical period. It seems to have been more variable during the depression and very recently. Also, bond returns have become substantially more variable in the past two decades. Does the market-consensus forecasting method take this into account?

A. In principle, it would be possible to take the changes in variability into account. But this would make the forecasting procedures much more complicated, with only limited benefits.

Choice of a Historical Period

22. Q. Why do you choose a 62-year period over which to measure your historical results?

A. The 62-year time period is arbitrary; it was selected because 1926 is the beginning date for the series that are based on data from CRSP. It is desirable to have a period long enough to include all types of events. The period is limited only because it is more difficult to obtain high-quality data prior to 1926.

Results of the Forecasts

Although numerical forecast results are not reported in this study, it is important to review the broad conclusions of the forecasts and to answer questions relating to these conclusions.

Stocks and Bonds

23. Q. Your historical results show that the stock market had a compound annual return of 9.9 percent over the past 62 years. The yield on high-quality corporate bonds is now at least that. What incentive is there to take the additional risk in buying stocks?

A. It is not correct to compare bond yields, which are a very close estimate of the expected return on a bond, with a historical average of stock returns. The historical average of stock returns includes many years in which the riskless part of the return—equivaient to the yield on a riskless bond—is very low. Today, the expected return on a stock is much higher because the riskless part of the return is much higher. The equity risk premium component has not visibly changed. Thus, the expected return on a stock, to which the bond yield should be compared, is higher than that of bonds by a substantial margin.

In general, the relevant relations are between risky and riskless asset returns, or between asset returns and inflation. Stocks have outperformed riskless U.S. Treasury bills by a geometric average of 6.2 percent per year, and have yielded a 6.6 percent compound annual return in excess of inflation. (The geometric average return on stocks is used in this context because bond yields are a geometric average of expected returns on the bond.) High-grade corporate bonds have compound returns of less than 2 percent in excess of either Treasury bills or inflation. Because these relations are expected to continue in the future, stocks are expected to outperform bonds. They also have more risk.

The Effect of Inflation

24. Q. Your method seems to imply that if the market's expectation of inflation is high, relative to the historical (1926-87) compound inflation rate of 3.0 percent, then nominal returns on common stocks will be higher than have been realized historically. Yet, the experience of the past two decades suggests the opposite: that high inflation rates are accompanied by poor stock market returns. How do you reconcile recent events with your forecasting procedure?

A. When high inflation rates are anticipated—that is, reflected in the yield curve—these higher rates tend to be impounded in the returns of common stocks. In some periods, such as the 1970s, however, increases in inflation are unanticipated. Evidence shows that unanticipated inflation tends to be detrimental to stock returns because unanticipated inflation generally occurs during periods of great uncertainty. Because the forecast model uses the yield curve to forecast inflation rates, only anticipated inflation rates are incorporated into the projected stock returns.

25. Q. The yield curve changes every day. Do your forecasts also change every day, and if so, what purpose do they serve?

   A. It is true that the yield curve changes every day, and it is also true that changes in the yield curve will change the forecast results every day. The yield curve reflects the changing anticipations of the marketplace, which continually revises its estimates. It is therefore necessary to incorporate the latest yield curve into the forecasts. As a practical matter, the yield curve changes are relatively small during short periods of time, so that it is not necessary to make abrupt changes in the forecasts.

   Furthermore, the forecasts are very stable in real terms because it is the inflation-rate component of the yield curve which is the most variable.

26. Q. Some government bonds have much lower yields than others, even though they have approximately the same maturity dates. Which bonds should be used to calculate the yield curve?

   A. A number of government bonds trade at unusual prices because of their special tax status. For example, some bonds, called flower bonds, enable the holder to pay estate taxes by tendering the bond at par value. Because these bonds are bought primarily for their tax benefits, not their yields, they are not included in the yield curve.

Forecast Errors on Interest and Inflation Rates

27. Q. Your forecast method uses the yield curve to forecast expected one-year interest and inflation rates each year into the future. How well has this procedure worked in the past?

A. Historically, yield-curve forecasts have had substantial forecast error. But, after allowing for horizon premiums, the interest-rate forecasts have been unbiased. After removing real interest rates, the inflation forecasts have also been unbiased. Furthermore, no reliable way to make more accurate forecasts exists. It is also possible to estimate the degree of the forecast error for both interest and inflation rates.

Behavior of the Real Riskless Rate

The real riskless rate is one of the most important components of the forecasts. An analysis of its behavior over time is germane to an understanding of the forecast process and results.

28. Q. Historically, the real rate of interest has been 0.5 percent and quite volatile (with an annual standard deviation of 4.4 percent), according to your data. The more traditional view is that the real rate of interest is stable and in the range of 1 to 2 percent. How do you reconcile this difference?

A. For about two decades following the 1951 U.S. Treasury-Federal Reserve Accord, real interest rates were low and stable, around 1 percent on average. This long experience convinced many economists that the "natural" real interest rate was 1 percent or perhaps somewhat higher. More recent experience indicates that real rates can turn sharply negative, as they did in the late 1970s, or sharply positive, as they did from mid-1981 to the end of 1986. That is, the low and stable real interest rate was simply one of various patterns that real rates could assume.

The behavior of real interest rates illustrates the value of studying lengthy historical periods. By looking at even a reasonably long period such as 1953-72, one could conclude incorrectly that real rates are not only stable, but close to a random walk; the longer view indicates that real rates are volatile and follow very distinct trends.

29. Q. The real riskless rate has averaged approximately 4 percent throughout most of the 1980s. How does this conform to your statement that the real riskless rate is near zero?

    A. The real riskless rate varies from year to year and may be positive, as from July 1980 to the present, or negative, as in most of the 1970s. On average, the rate has been near zero—0.5 percent. The real riskless rate seems to drift toward its long-term mean.

30. Q. How far into the future do you forecast?

    A. We can forecast as far out as the yield curve goes. For Treasury bonds, there is typically a 30-year bond, so that one could make 30-year forecasts.

Applications of the Forecast Method to Specific Investment Questions

The forecast method described here has implications for all types of specific investments; for portfolios of different investments; and for specific investment environments, such as the pension funding discipline mandated by Employee Retirement Income Security Act (ERISA) and various Financial Accounting Standards Board (FASB) standards. Forecasts can be constructed for stocks with high or low betas; for bonds of various maturities, durations, and quality ratings; and for other asset classes. These forecast distributions should be particularly useful to pension plans. The key to this flexibility is the component return approach, which regards the return on an asset as the sum of the returns on its components or elemental parts.

31. Q. In today's pension fund environment, wherein ERISA mandates that pension funds have to be actuarially funded, should your forecasts have any bearing on actuarial assumptions?

A. Any assumptions that affect the funding of pension plans should be based on realistic forecasts. In that regard, our forecasts and our forecasting procedure have an obvious bearing on the assumptions used in pension planning.

This question merits extensive treatment, because it subsumes many of the current controversial issues of pension-fund management. Such treatment is outside the scope of this book. Both the asset and liability sides of the pension equation should be estimated, for planning purposes, in accordance with the principles of forecasting set forth here.

32. Q. Most portfolios are made up of combinations of stocks, corporate bonds, government bonds, and so forth. How do you estimate returns associated with various portfolio mixes?

A. The forecast mean returns for a portfolio mix may be calculated by adding the forecast mean returns for the asset classes in the portfolio, for example, stocks, corporate bonds, and Treasury bills, each weighted by their weights in the portfolio.

It is not possible, however, to add sorted percentile distributions of portfolio components, because portfolios are more diversified than the individual asset classes comprising them. A number of commercially available asset allocation programs calculate probability distributions of expected returns for multiasset portfolios, taking into account the covariances between the assets held (i.e., the effects of portfolio diversification).

33. Q. Your stock market total returns are from investing in the S&P Composite Index. Suppose investors held high-beta or low-beta portfolios—how would this affect their historical and future returns?

A. Empirical evidence suggests that high-beta portfolios outperform low-beta portfolios on average. This has occurred over the past 62 years and it is reasonable to anticipate that it will continue in the future. The expected reward is not without its costs, because higher beta portfolios have higher risks, or wider distributions of returns.

34. Q. If an investor did not hold the market but rather held a highly undiversified portfolio, how would this have affected his or her returns?

A. In the past, on average, undiversified portfolios have neither outperformed nor underperformed diversified portfolios. The risks of undiversified portfolios, however, are larger than the risks of diversified portfolios. This will also be true in the future; that is, undiversified portfolios will have, on average, the same expected return, but wider distributions of return, or higher risk.

35. Q. Are your procedures useful in estimating the possible returns from superior money managers?

A. These procedures may be used to estimate returns for portfolios expected to outperform the market. If the belief that a portfolio can outperform the market is strong, then the model should be adjusted: The expectations input should be increased so that the expected return is increased by the amount that the portfolio is expected to outperform the market. The risks are also increased by the amount of the additional risk incurred as a result of holding a portfolio that is less diversified than the market.

36. Q. You have shown that, historically, the bond horizon premium is 1.1 percent. Do you expect investors to be paid this amount in the future for taking the additional risk of long-term bonds?

    A. Investors should expect to receive higher compensation for this risk. Over the post-World War II period, investors underestimated inflation. The result was that long-term bondholders suffered large unanticipated capital losses. Because these losses were both unanticipated and measurable as such, one can add back the annual rate of loss to the historical horizon premium to estimate what the expectancy was. The annual rate of capital loss, or addback, is 0.4 percent (arithmetic mean). Adding this to the historical horizon premium of 1.1 percent, it is reasonable to conclude that investors expect a somewhat larger horizon premium (1.5 percent) than was experienced over the period 1926-87.

37. Q. Are long-term bonds more risky now than in the past?

    A. In the past decade, long-term bonds have been considerably more risky than in earlier years. (From

1926 to 1932, annualized yields on long-term government bonds fluctuated within a 1 percentage point range.) This trend will not necessarily continue in the indefinite future. The volatility of bond returns follows distinct trends, so that long-term bonds are expected to be riskier in the near future than they were historically.

38. Q. What would have been the effect on returns of holding a portfolio of various duration bonds, not just short-term bills, or 20-year bonds?

A. Historically, yields across the entire spectrum of bond maturities have risen dramatically over the period 1926-87, resulting in greater capital losses on bonds, with longer durations. Thus, intermediate-term government bonds outperformed both long-term bonds and short-term bills over that historical period.

Looking forward, the returns from short-term bills should not be expected to reflect any horizon premium, whereas the returns on a 20-year bond should reflect a horizon premium, appropriate to the duration of a 20-year bond. The expected returns of intermediate-term bonds may reflect a partial horizon premium.

39. Q. Long-term bonds, Guaranteed Investment Contracts, and various immunization and dedication strategies are purported to reduce risk for investors with long-term time horizons. Do they work?

A. Investors frequently engage in "horizon matching." That is, they hold bond and bill portfolios with a duration equal or similar to the duration of the investor's future obligation. Thus, short-horizon investors hold short-term bills because they perceive bills as less risky than long-term bonds, which are subject to price fluctuation risk. Long-horizon investors may hold long-duration bonds, guaranteed investment contracts, or dedicated or immunized portfolios, all of which they perceive as less risky than short-term bills, which are subject to reinvestment risk. These long-horizon strategies work if structured properly, so that investors with a long time horizon and known nominal future obligations benefit from them.

Very few investors, however, have such known nominal needs and are interested in reducing risk in nominal (as opposed to real) terms. Pension funds that have obligations denominated in nominal terms with no inflation provison might be an exception. Most investors seek to reduce risk in nominal terms as a proxy for their primary, more difficult goal of reducing risk in real terms. Even if these investors have long-term time horizons, investing in short-term securities is a less risky strategy. If the market is dominated by investors who perceive short-term investments as less risky, then holders of long-term bonds should expect to be compensated for their taking on interest-rate risk.

40. Q. If one were to hold lower-quality bonds than the high-quality long-term corporate bonds listed in this study, how would this affect bondholder expected returns?

A. Lower-quality bonds have higher yields and higher default risks than high-quality bonds. Because investors are paid a premium for taking default risk, holders of lower-quality bonds have, in general, higher expected returns and higher variability than the holders of higher-quality bonds.

41. Q. On October 19, 1987, stock prices fell by more than 20 percent in one day. How does an event such as this crash affect your forecasts?

A. The crash of October 1987 broke new ground in terms of daily volatility: The crash was twice as large as the next largest decline in history, which occurred in 1929. In terms of monthly volatility, however, the crash has historical precedent. There were four months (in the 1920s, 1930s, and 1940s) that were worse. Thus, an investor with a sufficient base of historical knowledge would have known that such a crash was possible, although he or she could not have foreseen when it would occur.

This problem highlights the importance of a long historical time series in probabilistic forecasting—that is, in understanding the character of possible future risks and returns. An investor who looks only at the last half of the period will not perceive the possibility of months in which stock prices decline more than 20 percent. The crash of 1987 recalled the panics that punctuated the earlier, more turbulent half of the period studied, and shows the investor that history is indeed relevant to understanding the present.

APPENDIX

EXHIBIT A-1
COMMON STOCKS: TOTAL RETURNS
RATES OF RETURN FOR ALL YEARLY HOLDING PERIODS FROM 1926 TO 1987
(Percent Per Annum Compounded Annually)

TO THE END OF	FROM THE BEGINNING OF																				
	1926	1927	1928	1929	1930	1931	1932	1933	1934	1935	1936	1937	1938	1939	1940	1941	1942	1943	1944	1945	1946
1926	11.6																				
1927	23.9	37.5																			
1928	30.1	40.5	43.6																		
1929	19.2	21.8	14.7	-8.4																	
1930	8.7	8.0	-0.4	-17.1	-24.9																
1931	-2.5	-5.1	-13.5	-27.0	-34.8	-43.3															
1932	-3.3	-5.6	-12.5	-22.7	-26.9	-27.9	-8.2														
1933	2.5	1.2	-3.8	-11.2	-11.9	-7.1	18.9	54.0													
1934	2.0	0.9	-3.5	-9.7	-9.9	-5.7	11.7	23.2	-1.4												
1935	5.9	5.2	1.8	-3.1	-2.2	3.1	19.8	30.9	20.6	47.7											
1936	8.1	7.8	4.9	0.9	2.3	7.7	22.5	31.6	24.9	40.6	33.9										
1937	3.7	3.0	0.0	-3.9	-3.3	0.2	10.2	14.3	6.1	8.7	-6.7	-35.0									
1938	5.5	5.1	2.5	-0.9	-0.0	3.6	13.0	16.9	10.7	13.9	4.5	-7.7	31.1								
1939	5.1	4.6	2.3	-0.8	-0.1	3.2	11.2	14.3	8.7	10.9	3.2	-5.3	14.3	-0.4							
1940	4.0	3.5	1.3	-1.6	-1.0	1.8	8.6	11.0	5.9	7.2	0.5	-6.5	5.6	-5.2	-9.8						
1941	3.0	2.4	0.3	-2.4	-1.9	0.5	6.4	8.2	3.5	4.3	-1.6	-7.5	1.0	-7.4	-10.7	-11.6					
1942	3.9	3.5	1.5	-1.0	-0.4	2.0	7.6	9.3	5.3	6.1	1.2	-3.4	4.6	-1.1	-1.4	3.1	20.3				
1943	5.0	4.7	2.9	0.6	1.3	3.7	9.0	10.8	7.2	8.2	4.0	0.4	7.9	3.8	4.8	10.2	23.1	25.9			
1944	5.8	5.5	3.8	1.7	2.5	4.8	9.8	11.5	8.3	9.3	5.7	2.6	9.5	6.3	7.7	12.5	22.0	22.8	19.8		
1945	7.1	6.9	5.4	3.5	4.3	6.6	11.5	13.2	10.4	11.5	8.4	5.9	12.6	10.1	12.0	17.0	25.4	27.2	27.8	36.4	
1946	6.4	6.1	4.7	2.8	3.5	5.6	10.1	11.6	8.8	9.7	6.8	4.4	10.1	7.7	8.9	12.4	17.9	17.3	14.5	12.0	-8.1
1947	6.3	6.1	4.7	3.0	3.7	5.6	9.8	11.2	8.6	9.4	6.7	4.5	9.6	7.5	8.5	11.4	15.8	14.9	12.3	9.9	-1.4
1948	6.3	6.1	4.7	3.1	3.8	5.6	9.6	10.8	8.4	9.1	6.6	4.6	9.2	7.3	8.1	10.6	14.2	13.2	10.9	8.8	0.8
1949	6.8	6.6	5.3	3.8	4.5	6.3	10.1	11.2	9.0	9.7	7.4	5.6	10.0	8.3	9.2	11.5	14.8	14.0	12.2	10.7	5.1
1950	7.7	7.5	6.4	4.9	5.6	7.4	11.1	12.3	10.2	11.0	8.9	7.3	11.5	10.0	11.0	13.4	16.6	16.1	14.8	13.9	9.9
1951	8.3	8.1	7.1	5.7	6.4	8.2	11.7	12.9	11.0	11.7	9.8	8.4	12.4	11.1	12.1	14.3	17.3	16.9	15.9	15.3	12.1
1952	8.6	8.5	7.5	6.2	6.9	8.6	12.0	13.2	11.3	12.1	10.3	9.0	12.8	11.6	12.5	14.6	17.4	17.1	16.1	15.7	13.0
1953	8.3	8.1	7.2	5.9	6.5	8.2	11.4	12.4	10.7	11.4	9.6	8.3	11.9	10.7	11.5	13.4	15.7	15.3	14.3	13.7	11.2
1954	9.6	9.5	8.6	7.4	8.1	9.7	12.9	14.0	12.4	13.1	11.6	10.4	13.9	12.9	13.9	15.8	18.2	18.0	17.4	17.1	15.1
1955	10.2	10.2	9.3	8.2	8.9	10.5	13.7	14.7	13.1	13.9	12.5	11.4	14.8	13.9	14.9	16.8	19.1	19.0	18.5	18.4	16.7
1956	10.1	10.1	9.2	8.2	8.8	10.4	13.4	14.4	12.9	13.6	12.2	11.2	14.4	13.5	14.4	16.1	18.2	18.1	17.5	17.3	15.7
1957	9.4	9.3	8.5	7.4	8.1	9.5	12.3	13.2	11.8	12.4	11.0	10.0	13.0	12.1	12.8	14.3	16.2	15.9	15.2	14.9	13.2
1958	10.3	10.2	9.5	8.5	9.1	10.6	13.3	14.3	12.9	13.5	12.4	11.4	14.3	13.5	14.3	15.8	17.6	17.5	16.9	16.7	15.3
1959	10.3	10.3	9.5	8.6	9.2	10.6	13.3	14.2	12.9	13.5	12.3	11.4	14.2	13.4	14.1	15.6	17.3	17.1	16.6	16.4	15.1

EXHIBIT A-1 (Continued)

TO THE END OF	FROM THE BEGINNING OF																				
	1926	1927	1928	1929	1930	1931	1932	1933	1934	1935	1936	1937	1938	1939	1940	1941	1942	1943	1944	1945	1946
1960	10.0	10.0	9.3	8.3	8.9	10.3	12.8	13.7	12.4	13.0	11.8	10.9	13.5	12.8	13.5	14.8	16.4	16.1	15.6	15.3	14.0
1961	10.5	10.4	9.7	8.8	9.4	10.8	13.3	14.1	12.9	13.4	12.3	11.5	14.1	13.4	14.0	15.3	16.9	16.7	16.2	16.0	14.8
1962	9.9	9.9	9.2	8.3	8.8	10.1	12.5	13.2	12.1	12.6	11.4	10.7	13.0	12.3	12.9	14.1	15.5	15.3	14.7	14.4	13.3
1963	10.2	10.2	9.5	8.7	9.2	10.5	12.8	13.5	12.4	12.9	11.8	11.1	13.4	12.7	13.3	14.5	15.8	15.6	15.1	14.9	13.8
1964	10.4	10.4	9.7	8.9	9.4	10.6	12.9	13.6	12.5	13.0	12.0	11.3	13.5	12.9	13.5	14.5	15.7	15.5	15.2	14.9	13.9
1965	10.4	10.4	9.8	9.0	9.5	10.7	12.9	13.6	12.5	13.0	12.0	11.3	13.5	12.9	13.4	14.5	15.7	15.5	15.0	14.8	13.8
1966	9.9	9.8	9.2	8.4	8.9	10.1	12.2	12.8	11.8	12.2	11.2	10.5	12.6	12.0	12.4	13.4	14.5	14.3	13.8	13.6	12.6
1967	10.2	10.2	9.6	8.8	9.3	10.4	12.5	13.1	12.1	12.5	11.6	10.9	12.9	12.4	12.8	13.8	14.9	14.7	14.2	14.0	13.1
1968	10.2	10.2	9.6	8.9	9.3	10.4	12.4	13.1	12.1	12.5	11.6	10.9	12.9	12.3	12.8	13.7	14.7	14.5	14.1	13.9	13.0
1969	9.8	9.7	9.1	8.4	8.9	9.9	11.8	12.4	11.4	11.8	10.9	10.3	12.1	11.6	12.0	12.8	13.8	13.6	13.1	12.9	12.0
1970	9.6	9.6	9.0	8.3	8.7	9.7	11.6	12.2	11.2	11.6	10.7	10.1	11.9	11.3	11.7	12.5	13.5	13.2	12.8	12.5	11.7
1971	9.7	9.7	9.1	8.4	8.9	9.9	11.7	12.2	11.3	11.7	10.8	10.2	11.9	11.4	11.8	12.6	13.5	13.3	12.8	12.6	11.8
1972	9.9	9.9	9.3	8.7	9.1	10.1	11.9	12.4	11.5	11.9	11.0	10.5	12.1	11.6	12.0	12.8	13.7	13.5	13.0	12.8	12.0
1973	9.3	9.3	8.7	8.1	8.5	9.4	11.1	11.7	10.8	11.1	10.3	9.7	11.3	10.8	11.1	11.8	12.7	12.4	12.0	11.7	10.9
1974	8.5	8.4	7.8	7.2	7.5	8.4	10.1	10.6	9.7	10.0	9.1	8.5	10.1	9.5	9.8	10.5	11.2	10.9	10.5	10.2	9.4
1975	9.0	8.9	8.4	7.7	8.1	9.0	10.6	11.1	10.2	10.6	9.8	9.2	10.7	10.2	10.5	11.1	11.9	11.6	11.2	11.0	10.2
1976	9.2	9.2	8.7	8.0	8.4	9.3	10.9	11.4	10.5	10.9	10.1	9.5	11.0	10.5	10.8	11.5	12.2	12.0	11.6	11.3	10.6
1977	8.9	8.8	8.3	7.7	8.1	8.9	10.5	10.9	10.1	10.4	9.6	9.1	10.5	10.0	10.3	10.9	11.6	11.4	11.0	10.7	10.0
1978	8.9	8.8	8.3	7.7	8.0	8.9	10.4	10.8	10.0	10.3	9.6	9.0	10.4	9.9	10.2	10.8	11.5	11.3	10.9	10.6	9.9
1979	9.0	9.0	8.5	7.9	8.2	9.1	10.6	11.0	10.2	10.5	9.8	9.2	10.6	10.1	10.4	11.0	11.7	11.4	11.1	10.8	10.2
1980	9.4	9.4	8.9	8.3	8.7	9.5	11.0	11.4	10.6	10.9	10.2	9.7	11.1	10.6	10.9	11.5	12.2	11.9	11.6	11.4	10.7
1981	9.1	9.1	8.6	8.1	8.4	9.2	10.6	11.0	10.3	10.6	9.9	9.4	10.7	10.2	10.5	11.1	11.7	11.5	11.1	10.9	10.3
1982	9.3	9.3	8.8	8.3	8.6	9.4	10.8	11.2	10.5	10.8	10.1	9.6	10.9	10.5	10.8	11.3	11.9	11.7	11.4	11.2	10.6
1983	9.6	9.5	9.1	8.5	8.9	9.6	11.0	11.5	10.7	10.9	10.3	9.9	11.1	10.7	11.0	11.5	12.2	12.0	11.6	11.4	10.9
1984	9.5	9.5	9.0	8.5	8.8	9.6	10.9	11.3	10.6	10.9	10.3	9.8	11.0	10.6	10.9	11.4	12.0	11.8	11.5	11.3	10.7
1985	9.8	9.8	9.4	8.9	9.2	9.9	11.3	11.7	11.0	11.3	10.7	10.2	11.4	11.1	11.3	11.8	12.4	12.3	12.0	11.8	11.2
1986	10.0	9.9	9.5	9.0	9.4	10.1	11.4	11.8	11.2	11.4	10.8	10.4	11.6	11.2	11.5	12.0	12.6	12.4	12.1	11.9	11.4
1987	9.9	9.9	9.5	9.0	9.3	10.0	11.3	11.7	11.0	11.3	10.7	10.3	11.5	11.1	11.3	11.8	12.4	12.2	11.9	11.8	11.2

EXHIBIT A-1 (Continued)

TO THE END OF	FROM THE BEGINNING OF 1947	1948	1949	1950	1951	1952	1953	1954	1955	1956	1957	1958	1959	1960	1961	1962	1963	1964	1965	1966	1967
1947	5.7																				
1948	5.6	5.5																			
1949	9.8	11.9	18.8																		
1950	14.9	18.2	25.1	31.7																	
1951	16.7	19.6	24.7	27.8	24.0																
1952	17.0	19.4	23.1	24.6	21.2	18.4															
1953	14.2	15.7	17.9	17.6	13.3	8.3	-1.0														
1954	18.4	20.4	23.0	23.9	22.0	21.4	22.9	52.6													
1955	19.8	21.7	24.2	25.2	23.9	23.9	25.7	41.7	31.6												
1956	18.4	19.9	21.9	22.3	20.8	20.2	20.6	28.9	18.4	6.6											
1957	15.4	16.4	17.7	17.6	15.7	14.4	13.6	17.5	7.7	-2.5	-10.8										
1958	17.5	18.7	20.1	20.2	18.8	18.1	18.1	22.3	15.7	10.9	13.1	43.4									
1959	17.1	18.1	19.3	19.4	18.1	17.3	17.2	20.5	15.0	11.1	12.7	26.7	12.0								
1960	15.8	16.6	17.6	17.5	16.2	15.3	14.9	17.4	12.4	8.9	9.5	17.3	6.1	0.5							
1961	16.5	17.3	18.3	18.3	17.1	16.4	16.2	18.6	14.4	11.7	12.8	19.6	12.6	12.9	26.9						
1962	14.8	15.4	16.1	15.9	14.7	13.9	13.4	15.2	11.2	8.5	8.9	13.3	6.8	5.2	7.6	-8.7					
1963	15.2	15.8	16.6	16.4	15.3	14.6	14.3	16.0	12.4	10.2	10.8	14.8	9.3	9.3	12.5	5.9	22.8				
1964	15.3	15.9	16.6	16.4	15.4	14.7	14.4	16.0	12.8	10.9	11.5	15.1	10.9	10.7	13.5	9.3	19.6	16.5			
1965	15.1	15.7	16.3	16.2	15.2	14.6	14.3	15.7	12.8	11.1	11.6	14.7	11.1	11.0	13.2	10.1	17.2	14.4	12.5		
1966	13.7	14.2	14.7	14.4	13.4	12.7	12.4	13.4	10.7	9.0	9.2	11.7	8.2	7.7	9.0	5.7	9.7	5.6	0.6	-10.1	
1967	14.2	14.6	15.1	14.9	14.0	13.4	13.1	14.2	11.6	10.1	10.5	12.8	9.9	9.6	11.0	8.6	12.4	9.9	7.8	5.6	24.0
1968	14.0	14.5	14.9	14.7	13.8	13.3	13.0	14.0	11.6	10.2	10.5	12.7	10.0	9.8	11.0	8.9	12.2	10.2	8.6	7.4	17.3
1969	13.0	13.3	13.7	13.4	12.5	11.9	11.6	12.4	10.1	8.7	8.9	10.7	8.2	7.8	8.7	6.6	9.0	6.8	5.0	3.2	8.0
1970	12.6	12.9	13.2	13.0	12.1	11.5	11.1	11.9	9.7	8.4	8.6	10.2	7.8	7.5	8.2	6.3	8.3	6.4	4.8	3.3	7.0
1971	12.6	12.9	13.3	13.0	12.2	11.6	11.3	12.0	10.0	8.8	8.9	10.5	8.3	8.0	8.7	7.1	9.0	7.4	6.1	5.1	8.4
1972	12.8	13.2	13.5	13.3	12.5	12.0	11.7	12.4	10.5	9.4	9.5	11.0	9.0	8.8	9.5	8.1	9.9	8.6	7.6	7.0	10.1
1973	11.7	11.9	12.2	11.9	11.2	10.6	10.3	10.8	9.1	7.9	7.9	9.2	7.3	6.9	7.5	6.0	7.4	6.0	4.9	4.0	6.2
1974	10.1	10.2	10.4	10.1	9.3	8.7	8.2	8.7	6.9	5.7	5.7	6.7	4.8	4.3	4.6	3.0	4.1	2.5	1.2	0.1	1.4
1975	10.9	11.1	11.3	11.0	10.3	9.7	9.4	9.9	8.2	7.1	7.1	8.2	6.4	6.1	6.5	5.2	6.3	5.1	4.1	3.3	4.9
1976	10.9	11.5	11.7	11.5	10.8	10.3	9.9	10.4	8.8	7.8	7.9	9.0	7.3	7.1	7.5	6.3	7.5	6.4	5.6	5.0	6.6
1977	10.7	10.8	11.0	10.7	10.0	9.5	9.2	9.6	8.1	7.1	7.1	8.1	6.5	6.2	6.6	5.4	6.4	5.4	4.6	3.9	5.3
1978	10.5	10.7	10.9	10.6	9.9	9.4	9.1	9.5	8.0	7.1	7.1	8.0	6.5	6.2	6.6	5.5	6.5	5.4	4.7	4.1	5.4
1979	10.8	10.9	11.1	10.8	10.2	9.7	9.4	9.8	8.4	7.5	7.6	8.5	7.1	6.8	7.2	6.2	7.1	6.2	5.6	5.1	6.3
1980	11.3	11.5	11.7	11.5	10.9	10.4	10.2	10.6	9.2	8.4	8.5	9.4	8.1	7.9	8.3	7.4	8.4	7.6	7.1	6.7	8.0
1981	10.8	11.0	11.2	10.9	10.3	9.9	9.6	10.0	8.7	7.9	7.9	8.8	7.5	7.3	7.6	6.8	7.6	6.9	6.3	5.9	7.1
1982	11.1	11.3	11.5	11.2	10.7	10.2	10.0	10.4	9.1	8.4	8.4	9.3	8.1	7.9	8.2	7.4	8.3	7.6	7.1	6.8	8.0
1983	11.4	11.6	11.8	11.6	11.0	10.6	10.4	10.8	9.6	8.8	8.9	9.8	8.6	8.5	8.8	8.1	8.9	8.3	7.9	7.6	8.8
1984	11.3	11.4	11.6	11.4	10.9	10.5	10.2	10.6	9.4	8.7	8.8	9.6	8.5	8.4	8.7	8.0	8.8	8.2	7.8	7.5	8.6
1985	11.8	11.9	12.1	11.9	11.4	11.1	10.8	11.2	10.1	9.5	9.6	10.4	9.3	9.2	9.6	8.9	9.7	9.2	8.8	8.7	9.7
1986	11.9	12.1	12.3	12.1	11.6	11.3	11.1	11.4	10.4	9.7	9.8	10.6	9.6	9.5	9.9	9.3	10.1	9.6	9.3	9.1	10.2
1987	11.8	11.9	12.1	11.9	11.4	11.1	10.9	11.3	10.2	9.6	9.7	10.4	9.5	9.4	9.7	9.1	9.9	9.4	9.1	8.9	9.9

EXHIBIT A-1 (Continued)

TO THE END OF	FROM THE BEGINNING OF																			
	1968	1969	1970	1971	1972	1973	1974	1975	1976	1977	1978	1979	1980	1981	1982	1983	1984	1985	1986	1987
1968	11.1																			
1969	0.8	-8.5																		
1970	1.9	-2.4	4.0																	
1971	4.8	2.8	9.0	14.3																
1972	7.5	6.7	12.3	16.6	19.0															
1973	3.5	2.0	4.8	5.1	0.8	-14.7														
1974	-1.5	-3.4	-2.4	-3.9	-9.3	-20.8	-26.5													
1975	2.7	1.6	3.3	3.2	0.6	-4.9	0.4	37.2												
1976	4.9	4.1	6.0	6.4	4.9	1.6	7.7	30.4	23.8											
1977	3.6	2.8	4.3	4.3	2.8	-0.2	3.8	16.4	7.2	-7.2										
1978	3.9	3.2	4.5	4.6	3.3	0.9	4.3	13.9	7.0	-0.5	6.6									
1979	5.0	4.5	5.9	6.1	5.1	3.2	6.6	14.8	9.7	5.4	12.3	18.4								
1980	6.9	6.5	8.0	8.4	7.8	6.5	9.9	17.5	13.9	11.6	18.7	25.2	32.4							
1981	6.0	5.6	6.9	7.2	6.5	5.2	7.9	14.0	10.6	8.1	12.3	14.3	12.2	-4.9						
1982	7.0	6.7	7.9	8.3	7.7	6.7	9.4	14.9	12.1	10.2	14.0	16.0	15.2	7.4	21.4					
1983	7.9	7.7	8.9	9.3	8.9	8.0	10.6	15.7	13.3	11.9	15.4	17.3	17.0	12.3	22.0	22.5				
1984	7.8	7.6	8.7	9.1	8.7	7.9	10.2	14.8	12.5	11.2	14.1	15.4	14.8	10.7	16.5	14.1	6.3			
1985	9.0	8.9	10.1	10.5	10.2	9.6	11.9	16.2	14.3	13.3	16.2	17.6	17.5	14.7	20.2	19.8	18.5	32.2		
1986	9.5	9.4	10.6	11.0	10.8	10.2	12.4	16.4	14.7	13.8	16.4	17.7	17.6	15.3	19.9	19.5	18.5	25.1	18.5	
1987	9.3	9.2	10.3	10.6	10.4	9.9	11.9	15.5	13.9	13.0	15.3	16.3	16.0	13.8	17.3	16.5	15.0	18.1	11.7	5.2

EXHIBIT A-2
SMALL-COMPANY STOCKS: TOTAL RETURNS
RATES OF RETURN FOR ALL YEARLY HOLDING PERIODS FROM 1926 TO 1987
(Percent Per Annum Compounded Annually)

TO THE END OF	1926	1927	1928	1929	1930	1931	1932	1933	1934	1935	1936	1937	1938	1939	1940	1941	1942	1943	1944	1945	1946
1926	0.3																				
1927	10.7	22.1																			
1928	19.6	30.6	39.7																		
1929	-4.5	-6.0	-17.6	-51.4																	
1930	-12.4	-15.4	-25.1	-45.1	-38.1																
1931	-20.2	-23.7	-32.2	-46.7	-44.3	-49.8															
1932	-18.2	-21.0	-27.5	-38.5	-33.5	-31.1	-5.4														
1933	-6.3	-7.2	-11.4	-19.1	-8.1	4.9	51.6	142.9													
1934	-3.3	-3.8	-7.0	-13.1	-2.4	9.4	41.9	73.7	24.2												
1935	0.3	0.3	-2.1	-6.9	3.7	15.0	41.4	61.7	32.0	40.2											
1936	5.0	5.5	3.7	-0.0	10.8	22.1	45.8	62.5	42.1	52.0	64.8										
1937	-2.7	-3.0	-5.2	-9.2	-1.9	4.8	18.5	24.0	4.8	-1.0	-16.8	-58.0									
1938	-0.4	-0.4	-2.3	-5.7	1.5	8.0	20.4	25.4	9.9	6.5	-2.8	-25.3	32.8								
1939	-0.3	-0.4	-2.1	-5.2	1.4	7.1	17.7	21.5	8.2	5.3	-2.0	-17.6	15.4	0.3							
1940	-0.7	-0.7	-2.3	-5.2	0.8	5.8	14.9	17.8	6.2	3.5	-2.6	-14.6	8.1	-2.4	-5.2						
1941	-1.2	-1.3	-2.8	-5.5	-0.1	4.4	12.3	14.4	4.2	1.6	-3.7	-13.5	3.6	-4.7	-7.1	-9.0					
1942	1.0	1.1	-0.2	-2.6	2.8	7.2	14.9	17.1	8.0	6.2	2.0	-5.8	10.7	5.8	7.6	14.7	44.5				
1943	4.6	4.8	3.9	1.8	7.3	12.0	19.7	22.3	14.2	13.1	10.1	4.0	21.0	18.7	23.8	35.3	65.0	88.4			
1944	6.7	7.1	6.3	4.5	9.9	14.5	22.0	24.7	17.3	16.7	14.3	9.2	25.2	23.9	29.3	39.7	61.1	70.2	53.7		
1945	9.4	9.9	9.2	7.6	13.1	17.8	25.2	27.9	21.2	21.0	19.2	15.0	30.4	30.1	35.8	45.9	64.2	71.3	63.4	73.6	
1946	8.3	8.7	8.0	6.5	11.5	15.7	22.3	24.5	18.3	17.8	16.0	12.0	24.9	23.9	27.7	34.2	45.0	45.2	33.1	23.9	-11.6
1947	7.9	8.3	7.6	6.2	11.1	14.8	20.8	22.8	17.0	16.4	14.6	10.9	22.2	21.1	24.0	28.8	36.5	35.0	24.2	15.7	-5.6
1948	7.5	7.8	7.2	5.7	10.2	13.7	19.3	21.1	15.6	15.0	13.3	9.8	19.8	18.6	20.8	24.5	30.2	28.0	18.4	11.0	-4.4
1949	7.9	8.3	7.7	6.4	10.6	14.1	19.4	21.0	15.9	15.3	13.7	10.5	19.8	18.7	20.7	24.0	28.8	26.7	18.7	12.7	1.1
1950	9.0	9.3	8.9	7.7	11.8	15.2	20.3	21.9	17.1	16.7	15.2	12.3	21.2	20.2	22.2	25.4	29.9	28.2	21.3	16.6	7.7
1951	9.0	9.3	8.8	7.7	11.6	14.8	19.7	21.1	16.5	16.1	14.8	12.0	20.1	19.2	21.0	23.7	27.5	25.7	19.6	15.3	7.7
1952	8.8	9.1	8.6	7.5	11.2	14.2	18.8	20.2	15.8	15.3	14.0	11.4	18.9	18.0	19.5	21.8	25.1	23.3	17.6	13.7	7.0
1953	8.2	8.5	8.0	6.9	10.4	13.3	17.5	18.7	14.6	14.1	12.8	10.3	17.2	16.2	17.4	19.3	22.1	20.2	14.9	11.3	5.3
1954	9.7	10.0	9.6	8.6	12.1	14.9	19.1	20.4	16.2	16.0	14.9	12.6	19.3	18.6	19.9	21.9	24.7	23.1	18.5	15.4	10.3
1955	10.0	10.3	9.9	9.0	12.4	15.1	19.2	20.4	16.3	16.3	15.2	13.0	19.4	18.7	19.9	21.8	24.4	22.9	18.6	15.9	11.3
1956	9.8	10.1	9.7	8.8	12.1	14.7	18.5	19.7	16.0	15.7	14.6	12.6	18.6	17.8	18.9	20.6	22.9	21.5	17.5	14.9	10.6
1957	8.9	9.2	8.8	7.9	11.0	13.4	17.1	18.1	14.6	14.2	13.1	11.1	16.6	15.8	16.8	18.2	20.1	18.7	14.8	12.3	8.3
1958	10.3	10.7	10.3	9.4	12.5	15.0	18.6	19.6	16.2	15.9	15.0	13.1	18.6	17.9	18.9	20.4	22.4	21.1	17.6	15.4	11.8
1959	10.5	10.8	10.5	9.7	12.7	15.0	18.5	19.5	16.3	15.9	15.0	13.2	18.5	17.8	18.8	20.2	22.1	20.9	17.6	15.5	12.2

FROM THE BEGINNING OF

EXHIBIT A-2 (Continued)

TO THE END OF	FROM THE BEGINNING OF 1926	1927	1928	1929	1930	1931	1932	1933	1934	1935	1936	1937	1938	1939	1940	1941	1942	1943	1944	1945	1946
1960	10.1	10.4	10.0	9.2	12.1	14.4	17.7	18.6	15.5	15.1	14.2	12.5	17.4	16.8	17.6	18.9	20.6	19.4	16.2	14.2	11.1
1961	10.6	10.9	10.6	9.9	12.7	14.9	18.1	19.0	16.0	15.7	14.9	13.2	18.0	17.4	18.2	19.5	21.1	20.0	17.0	15.2	12.3
1962	10.0	10.2	9.9	9.1	11.9	13.9	17.0	17.8	14.9	14.6	13.8	12.1	16.6	16.0	16.7	17.8	19.3	18.2	15.3	13.5	10.7
1963	10.3	10.6	10.3	9.5	12.2	14.2	17.2	18.0	15.2	14.9	14.1	12.5	16.9	16.3	17.0	18.1	19.5	18.4	15.7	14.0	11.4
1964	10.6	10.9	10.6	9.9	12.5	14.5	17.4	18.2	15.5	15.2	14.4	12.9	17.1	16.6	17.3	18.3	19.7	18.6	16.1	14.4	12.0
1965	11.3	11.6	11.3	10.7	13.2	15.2	18.0	18.8	16.2	16.0	15.2	13.8	17.9	17.4	18.1	19.2	20.5	19.6	17.1	15.6	13.3
1966	10.8	11.1	10.8	10.2	12.6	14.5	17.2	18.0	15.4	15.2	14.4	13.0	17.0	16.4	17.1	18.0	19.3	18.3	16.0	14.5	12.2
1967	12.2	12.5	12.2	11.6	14.1	16.0	18.7	19.5	17.0	16.8	16.1	14.8	18.7	18.3	19.0	20.0	21.3	20.4	18.2	16.9	14.8
1968	12.7	13.0	12.8	12.2	14.6	16.5	19.1	19.9	17.5	17.3	16.7	15.4	19.3	18.8	19.5	20.5	21.8	21.0	18.9	17.6	15.6
1969	11.6	11.9	11.7	11.1	13.4	15.2	17.7	18.4	16.1	15.8	15.2	13.9	17.5	17.1	17.7	18.6	19.7	18.9	16.8	15.5	13.5
1970	10.9	11.1	10.9	10.3	12.5	14.2	16.6	17.3	15.0	14.7	14.1	12.9	16.3	15.8	16.3	17.1	18.1	17.3	15.3	14.0	12.1
1971	11.0	11.2	11.0	10.4	12.6	14.3	16.6	17.3	15.0	14.8	14.2	13.0	16.3	15.8	16.4	17.1	18.1	17.3	15.3	14.1	12.3
1972	10.9	11.1	10.9	10.3	12.4	14.0	16.3	16.9	14.7	14.5	13.9	12.7	15.9	15.5	16.0	16.7	17.6	16.8	14.9	13.7	12.0
1973	9.8	10.0	9.7	9.1	11.2	12.7	14.9	15.4	13.3	13.0	12.4	11.2	14.3	13.8	14.2	14.9	15.7	14.9	13.0	11.8	10.1
1974	9.1	9.3	9.0	8.4	10.4	11.8	13.9	14.4	12.3	12.1	11.4	10.3	13.2	12.7	13.1	13.6	14.4	13.6	11.7	10.6	8.9
1975	9.8	10.0	9.8	9.2	11.1	12.6	14.7	15.2	13.2	12.9	12.3	11.2	14.1	13.6	14.0	14.6	15.4	14.6	12.8	11.7	10.1
1976	10.6	10.8	10.6	10.0	12.0	13.4	15.5	16.0	14.0	13.8	13.2	12.2	15.0	14.6	15.0	15.6	16.4	15.7	14.0	12.9	11.4
1977	10.8	11.1	10.9	10.3	12.2	13.7	15.7	16.2	14.3	14.1	13.5	12.5	15.3	14.9	15.3	15.9	16.7	16.0	14.3	13.3	11.8
1978	11.1	11.3	11.1	10.6	12.4	13.9	15.9	16.4	14.5	14.3	13.7	12.7	15.5	15.1	15.5	16.1	16.8	16.2	14.6	13.6	12.1
1979	11.6	11.8	11.6	11.1	13.0	14.4	16.4	16.9	15.0	14.8	14.3	13.4	16.1	15.7	16.1	16.7	17.5	16.8	15.3	14.3	12.9
1980	12.1	12.3	12.1	11.6	13.5	14.9	16.8	17.3	15.5	15.3	14.8	13.9	16.6	16.2	16.6	17.2	18.0	17.4	15.9	15.0	13.6
1981	12.1	12.3	12.1	11.7	13.5	14.8	16.8	17.3	15.5	15.3	14.8	13.9	16.5	16.2	16.6	17.2	17.9	17.3	15.8	14.9	13.6
1982	12.4	12.6	12.4	12.0	13.7	15.1	17.0	17.5	15.7	15.6	15.1	14.2	16.8	16.4	16.8	17.4	18.1	17.5	16.1	15.3	14.0
1983	12.8	13.0	12.9	12.4	14.2	15.5	17.4	17.9	16.2	16.0	15.6	14.7	17.2	16.9	17.3	17.9	18.6	18.0	16.7	15.8	14.6
1984	12.4	12.6	12.5	12.0	13.8	15.0	16.9	17.3	15.7	15.5	15.0	14.4	16.6	16.3	16.7	17.3	17.9	17.4	16.0	15.2	14.0
1985	12.6	12.8	12.7	12.3	13.9	15.2	17.0	17.5	15.8	15.7	15.2	14.4	16.8	16.5	16.9	17.4	18.1	17.5	16.2	15.4	14.3
1986	12.5	12.7	12.6	12.2	13.8	15.1	16.8	17.3	15.7	15.5	15.1	14.2	16.6	16.3	16.6	17.2	17.8	17.3	16.0	15.2	14.1
1987	12.1	12.3	12.2	11.8	13.4	14.6	16.3	16.7	15.1	15.0	14.5	13.7	16.0	15.7	16.0	16.5	17.2	16.6	15.4	14.6	13.5

EXHIBIT A-2 (Continued)

TO THE END OF	1947	1948	1949	1950	1951	1952	1953	1954	1955	1956	1957	1958	1959	1960	1961	1962	1963	1964	1965	1966	1967
																					FROM THE BEGINNING OF
1947	0.9																				
1948	-0.6	-2.1																			
1949	5.8	8.3	19.7																		
1950	13.2	17.6	28.9	38.7																	
1951	12.1	15.1	21.4	22.3	7.8																
1952	10.5	12.6	16.6	15.5	5.4	3.0															
1953	7.9	9.1	11.5	9.6	1.3	-1.8	-6.5														
1954	13.4	15.3	18.8	18.3	13.6	15.7	22.5	60.6													
1955	14.2	15.9	18.8	18.6	15.0	16.8	21.8	39.1	20.4												
1956	13.1	14.6	16.9	16.5	13.1	14.2	17.2	26.3	12.1	4.3											
1957	10.3	11.3	12.9	12.0	8.7	8.8	10.0	14.6	2.4	-5.6	-14.6										
1958	14.0	15.4	17.2	17.0	14.5	15.5	17.7	23.2	15.3	13.7	18.7	64.9									
1959	14.2	15.4	17.2	16.9	14.7	15.6	17.5	22.1	15.5	14.4	17.9	38.5	16.4								
1960	12.9	13.9	15.3	14.9	12.8	13.3	14.7	18.1	12.2	10.6	12.2	22.9	6.1	-3.3							
1961	14.1	15.1	16.5	16.2	14.4	15.1	16.5	19.7	14.8	13.9	15.9	25.1	14.1	13.0	32.1						
1962	12.2	13.0	14.2	13.8	11.9	12.3	13.3	15.7	11.1	9.8	10.7	16.6	7.0	4.0	7.9	-11.9					
1963	12.9	13.7	14.8	14.5	12.8	13.2	14.2	16.5	12.4	11.4	12.5	17.8	10.1	8.6	12.9	4.3	23.6				
1964	13.4	14.2	15.3	15.0	13.5	14.0	14.9	17.1	13.3	12.7	13.8	18.6	12.2	11.4	15.4	10.4	23.5	23.5			
1965	14.8	15.6	16.7	16.6	15.2	15.8	16.8	19.0	15.8	15.3	16.6	21.3	16.0	16.0	20.3	17.5	29.3	32.3	41.8		
1966	13.6	14.3	15.3	15.0	13.7	14.1	14.9	16.7	13.7	13.1	14.0	17.7	12.9	12.4	15.2	12.1	19.1	17.6	14.8	-7.0	
1967	16.2	17.0	18.1	18.0	16.9	17.5	18.6	20.6	18.0	17.8	19.1	23.1	19.1	19.5	23.2	21.7	29.9	31.5	34.3	30.7	83.6
1968	17.0	17.9	19.0	18.9	17.9	18.5	19.6	21.6	19.2	19.1	20.4	24.2	20.7	21.2	24.7	23.7	30.9	32.4	34.7	32.4	58.0
1969	14.8	15.5	16.4	16.2	15.1	15.6	16.3	17.9	15.5	15.2	16.1	19.1	15.6	15.5	17.8	16.2	20.8	20.4	19.8	14.8	23.2
1970	13.2	13.8	14.6	14.3	13.2	13.5	14.1	15.5	13.1	12.7	13.3	15.8	12.4	12.1	13.7	11.8	15.2	14.1	12.6	7.5	11.5
1971	13.4	13.9	14.7	14.4	13.4	13.7	14.3	15.5	13.3	12.9	13.5	15.8	12.7	12.4	14.0	12.3	15.4	14.4	13.1	9.0	12.5
1972	13.0	13.5	14.2	14.0	13.0	13.2	13.8	14.9	12.8	12.4	12.9	15.0	12.1	11.8	13.1	11.6	14.2	13.2	12.0	8.3	11.1
1973	11.0	11.4	11.5	11.6	10.6	10.7	11.1	12.0	9.9	9.4	9.7	11.4	8.5	8.0	8.9	7.2	9.1	7.8	6.2	2.4	3.8
1974	9.7	10.0	10.1	10.2	9.1	9.2	9.4	10.3	8.2	7.6	7.8	9.3	6.5	5.9	6.6	4.8	6.3	4.9	3.2	-0.4	0.5
1975	10.9	11.3	11.4	11.5	10.6	10.7	11.0	11.9	10.0	9.5	9.8	11.3	8.8	8.3	9.2	7.7	9.3	8.2	6.9	4.0	5.3
1976	12.2	12.6	13.2	13.0	12.1	12.3	12.7	13.6	11.8	11.4	11.8	13.4	11.0	10.7	11.7	10.4	12.2	11.4	10.4	8.0	9.6
1977	12.6	13.1	13.6	13.4	12.6	12.7	13.1	14.1	12.4	12.0	12.4	13.9	11.8	11.5	12.4	11.3	13.1	12.3	11.5	9.3	10.9
1978	13.0	13.4	13.9	13.7	12.9	13.1	13.5	14.4	12.8	12.5	12.9	14.4	12.3	12.1	13.0	12.0	13.7	13.1	12.3	10.4	11.9
1979	13.8	14.2	14.8	14.6	13.9	14.1	14.5	15.4	13.9	13.6	14.1	15.6	13.6	13.5	14.5	13.5	15.3	14.8	14.2	12.4	14.1
1980	14.5	14.9	15.5	15.4	14.6	14.9	15.3	16.2	14.8	14.6	15.0	16.5	14.7	14.6	15.6	14.8	16.5	16.1	15.6	14.1	15.8
1981	14.5	14.9	15.4	15.3	14.6	14.9	15.3	16.2	14.8	14.6	15.0	16.4	14.7	14.6	15.5	14.8	16.4	16.0	15.5	14.1	15.6
1982	14.8	15.2	15.8	15.7	15.0	15.3	15.7	16.5	15.2	15.0	15.5	16.9	15.2	15.1	16.1	15.4	16.9	16.6	16.2	14.9	16.4
1983	15.4	15.9	16.4	16.3	15.7	16.0	16.4	17.2	16.0	15.8	16.3	17.7	16.1	16.1	16.9	16.4	17.9	17.6	17.3	16.1	17.6
1984	14.8	15.2	15.7	15.6	15.0	15.2	15.6	16.4	15.1	15.0	15.4	16.7	15.1	15.1	15.9	15.2	16.7	16.3	16.0	14.8	16.1
1985	15.0	15.4	15.9	15.8	15.2	15.5	15.9	16.6	15.4	15.3	15.7	16.9	15.5	15.4	16.2	15.6	17.0	16.7	16.4	15.3	16.6
1986	14.8	15.2	15.7	15.6	15.0	15.2	15.6	16.3	15.2	15.0	15.4	16.6	15.1	15.1	15.9	15.3	16.6	16.3	15.9	14.8	16.1
1987	14.2	14.5	15.0	14.8	14.3	14.4	14.8	15.5	14.3	14.1	14.5	15.6	14.2	14.1	14.8	14.2	15.4	15.1	14.7	13.6	14.7

EXHIBIT A-2 (Continued)

TO THE END OF	FROM THE BEGINNING OF 1968	1969	1970	1971	1972	1973	1974	1975	1976	1977	1978	1979	1980	1981	1982	1983	1984	1985	1986	1987
1968	36.0																			
1969	0.9	-25.1																		
1970	-5.6	-21.3	-17.4																	
1971	-0.5	-10.3	-1.9	16.5																
1972	0.5	-6.9	0.2	10.3	4.4															
1973	-5.6	-12.3	-8.7	-5.6	-15.1	-30.9														
1974	-7.8	-13.6	-11.1	-9.4	-16.7	-25.6	-19.9													
1975	-1.8	-6.3	-2.7	0.6	-3.1	-5.4	10.6	52.8												
1976	3.5	0.0	4.2	8.4	6.8	7.4	24.4	55.1	57.4											
1977	5.5	2.6	6.7	10.6	9.7	10.8	24.6	44.5	40.5	25.4										
1978	7.0	4.5	8.4	12.2	11.6	12.8	24.4	38.9	34.6	24.4	23.5									
1979	9.7	7.5	11.5	15.3	15.1	16.7	27.4	39.8	36.7	30.5	33.1	43.5								
1980	11.7	9.9	13.8	17.5	17.6	19.4	29.1	39.8	37.4	32.8	35.3	41.7	39.9							
1981	11.9	10.2	13.8	17.2	17.3	18.8	27.1	35.8	33.1	28.7	29.6	31.7	26.2	13.9						
1982	12.9	11.4	14.9	18.1	18.2	19.7	27.2	34.8	32.4	26.6	29.3	30.8	26.8	20.7	28.0					
1983	14.4	13.1	16.5	19.6	19.9	21.4	28.4	35.3	33.3	30.1	31.0	32.5	29.9	26.7	33.7	39.7				
1984	13.0	11.7	14.8	17.5	17.6	18.7	24.7	30.4	28.1	24.8	24.8	25.0	21.6	17.4	18.6	14.2	-6.7			
1985	13.7	12.5	15.4	18.0	18.1	19.2	24.7	29.9	27.8	24.8	24.8	24.9	22.1	18.8	20.1	17.6	7.9	24.7		
1986	13.3	12.1	14.8	17.2	17.3	18.3	23.2	27.8	25.7	22.9	22.6	22.5	19.8	16.7	17.3	14.8	7.5	15.4	6.9	
1987	12.0	10.9	13.3	15.5	15.4	16.2	20.6	24.4	22.3	19.6	19.0	18.5	15.7	12.6	12.4	9.5	3.0	6.5	-1.6	-9.3

EXHIBIT A-3
LONG-TERM CORPORATE BONDS: TOTAL RETURNS
RATES OF RETURN FOR ALL YEARLY HOLDING PERIODS FROM 1926 TO 1987
(Percent Per Annum Compounded Annually)

TO THE END OF	FROM THE BEGINNING OF																				
	1926	1927	1928	1929	1930	1931	1932	1933	1934	1935	1936	1937	1938	1939	1940	1941	1942	1943	1944	1945	1946
1926	7.4																				
1927	7.4	7.4																			
1928	5.9	5.1	2.8																		
1929	5.2	4.5	3.1	3.3																	
1930	5.8	5.4	4.7	5.6	8.0																
1931	4.4	3.9	3.0	3.1	2.9	-1.9															
1932	5.3	5.0	4.5	4.9	5.5	4.3	10.8														
1933	6.0	5.8	5.5	6.0	6.7	6.3	10.6	10.4													
1934	6.8	6.7	6.6	7.3	8.1	8.1	11.7	12.1	13.8												
1935	7.1	7.0	7.0	7.6	8.3	8.4	11.2	11.3	11.7	9.6											
1936	7.1	7.0	7.0	7.5	8.1	8.1	10.3	10.1	10.0	8.2	6.7										
1937	6.7	6.6	6.5	7.0	7.4	7.4	9.0	8.6	8.2	6.3	4.7	2.7									
1938	6.6	6.6	6.5	6.9	7.3	7.2	8.6	8.2	7.8	6.3	5.2	4.4	6.1								
1939	6.4	6.4	6.3	6.6	6.9	6.8	8.0	7.6	7.1	5.8	4.9	4.3	5.0	4.0							
1940	6.2	6.2	6.1	6.3	6.6	6.5	7.5	7.0	6.6	5.4	4.6	4.1	4.5	3.7	3.4						
1941	6.0	5.9	5.8	6.1	6.3	6.1	7.0	6.6	6.1	5.0	4.3	3.8	4.0	3.4	3.1	2.7					
1942	5.8	5.7	5.6	5.8	6.0	5.8	6.6	6.2	5.7	4.7	4.0	3.6	3.8	3.2	2.9	2.7	2.6				
1943	5.6	5.5	5.4	5.6	5.8	5.6	6.3	5.8	5.4	4.5	3.9	3.5	3.6	3.1	3.1	2.9	2.7	2.8			
1944	5.6	5.5	5.4	5.6	5.7	5.5	6.1	5.8	5.3	4.5	4.0	3.6	3.8	3.4	3.4	3.2	3.4	3.8	4.7		
1945	5.5	5.4	5.3	5.5	5.6	5.4	6.0	5.6	5.2	4.5	4.0	3.7	3.8	3.5	3.4	3.4	3.6	3.9	4.4	4.1	
1946	5.3	5.2	5.1	5.3	5.4	5.2	5.7	5.3	5.0	4.3	3.8	3.5	3.6	3.3	3.2	3.1	3.3	3.3	3.5	2.9	1.7
1947	5.0	4.9	4.7	4.8	4.9	4.7	5.2	4.8	4.4	3.7	3.3	2.9	3.0	2.6	2.4	2.3	2.2	2.0	2.0	1.1	-0.3
1948	4.9	4.8	4.7	4.8	4.9	4.7	5.1	4.8	4.4	3.8	3.3	3.0	3.1	2.8	2.6	2.5	2.5	2.4	2.4	1.9	1.1
1949	4.9	4.8	4.6	4.7	4.8	4.6	5.0	4.7	4.3	3.7	3.3	3.1	3.1	2.8	2.7	2.6	2.6	2.6	2.6	2.2	1.7
1950	4.8	4.7	4.5	4.6	4.7	4.5	4.9	4.5	4.2	3.6	3.2	3.0	3.0	2.8	2.2	2.6	2.6	2.6	2.5	2.1	1.8
1951	4.5	4.5	4.2	4.3	4.3	4.2	4.5	4.1	3.8	3.3	2.9	2.6	2.6	2.3	2.2	2.1	2.0	2.0	1.8	1.4	1.0
1952	4.4	4.3	4.2	4.2	4.3	4.1	4.4	4.1	3.8	3.3	2.9	2.7	2.7	2.4	2.3	2.2	2.2	2.1	2.0	1.7	1.4
1953	4.4	4.3	4.2	4.2	4.3	4.1	4.4	4.1	3.8	3.3	2.9	2.7	2.7	2.5	2.4	2.3	2.3	2.3	2.2	1.9	1.6
1954	4.4	4.3	4.2	4.2	4.4	4.2	4.4	4.1	3.8	3.4	3.1	2.9	2.9	2.7	2.6	2.4	2.5	2.4	2.5	2.2	2.0
1955	4.3	4.2	4.1	4.1	4.2	4.0	4.3	4.0	3.7	3.2	2.9	2.7	2.7	2.5	2.4	2.4	2.5	2.4	2.3	2.1	1.9
1956	3.9	3.8	3.7	3.7	3.7	3.6	3.8	3.5	3.2	2.8	2.4	2.2	2.2	2.0	1.9	1.8	1.7	1.7	1.6	1.3	1.1
1957	4.1	4.0	3.8	3.9	3.9	3.7	4.0	3.7	3.4	3.0	2.7	2.5	2.5	2.3	2.2	2.2	2.1	2.1	2.1	1.9	1.7
1958	3.9	3.8	3.6	3.7	3.7	3.5	3.7	3.5	3.2	2.8	2.5	2.3	2.3	2.1	2.0	1.9	1.9	1.9	1.8	1.6	1.4
1959	3.7	3.6	3.5	3.5	3.5	3.4	3.6	3.3	3.0	2.6	2.3	2.2	2.1	1.9	1.8	1.8	1.7	1.7	1.6	1.4	1.2

EXHIBIT A-3 (Continued)

FROM THE BEGINNING OF

TO THE END OF	1926	1927	1928	1929	1930	1931	1932	1933	1934	1935	1936	1937	1938	1939	1940	1941	1942	1943	1944	1945	1946
1960	3.9	3.8	3.7	3.7	3.7	3.6	3.7	3.5	3.3	2.9	2.6	2.4	2.4	2.3	2.2	2.1	2.1	2.1	2.0	1.8	1.7
1961	3.9	3.8	3.7	3.7	3.7	3.6	3.8	3.5	3.3	2.9	2.7	2.5	2.5	2.4	2.3	2.2	2.2	2.2	2.2	2.0	1.9
1962	4.0	3.9	3.8	3.8	3.9	3.7	3.9	3.7	3.5	3.1	2.9	2.7	2.7	2.6	2.5	2.5	2.5	2.5	2.5	2.3	2.2
1963	4.0	3.9	3.8	3.8	3.8	3.7	3.9	3.6	3.4	3.1	2.9	2.7	2.7	2.6	2.6	2.6	2.5	2.5	2.5	2.3	2.2
1964	4.0	3.9	3.8	3.8	3.8	3.7	3.9	3.7	3.5	3.1	2.9	2.8	2.8	2.7	2.6	2.6	2.6	2.6	2.6	2.5	2.4
1965	3.9	3.8	3.7	3.7	3.7	3.6	3.8	3.6	3.3	3.0	2.8	2.7	2.7	2.5	2.5	2.5	2.4	2.4	2.4	2.3	2.2
1966	3.8	3.7	3.6	3.6	3.6	3.5	3.7	3.5	3.2	2.9	2.7	2.6	2.6	2.5	2.4	2.4	2.4	2.3	2.3	2.2	2.1
1967	3.6	3.5	3.4	3.4	3.4	3.3	3.4	3.2	3.0	2.7	2.5	2.3	2.3	2.2	2.2	2.1	2.1	2.0	2.0	1.9	1.8
1968	3.5	3.4	3.3	3.4	3.4	3.2	3.4	3.2	3.0	2.7	2.5	2.3	2.3	2.2	2.2	2.1	2.1	2.1	2.0	1.9	1.8
1969	3.3	3.2	3.1	3.1	3.1	2.9	3.1	2.9	2.7	2.4	2.2	2.0	2.0	1.9	1.8	1.7	1.7	1.7	1.6	1.5	1.4
1970	3.6	3.5	3.4	3.4	3.4	3.3	3.4	3.2	3.1	2.8	2.6	2.5	2.5	2.3	2.3	2.3	2.2	2.2	2.2	2.1	2.0
1971	3.7	3.6	3.6	3.6	3.6	3.5	3.6	3.4	3.3	3.0	2.8	2.7	2.7	2.6	2.6	2.5	2.5	2.5	2.5	2.4	2.4
1972	3.8	3.7	3.6	3.7	3.7	3.6	3.7	3.5	3.4	3.1	2.9	2.8	2.8	2.7	2.6	2.7	2.7	2.7	2.7	2.6	2.5
1973	3.7	3.5	3.4	3.4	3.5	3.4	3.6	3.3	3.1	3.0	2.9	2.8	2.8	2.7	2.6	2.6	2.6	2.6	2.6	2.5	2.5
1974	3.6	3.5	3.4	3.4	3.5	3.4	3.5	3.3	3.1	2.9	2.7	2.6	2.6	2.5	2.5	2.4	2.4	2.4	2.4	2.3	2.3
1975	3.8	3.7	3.7	3.7	3.7	3.6	3.7	3.6	3.4	3.2	3.0	2.9	2.9	2.8	2.8	2.8	2.8	2.8	2.8	2.7	2.7
1976	4.1	4.0	3.9	4.0	4.0	3.9	4.0	3.9	3.7	3.5	3.4	3.3	3.3	3.2	3.2	3.2	3.2	3.2	3.2	3.1	3.1
1977	4.0	4.0	3.9	3.9	3.9	3.9	4.0	3.8	3.7	3.5	3.3	3.2	3.2	3.2	3.2	3.1	3.2	3.2	3.2	3.1	3.1
1978	4.0	3.9	3.8	3.8	3.9	3.8	3.9	3.7	3.6	3.4	3.2	3.2	3.2	3.1	3.1	3.1	3.1	3.1	3.1	3.0	3.0
1979	3.8	3.7	3.7	3.7	3.7	3.6	3.7	3.6	3.4	3.2	3.1	3.0	3.0	2.9	2.9	2.9	2.9	2.9	2.9	2.8	2.8
1980	3.7	3.6	3.5	3.6	3.6	3.5	3.6	3.4	3.3	3.1	2.9	2.8	2.9	2.8	2.7	2.7	2.7	2.7	2.7	2.7	2.6
1981	3.6	3.5	3.5	3.5	3.5	3.4	3.5	3.3	3.2	3.0	2.8	2.8	2.8	2.7	2.7	2.6	2.6	2.6	2.6	2.6	2.5
1982	4.2	4.1	4.1	4.1	4.1	4.0	4.2	4.0	3.9	3.7	3.6	3.5	3.5	3.5	3.5	3.5	3.5	3.5	3.5	3.5	3.5
1983	4.2	4.1	4.1	4.1	4.3	4.1	4.4	4.3	3.9	3.7	3.6	3.5	3.6	3.5	3.5	3.5	3.5	3.5	3.6	3.5	3.5
1984	4.4	4.3	4.3	4.3	4.3	4.3	4.4	4.3	4.2	4.0	3.9	3.8	3.8	3.8	3.8	3.8	3.8	3.8	3.8	3.8	3.8
1985	4.8	4.7	4.7	4.7	4.8	4.7	4.8	4.7	4.6	4.4	4.3	4.3	4.3	4.3	4.3	4.3	4.3	4.4	4.4	4.4	4.4
1986	5.0	5.0	4.9	5.0	5.0	5.0	5.1	5.0	4.9	4.7	4.5	4.6	4.6	4.6	4.6	4.6	4.7	4.7	4.8	4.8	4.8
1987	4.9	4.9	4.9	4.9	4.9	4.9	5.0	4.9	4.8	4.6	4.5	4.5	4.5	4.5	4.5	4.5	4.6	4.6	4.6	4.6	4.7

EXHIBIT A-3 (Continued)

TO THE END OF	| FROM THE BEGINNING OF 1947	1948	1949	1950	1951	1952	1953	1954	1955	1956	1957	1958	1959	1960	1961	1962	1963	1964	1965	1966	1967
1947	-2.3																				
1948	0.8	4.1																			
1949	1.7	3.7	3.3																		
1950	1.8	3.2	2.7	2.1																	
1951	0.9	1.7	0.9	-0.3	-2.7																
1952	1.3	2.0	1.5	0.9	0.4	3.5															
1953	1.6	2.3	1.9	1.6	1.4	3.5	3.4														
1954	2.1	2.7	2.5	2.3	2.4	4.1	4.4	5.4													
1955	1.9	2.4	2.2	2.0	2.0	3.2	3.1	2.9	0.5												
1956	1.0	1.4	1.0	0.7	0.5	1.1	0.5	-0.4	-3.2	-6.8											
1957	1.7	2.1	1.8	1.7	1.6	2.3	2.1	1.8	0.6	0.7	8.7										
1958	1.3	1.7	1.4	1.2	1.1	1.7	1.4	1.0	-0.1	-0.3	3.1	-2.2									
1959	1.2	1.5	1.2	1.0	0.9	1.3	1.0	0.6	-0.3	-0.5	1.7	-1.6	-1.0								
1960	1.7	2.0	1.8	1.7	1.7	2.2	2.0	1.8	1.2	1.4	3.5	1.8	3.9	9.1							
1961	1.9	2.2	2.1	2.0	2.0	2.4	2.3	2.2	1.7	1.9	3.8	2.6	4.2	6.9	4.8						
1962	2.3	2.6	2.5	2.4	2.4	2.9	2.9	2.8	2.5	2.8	4.5	3.6	5.1	7.3	6.4	7.9					
1963	2.3	2.6	2.5	2.4	2.6	2.9	2.8	2.7	2.4	2.7	4.1	3.4	4.5	6.0	5.0	5.0	2.2				
1964	2.4	2.7	2.6	2.6	2.6	3.0	3.0	2.9	2.7	2.9	4.2	3.6	4.6	5.7	4.9	4.9	3.5	4.8			
1965	2.3	2.5	2.4	2.4	2.4	2.8	2.7	2.6	2.4	2.6	3.7	3.1	3.8	4.7	3.8	3.6	2.1	2.1	-0.5		
1966	2.1	2.4	2.3	2.2	2.2	2.6	2.5	2.4	2.2	2.4	3.3	2.7	3.4	4.0	3.2	2.9	1.7	1.5	-0.1	0.2	
1967	1.8	2.0	1.9	1.8	1.8	2.1	2.0	1.9	1.6	1.7	2.5	1.9	2.4	2.9	2.0	1.5	0.3	-0.2	-1.8	-2.4	-5.0
1968	1.8	2.0	1.9	1.9	1.8	2.1	2.0	1.9	1.7	1.8	2.5	2.0	2.4	2.8	2.1	1.7	0.7	0.4	-0.7	-0.8	-1.3
1969	1.4	1.6	1.4	1.3	1.3	1.5	1.4	1.3	1.0	1.1	1.7	1.1	1.4	1.7	0.9	0.4	-0.6	-1.1	-2.2	-2.7	-3.6
1970	2.0	2.2	2.1	2.1	2.1	2.3	2.3	2.2	2.0	2.1	2.8	2.4	2.7	3.1	2.5	2.3	1.6	1.5	0.9	1.2	1.5
1971	2.4	2.6	2.5	2.5	2.5	2.8	2.7	2.7	2.5	2.7	3.3	3.0	3.4	3.7	3.3	3.1	2.6	2.6	2.3	2.8	3.3
1972	2.6	2.8	2.7	2.7	2.7	3.0	2.9	2.9	2.8	2.9	3.6	3.2	3.6	4.0	3.6	3.5	3.0	3.1	2.9	3.4	4.0
1973	2.5	2.7	2.6	2.6	2.6	2.9	2.9	2.8	2.7	2.8	3.4	3.1	3.5	3.8	3.4	3.3	2.9	2.9	2.7	3.1	3.6
1974	2.3	2.5	2.4	2.4	2.4	2.6	2.6	2.5	2.4	2.5	3.1	2.7	3.0	3.3	2.9	2.8	2.4	2.4	2.1	2.4	2.7
1975	2.7	2.9	2.8	2.8	2.8	3.1	3.1	3.1	3.0	3.1	3.6	3.4	3.7	4.0	3.7	3.6	3.3	3.3	3.2	3.6	4.0
1976	3.2	3.4	3.4	3.4	3.4	3.7	3.7	3.7	3.6	3.8	4.3	4.1	4.5	4.8	4.5	4.5	4.3	4.4	4.4	4.9	5.4
1977	3.2	3.3	3.3	3.3	3.4	3.6	3.6	3.6	3.5	3.7	4.2	4.0	4.3	4.6	4.4	4.3	4.1	4.2	4.2	4.6	5.0
1978	3.1	3.2	3.2	3.2	3.2	3.5	3.5	3.5	3.4	3.5	4.0	3.8	4.1	4.4	4.1	4.1	3.8	4.0	3.9	4.2	4.6
1979	2.8	3.0	3.0	2.9	3.0	3.2	3.2	3.2	3.1	3.2	3.6	3.4	3.7	3.9	3.7	3.6	3.4	3.4	3.3	3.6	3.9
1980	2.7	2.8	2.8	2.8	2.8	3.0	3.0	2.9	2.8	2.9	3.4	3.1	3.4	3.6	3.3	3.3	3.0	3.1	3.0	3.2	3.4
1981	2.6	2.7	2.7	2.6	2.7	2.8	2.8	2.8	2.7	2.8	3.2	3.0	3.2	3.4	3.1	3.1	2.8	2.8	2.7	2.9	3.1
1982	3.5	3.7	3.7	3.7	3.7	4.0	4.0	4.0	3.9	4.1	4.5	4.4	4.6	4.9	4.7	4.7	4.5	4.7	4.7	5.0	5.3
1983	3.6	3.7	3.7	3.7	3.8	4.0	4.0	4.0	4.0	4.1	4.5	4.4	4.6	4.9	4.7	4.7	4.5	4.7	4.7	5.0	5.2
1984	3.9	4.0	4.0	4.1	4.1	4.3	4.4	4.4	4.4	4.5	4.9	4.8	5.1	5.3	5.2	5.2	5.1	5.2	5.3	5.5	5.8
1985	4.5	4.7	4.7	4.7	4.8	5.0	5.1	5.1	5.1	5.3	5.7	5.6	5.9	6.2	6.1	6.1	6.1	6.2	6.3	6.7	7.0
1986	4.9	5.0	5.1	5.1	5.2	5.4	5.5	5.6	5.6	5.7	6.2	6.1	6.4	6.7	6.6	6.7	6.6	6.8	6.9	7.3	7.6
1987	4.7	4.9	4.9	5.0	5.0	5.3	5.3	5.4	5.4	5.5	6.0	5.9	6.2	6.4	6.3	6.4	6.3	6.5	6.6	6.9	7.2

EXHIBIT A-3 (Continued)

FROM THE BEGINNING OF

TO THE END OF	1968	1969	1970	1971	1972	1973	1974	1975	1976	1977	1978	1979	1980	1981	1982	1983	1984	1985	1986	1987
1968	2.6																			
1969	-2.9	-8.1																		
1970	3.7	4.3	18.4																	
1971	5.5	6.5	14.6	11.0																
1972	5.8	6.7	12.1	9.1	7.3															
1973	5.0	5.6	9.3	6.4	4.2	1.1														
1974	3.9	4.1	6.7	3.9	1.7	-1.0	-3.1													
1975	5.1	5.5	8.0	6.0	4.8	4.0	5.4	14.6												
1976	6.6	7.1	9.4	8.0	7.4	7.5	9.7	16.6	18.6											
1977	6.1	6.5	8.4	7.1	6.4	6.3	7.6	11.4	9.9	1.7										
1978	5.5	5.8	7.5	6.2	5.5	5.2	6.0	8.4	6.4	0.8	-0.1									
1979	4.7	4.8	6.2	5.0	4.2	3.8	4.3	5.8	3.7	-0.9	-2.1	-4.2								
1980	4.1	4.2	5.4	4.2	3.4	3.0	3.2	4.3	2.4	-1.3	-2.3	-3.4	-2.6							
1981	3.7	3.8	4.9	3.7	3.0	2.5	2.7	3.6	1.8	-1.2	-2.0	-2.6	-1.8	-1.0						
1982	6.0	6.2	7.4	6.6	6.2	6.1	6.6	7.9	7.0	5.1	5.8	7.4	11.5	19.3	43.8					
1983	5.9	6.1	7.2	6.4	6.0	5.9	6.4	7.5	6.7	5.1	5.6	6.8	9.8	14.2	22.7	4.7				
1984	6.5	6.7	7.8	7.1	6.8	6.8	7.3	8.4	7.7	6.4	7.1	8.4	11.1	14.8	20.6	10.4	16.4			
1985	7.7	8.0	9.1	8.5	8.4	8.5	9.1	10.3	9.8	8.9	9.8	11.3	14.1	17.8	23.1	16.8	23.4	30.9		
1986	8.3	8.7	9.7	9.2	9.1	9.2	9.9	11.0	10.7	10.0	10.9	12.4	14.9	18.2	22.4	17.6	22.2	25.3	19.8	
1987	7.9	8.2	9.2	8.6	8.5	8.6	9.1	10.1	9.8	9.0	9.7	10.9	12.9	15.3	18.3	13.8	16.2	16.1	9.3	-0.3

EXHIBIT A-4
LONG-TERM GOVERNMENT BONDS: TOTAL RETURNS
RATES OF RETURN FOR ALL YEARLY HOLDING PERIODS FROM 1926 TO 1987
(Percent Per Annum Compounded Annually)

TO THE END OF	FROM THE BEGINNING OF 1926	1927	1928	1929	1930	1931	1932	1933	1934	1935	1936	1937	1938	1939	1940	1941	1942	1943	1944	1945	1946
1926	7.8																				
1927	8.3	8.9																			
1928	5.5	4.4	0.1																		
1929	5.0	4.1	1.7	3.4																	
1930	4.9	4.2	2.7	4.0	4.7																
1931	3.1	2.2	0.6	0.8	-0.5	-5.3															
1932	5.0	4.5	3.7	4.6	5.0	5.2	16.8														
1933	4.4	3.9	3.1	3.7	3.7	3.4	8.1	-0.1													
1934	5.0	4.6	4.0	4.7	4.9	5.0	8.7	4.9	10.0												
1935	5.0	4.7	4.1	4.7	5.0	5.0	7.8	4.9	7.5	5.0											
1936	5.2	4.9	4.5	5.1	5.3	5.4	7.7	5.5	7.5	6.2	7.5										
1937	4.8	4.5	4.1	4.5	4.7	4.7	6.4	4.5	5.6	4.2	3.8	0.2									
1938	4.8	4.6	4.2	4.6	4.7	4.8	6.3	4.6	5.6	4.5	4.4	2.8	5.5								
1939	4.9	4.7	4.3	4.7	4.9	4.9	6.3	4.8	5.7	4.8	4.8	3.9	5.7	5.9							
1940	5.0	4.8	4.5	4.9	5.0	5.0	6.2	5.0	5.7	5.0	5.0	4.4	5.9	6.0	6.1						
1941	4.7	4.5	4.2	4.5	4.6	4.6	5.7	4.5	5.1	4.4	4.3	3.7	4.6	4.3	3.5	0.9					
1942	4.6	4.4	4.2	4.5	4.5	4.5	5.5	4.4	4.9	4.3	4.2	3.6	4.3	4.0	3.4	2.1	3.2				
1943	4.5	4.3	4.0	4.3	4.4	4.3	5.2	4.2	4.6	4.0	3.9	3.4	3.9	3.6	3.1	2.1	2.6	2.1			
1944	4.4	4.2	4.0	4.2	4.3	4.2	5.0	4.1	4.4	3.9	3.8	3.3	3.8	3.5	3.0	2.3	2.7	2.4	2.8		
1945	4.7	4.6	4.3	4.6	4.6	4.6	5.4	4.6	5.0	4.5	4.5	4.1	4.6	4.5	4.3	3.9	4.7	5.1	6.7	10.7	
1946	4.5	4.3	4.1	4.3	4.4	4.3	5.0	4.2	4.6	4.1	4.0	3.7	4.1	3.9	3.6	3.2	3.7	3.8	4.4	5.2	-0.1
1947	4.1	4.0	3.7	3.9	4.0	3.9	4.5	3.8	4.0	3.6	3.5	3.1	3.4	3.2	2.8	2.4	2.6	2.5	2.6	2.5	-1.4
1948	4.1	4.0	3.7	3.9	3.9	3.9	4.5	3.7	4.0	3.6	3.5	3.1	3.4	3.2	2.9	2.5	2.7	2.6	2.7	2.7	0.2
1949	4.2	4.1	3.8	4.0	4.1	4.0	4.6	3.9	4.1	3.8	3.7	3.4	3.6	3.5	3.2	2.9	3.2	3.2	3.4	3.5	1.7
1950	4.0	3.9	3.7	3.8	3.9	3.8	4.3	3.7	3.9	3.5	3.4	3.1	3.4	3.2	2.9	2.6	2.8	2.8	2.9	2.9	1.4
1951	3.7	3.6	3.3	3.5	3.5	3.4	3.9	3.3	3.4	3.1	3.0	2.7	2.8	2.6	2.4	2.0	2.1	2.0	2.0	1.9	0.5
1952	3.6	3.5	3.3	3.4	3.4	3.3	3.8	3.1	3.3	3.0	2.8	2.6	2.7	2.5	2.3	1.9	2.0	1.9	1.9	1.8	0.6
1953	3.6	3.5	3.3	3.4	3.4	3.3	3.8	3.2	3.3	3.0	2.9	2.6	2.8	2.6	2.4	2.1	2.2	2.1	2.1	2.0	1.0
1954	3.7	3.6	3.4	3.5	3.5	3.5	3.9	3.4	3.5	3.2	3.1	2.9	3.0	2.9	2.7	2.4	2.5	2.5	2.5	2.5	1.6
1955	3.6	3.4	3.2	3.4	3.4	3.3	3.7	3.1	3.3	3.0	2.9	2.6	2.8	2.6	2.4	2.2	2.3	2.2	2.2	2.2	1.3
1956	3.3	3.1	2.9	3.0	3.0	2.9	3.3	2.8	2.9	2.6	2.5	2.2	2.3	2.1	1.9	1.7	1.7	1.6	1.6	1.5	0.7
1957	3.4	3.3	3.1	3.2	3.2	3.1	3.5	2.9	3.1	2.8	2.7	2.5	2.6	2.4	2.2	2.0	2.1	2.0	2.0	1.9	1.2
1958	3.1	3.0	2.8	2.9	2.8	2.8	3.1	2.6	2.7	2.4	2.3	2.1	2.1	2.0	1.8	1.5	1.6	1.5	1.4	1.3	0.6
1959	2.9	2.8	2.6	2.7	2.7	2.6	2.9	2.4	2.5	2.2	2.1	1.9	1.9	1.8	1.6	1.3	1.4	1.2	1.2	1.1	0.4

EXHIBIT A-4 (Continued)

TO THE END OF	FROM THE BEGINNING OF 1926	1927	1928	1929	1930	1931	1932	1933	1934	1935	1936	1937	1938	1939	1940	1941	1942	1943	1944	1945	1946
1960	3.2	3.1	2.9	3.0	3.0	2.9	3.2	2.8	2.9	2.6	2.5	2.3	2.4	2.3	2.1	1.9	2.0	1.9	1.9	1.8	1.3
1961	3.2	3.0	2.9	3.0	2.9	2.9	3.2	2.7	2.8	2.6	2.5	2.3	2.4	2.2	2.1	1.9	1.9	1.9	1.8	1.8	1.3
1962	3.3	3.1	3.0	3.1	3.1	3.0	3.3	2.9	3.0	2.7	2.6	2.5	2.5	2.4	2.3	2.1	2.2	2.1	2.1	2.1	1.6
1963	3.2	3.1	2.9	3.0	3.0	2.9	3.2	2.8	2.9	2.7	2.6	2.4	2.5	2.4	2.2	2.1	2.1	2.1	2.1	2.0	1.6
1964	3.2	3.1	2.9	3.0	3.0	3.0	3.2	2.8	2.9	2.7	2.6	2.4	2.5	2.4	2.3	2.1	2.1	2.1	2.1	2.1	1.7
1965	3.2	3.0	2.9	3.0	2.9	3.0	3.2	2.8	2.9	2.6	2.6	2.4	2.5	2.4	2.2	2.1	2.1	2.1	2.1	2.0	1.6
1966	3.2	3.1	2.9	3.0	3.0	2.9	3.2	2.8	2.9	2.7	2.6	2.4	2.5	2.4	2.3	2.1	2.2	2.1	2.1	2.1	1.7
1967	2.9	2.7	2.6	2.6	2.6	2.6	2.8	2.4	2.5	2.3	2.2	2.0	2.1	2.0	1.8	1.7	1.7	1.7	1.6	1.6	1.2
1968	2.8	2.7	2.5	2.6	2.6	2.5	2.7	2.4	2.4	2.2	2.1	2.0	2.0	1.9	1.8	1.6	1.6	1.6	1.6	1.5	1.1
1969	2.6	2.5	2.3	2.4	2.4	2.3	2.5	2.1	2.2	2.0	1.9	1.7	1.8	1.7	1.5	1.4	1.4	1.3	1.3	1.2	0.9
1970	2.8	2.7	2.5	2.6	2.6	2.5	2.7	2.4	2.5	2.3	2.2	2.0	2.1	2.0	1.9	1.7	1.7	1.7	1.7	1.6	1.3
1971	3.0	2.9	2.8	2.8	2.8	2.8	3.0	2.7	2.7	2.5	2.5	2.3	2.4	2.3	2.2	2.1	2.1	2.1	2.1	2.0	1.7
1972	3.1	3.0	2.8	2.9	2.9	2.8	3.1	2.7	2.8	2.6	2.6	2.4	2.5	2.4	2.3	2.2	2.2	2.2	2.2	2.2	1.9
1973	3.0	2.9	2.8	2.8	2.8	2.8	3.0	2.6	2.7	2.5	2.5	2.3	2.4	2.3	2.2	2.1	2.1	2.1	2.1	2.1	1.8
1974	3.0	2.9	2.8	2.8	2.8	2.8	3.0	2.7	2.7	2.6	2.5	2.4	2.4	2.4	2.3	2.1	2.2	2.1	2.1	2.1	1.8
1975	3.1	3.0	2.9	3.0	3.0	2.9	3.1	2.8	2.9	2.7	2.7	2.5	2.6	2.5	2.4	2.3	2.4	2.4	2.4	2.3	2.1
1976	3.4	3.3	3.2	3.2	3.2	3.2	3.4	3.1	3.2	3.0	3.0	2.9	3.0	2.9	2.8	2.7	2.8	2.8	2.8	2.8	2.5
1977	3.3	3.2	3.1	3.2	3.2	3.1	3.3	3.0	3.1	3.0	2.9	2.8	2.9	2.8	2.7	2.6	2.7	2.7	2.7	2.7	2.4
1978	3.2	3.1	3.0	3.1	3.1	3.0	3.2	2.9	3.0	2.9	2.8	2.7	2.8	2.7	2.6	2.5	2.6	2.5	2.6	2.5	2.3
1979	3.1	3.0	2.9	3.0	3.0	2.9	3.1	2.9	2.9	2.8	2.7	2.6	2.7	2.6	2.5	2.4	2.5	2.4	2.5	2.4	2.2
1980	3.0	2.9	2.8	2.9	2.8	2.8	3.0	2.7	2.8	2.6	2.6	2.5	2.5	2.4	2.3	2.3	2.3	2.3	2.3	2.3	2.0
1981	3.0	2.9	2.8	2.8	2.8	2.8	3.0	2.7	2.7	2.6	2.5	2.4	2.5	2.4	2.3	2.2	2.3	2.3	2.3	2.2	2.0
1982	3.5	3.5	3.4	3.4	3.4	3.4	3.6	3.3	3.4	3.3	3.2	3.1	3.2	3.2	3.1	3.0	3.1	3.1	3.1	3.1	2.9
1983	3.5	3.4	3.3	3.4	3.4	3.4	3.5	3.3	3.3	3.2	3.2	3.1	3.2	3.1	3.0	3.0	3.0	3.0	3.0	3.0	2.8
1984	3.7	3.6	3.5	3.6	3.6	3.6	3.7	3.5	3.6	3.4	3.4	3.3	3.4	3.4	3.3	3.2	3.3	3.3	3.3	3.3	3.1
1985	4.1	4.0	3.9	4.0	4.0	4.0	4.2	4.0	4.0	3.9	3.9	3.8	3.9	3.9	3.8	3.8	3.8	3.9	3.9	3.9	3.8
1986	4.4	4.3	4.3	4.3	4.3	4.3	4.5	4.3	4.4	4.3	4.3	4.2	4.3	4.3	4.2	4.2	4.3	4.3	4.3	4.4	4.2
1987	4.3	4.2	4.1	4.2	4.2	4.2	4.4	4.2	4.3	4.2	4.1	4.1	4.1	4.1	4.1	4.0	4.1	4.1	4.2	4.2	4.1

EXHIBIT A-4 (Continued)

TO THE END OF	FROM THE BEGINNING OF																				
	1947	1948	1949	1950	1951	1952	1953	1954	1955	1956	1957	1958	1959	1960	1961	1962	1963	1964	1965	1966	1967
1947	-2.6																				
1948	0.3	3.4																			
1949	2.3	4.9	6.4																		
1950	1.8	3.3	3.2	0.1																	
1951	0.6	1.4	0.8	-2.0	-3.9																
1952	0.7	1.4	0.9	-0.9	-1.4	1.2															
1953	1.1	1.7	1.4	0.2	0.2	2.4	3.6														
1954	1.8	2.5	2.4	1.6	1.9	4.0	5.4	7.2													
1955	1.5	2.0	1.8	1.1	1.3	2.6	3.1	2.9	-1.3												
1956	0.8	1.1	0.9	0.1	0.1	0.9	0.9	-0.0	-3.5	-5.6											
1957	1.4	1.8	1.6	1.0	1.1	2.0	2.2	1.8	0.0	0.7	7.5										
1958	0.7	1.0	0.8	0.2	0.2	0.8	0.7	0.2	-1.5	-1.6	0.5	-6.1									
1959	0.5	0.7	0.5	-0.1	-0.1	0.4	0.3	-0.3	-1.7	-1.8	-0.5	-4.2	-2.3								
1960	1.4	1.7	1.5	1.1	1.2	1.8	1.9	1.6	0.7	1.2	2.9	1.5	5.5	13.8							
1961	1.3	1.6	1.5	1.1	1.2	1.7	1.8	1.6	0.8	1.1	2.5	1.3	3.9	7.2	1.0						
1962	1.7	2.0	1.9	1.5	1.7	2.2	2.3	2.1	1.5	1.9	3.2	2.4	4.7	7.1	3.9	6.9					
1963	1.7	1.9	1.8	1.5	1.6	2.1	2.2	2.0	1.5	1.8	2.9	2.2	4.0	5.6	3.0	4.0	1.2				
1964	1.8	2.0	1.9	1.6	1.8	2.2	2.3	2.2	1.7	2.0	3.0	2.4	3.9	5.2	3.1	3.8	2.4	3.5			
1965	1.7	1.9	1.9	1.6	1.7	2.1	2.2	2.1	1.6	1.9	2.8	2.2	3.4	4.4	2.6	3.0	1.8	2.1	0.7		
1966	1.8	2.0	2.0	1.7	1.8	2.2	2.3	2.2	1.8	2.1	2.8	2.3	3.5	4.3	2.8	3.2	2.3	2.6	2.2	3.6	
1967	1.2	1.4	1.3	1.1	1.1	1.5	1.5	1.3	0.9	1.1	1.7	1.1	2.0	2.5	1.0	1.0	-0.1	-0.5	-1.8	-3.0	-9.2
1968	1.2	1.4	1.3	1.0	1.0	1.3	1.4	1.2	0.8	1.0	1.5	1.0	1.7	2.2	0.8	0.8	-0.2	-0.4	-1.4	-2.1	-4.8
1969	0.9	1.1	1.0	0.7	0.7	1.0	1.0	0.8	0.4	0.5	1.0	0.5	1.1	1.4	0.2	0.1	-0.9	-1.2	-2.1	-2.8	-4.9
1970	1.3	1.5	1.4	1.2	1.3	1.5	1.6	1.4	1.1	1.2	1.8	1.3	2.0	2.4	1.3	1.3	0.7	0.6	0.1	-0.0	-0.9
1971	1.8	2.0	1.9	1.7	1.8	2.1	2.1	2.1	1.8	2.0	2.5	2.1	2.8	3.2	2.3	2.5	2.0	2.1	1.9	2.1	1.8
1972	1.9	2.1	2.1	1.9	2.0	2.3	2.3	2.2	2.0	2.2	2.7	2.4	3.0	3.4	2.6	2.8	2.3	2.5	2.3	2.6	2.4
1973	1.8	2.0	1.9	1.8	1.8	2.1	2.2	2.1	1.8	2.0	2.5	2.2	2.7	3.1	2.3	2.4	2.0	2.1	2.0	2.1	1.9
1974	1.9	2.1	2.0	1.9	1.9	2.2	2.2	2.2	1.9	2.1	2.6	2.3	2.8	3.2	2.5	2.6	2.2	2.3	2.2	2.4	2.2
1975	2.2	2.3	2.3	2.1	2.2	2.5	2.5	2.5	2.3	2.5	2.9	2.7	3.2	3.5	2.9	3.0	2.7	2.9	2.8	3.0	3.0
1976	2.6	2.8	2.8	2.6	2.7	3.0	3.1	3.1	2.9	3.1	3.6	3.3	3.9	4.3	3.7	3.9	3.7	3.9	3.9	4.2	4.3
1977	2.5	2.7	2.7	2.5	2.6	2.9	2.9	2.9	2.7	2.9	3.3	3.1	3.7	4.0	3.4	3.6	3.4	3.5	3.5	3.8	3.8
1978	2.4	2.6	2.5	2.4	2.5	2.7	2.8	2.8	2.6	2.7	3.1	2.9	3.4	3.7	3.2	3.3	3.1	3.2	3.2	3.4	3.4
1979	2.3	2.4	2.4	2.3	2.3	2.6	2.6	2.6	2.4	2.6	2.9	2.7	3.2	3.5	2.9	3.1	2.8	2.9	2.9	3.1	3.0
1980	2.1	2.2	2.2	2.1	2.1	2.3	2.4	2.3	2.2	2.3	2.6	2.4	2.8	3.1	2.6	2.7	2.4	2.5	2.5	2.6	2.5
1981	2.1	2.2	2.2	2.1	2.1	2.3	2.4	2.3	2.2	2.3	2.6	2.4	2.8	3.0	2.6	2.6	2.4	2.4	2.4	2.5	2.5
1982	3.0	3.2	3.1	3.0	3.1	3.4	3.5	3.4	3.3	3.5	3.9	3.7	4.1	4.4	4.0	4.2	4.0	4.2	4.2	4.4	4.5
1983	2.9	3.1	3.1	3.0	3.1	3.3	3.4	3.4	3.2	3.4	3.7	3.6	4.0	4.3	3.9	4.0	3.9	4.0	4.0	4.2	4.3
1984	3.2	3.4	3.4	3.3	3.4	3.6	3.7	3.7	3.6	3.8	4.1	4.0	4.4	4.7	4.3	4.5	4.4	4.5	4.6	4.8	4.9
1985	3.9	4.0	4.1	4.0	4.1	4.4	4.5	4.5	4.4	4.6	5.0	4.9	5.3	5.6	5.3	5.5	5.4	5.6	5.7	6.0	6.1
1986	4.3	4.5	4.6	4.5	4.6	4.9	5.0	5.0	5.0	5.2	5.6	5.5	5.9	6.2	6.0	6.2	6.1	6.4	6.5	6.8	6.9
1987	4.2	4.3	4.4	4.3	4.4	4.7	4.8	4.8	4.7	4.9	5.3	5.2	5.6	5.9	5.6	5.8	5.8	6.0	6.1	6.3	6.5

EXHIBIT A-4 (Continued)

TO THE END OF	FROM THE BEGINNING OF 1968	1969	1970	1971	1972	1973	1974	1975	1976	1977	1978	1979	1980	1981	1982	1983	1984	1985	1986	1987
1968	-0.3																			
1969	-2.7	-5.1																		
1970	2.0	3.2	12.1																	
1971	4.7	6.4	12.7	13.2																
1972	4.9	6.2	10.3	9.4	5.7															
1973	3.9	4.7	7.3	5.8	2.2	-1.1														
1974	3.9	4.7	6.7	5.4	2.9	1.6	4.4													
1975	4.6	5.3	7.1	6.2	4.5	4.1	6.7	9.2												
1976	5.9	6.7	8.5	7.9	6.8	7.1	10.0	12.9	16.8											
1977	5.2	5.8	7.3	6.6	5.5	5.5	7.2	8.2	7.7	-0.7										
1978	4.6	5.1	6.3	5.6	4.5	4.4	5.5	5.8	4.7	-0.9	-1.2									
1979	4.1	4.5	5.5	4.8	3.8	3.5	4.3	4.3	3.2	-1.0	-1.2	-1.2								
1980	3.5	3.8	4.6	3.9	2.9	2.6	3.1	2.9	1.7	-1.8	-2.1	-2.6	-4.0							
1981	3.3	3.6	4.4	3.7	2.8	2.5	3.0	2.8	1.7	-1.0	-1.1	-1.1	-1.1	1.8						
1982	5.5	5.9	6.8	6.4	5.8	5.8	6.6	6.8	6.5	4.9	6.0	7.9	11.1	19.6	40.3					
1983	5.2	5.5	6.3	5.6	5.3	5.3	6.0	6.1	5.8	4.3	5.1	6.4	8.4	12.9	18.9	0.7				
1984	5.7	6.1	6.9	6.6	6.1	6.1	6.8	7.0	6.8	5.6	6.5	7.9	9.8	13.5	17.7	7.8	15.4			
1985	7.0	7.5	8.3	8.0	7.7	7.8	8.6	9.0	9.0	8.2	9.3	10.9	13.1	16.8	20.9	15.0	23.0	31.0		
1986	7.9	8.3	9.2	9.0	8.7	8.9	9.8	10.2	10.3	9.7	10.9	12.5	14.6	18.1	21.6	17.3	23.4	27.7	24.4	
1987	7.3	7.7	8.5	8.3	8.0	8.1	8.8	9.2	9.2	8.5	9.5	10.7	12.3	14.8	17.2	13.0	16.3	16.6	10.0	-2.7

EXHIBIT A-5
INTERMEDIATE-TERM GOVERNMENT BONDS: TOTAL RETURNS
RATES OF RETURN FOR ALL YEARLY HOLDING PERIODS FROM 1926 TO 1987
(Percent Per Annum Compounded Annually)

TO THE END OF	FROM THE BEGINNING OF																				
	1926	1927	1928	1929	1930	1931	1932	1933	1934	1935	1936	1937	1938	1939	1940	1941	1942	1943	1944	1945	1946
1926	5.4																				
1927	4.9	4.5																			
1928	3.6	2.7	0.9																		
1929	4.2	3.8	3.4	6.0																	
1930	4.7	4.5	4.5	6.4	6.7																
1931	3.5	3.1	2.8	3.4	2.1	-2.3															
1932	4.2	4.0	3.9	4.7	4.3	3.1	8.8														
1933	3.9	3.7	3.6	4.1	3.7	2.7	5.3	1.8													
1934	4.5	4.4	4.3	4.9	4.7	4.2	6.5	5.3	9.0												
1935	4.7	4.7	4.7	5.2	5.1	4.8	6.6	5.9	8.0	7.0											
1936	4.6	4.5	4.5	4.9	4.8	4.5	5.9	5.2	6.3	5.0	3.1										
1937	4.3	4.2	4.2	4.6	4.4	4.1	5.2	4.4	5.1	3.8	2.3	1.6									
1938	4.5	4.4	4.4	4.7	4.6	4.3	5.3	4.7	5.3	4.4	3.6	3.9	6.2								
1939	4.5	4.4	4.4	4.7	4.6	4.3	5.2	4.7	5.2	4.5	3.8	4.1	5.4	4.5							
1940	4.4	4.3	4.3	4.6	4.4	4.2	5.0	4.5	4.9	4.2	3.7	3.8	4.6	3.7	3.0						
1941	4.1	4.0	4.0	4.2	4.1	3.9	4.5	4.0	4.3	3.7	3.1	3.1	3.5	2.6	1.7	0.5					
1942	4.0	3.9	3.9	4.1	3.9	3.7	4.3	3.8	4.1	3.4	2.9	2.9	3.2	2.5	1.8	1.2	1.9				
1943	3.9	3.8	3.8	4.0	3.9	3.6	4.1	3.7	3.9	3.4	2.9	2.9	3.1	2.5	2.0	1.7	2.4	2.8			
1944	3.8	3.7	3.7	3.9	3.7	3.5	4.0	3.6	3.7	3.2	2.8	2.8	2.9	2.4	2.0	1.8	2.2	2.3	1.8		
1945	3.7	3.6	3.6	3.8	3.6	3.4	3.8	3.5	3.6	3.1	2.7	2.7	2.9	2.4	2.0	1.8	2.2	2.3	2.0	2.2	
1946	3.6	3.5	3.5	3.6	3.5	3.3	3.6	3.3	3.4	2.9	2.6	2.5	2.6	2.2	1.9	1.7	2.0	2.0	1.7	1.6	1.0
1947	3.5	3.4	3.3	3.5	3.3	3.1	3.5	3.1	3.2	2.8	2.4	2.4	2.5	2.1	1.8	1.6	1.8	1.7	1.5	1.4	1.0
1948	3.4	3.3	3.3	3.4	3.2	3.1	3.4	3.0	3.1	2.7	2.4	2.3	2.4	2.0	1.8	1.6	1.8	1.8	1.6	1.5	1.3
1949	3.4	3.3	3.2	3.3	3.2	3.0	3.3	3.0	3.1	2.7	2.4	2.3	2.4	2.1	1.8	1.7	1.9	1.8	1.7	1.7	1.5
1950	3.3	3.2	3.1	3.2	3.1	2.9	3.2	2.9	2.9	2.6	2.3	2.2	2.3	2.0	1.7	1.6	1.7	1.7	1.5	1.5	1.4
1951	3.1	3.1	3.0	3.1	2.9	2.8	3.0	2.7	2.8	2.4	2.2	2.1	2.1	1.8	1.6	1.5	1.6	1.5	1.4	1.3	1.2
1952	3.1	3.0	2.9	3.0	2.9	2.7	3.0	2.7	2.7	2.4	2.1	2.1	2.1	1.8	1.6	1.5	1.6	1.6	1.4	1.4	1.3
1953	3.1	3.0	2.9	3.0	2.9	2.7	3.0	2.7	2.8	2.4	2.2	2.1	2.2	1.9	1.7	1.6	1.7	1.7	1.6	1.6	1.5
1954	3.1	3.0	2.9	2.9	2.9	2.7	3.0	2.7	2.8	2.4	2.2	2.2	2.2	2.0	1.8	1.7	1.8	1.8	1.7	1.6	1.6
1955	2.9	2.9	2.8	2.9	2.8	2.6	2.8	2.6	2.6	2.3	2.1	2.0	2.0	1.8	1.5	1.5	1.6	1.5	1.5	1.5	1.4
1956	2.8	2.8	2.7	2.8	2.6	2.5	2.7	2.4	2.5	2.2	1.9	1.9	1.9	1.7	1.5	1.4	1.5	1.5	1.3	1.3	1.2
1957	3.0	2.9	2.9	2.9	2.8	2.7	2.9	2.6	2.7	2.4	2.2	2.2	2.2	2.0	1.8	1.8	1.9	1.9	1.8	1.8	1.8
1958	2.9	2.8	2.7	2.8	2.7	2.5	2.7	2.5	2.5	2.3	2.1	2.0	2.0	1.8	1.7	1.6	1.7	1.7	1.6	1.6	1.5
1959	2.8	2.7	2.6	2.7	2.6	2.4	2.6	2.4	2.4	2.1	2.0	1.9	1.9	1.7	1.6	1.5	1.6	1.5	1.5	1.4	1.4

EXHIBIT A-5 (Continued)

FROM THE BEGINNING OF

TO THE END OF	1926	1927	1928	1929	1930	1931	1932	1933	1934	1935	1936	1937	1938	1939	1940	1941	1942	1943	1944	1945	1946
1960	3.0	2.9	2.9	3.0	2.9	2.7	2.9	2.7	2.7	2.5	2.3	2.3	2.3	2.2	2.0	2.0	2.1	2.1	2.0	2.1	2.0
1961	3.0	2.9	2.9	2.9	2.8	2.7	2.9	2.7	2.7	2.5	2.3	2.3	2.3	2.1	2.0	2.0	2.1	2.1	2.0	2.0	2.0
1962	3.0	3.0	2.9	3.0	2.9	2.8	3.0	2.8	2.8	2.6	2.4	2.4	2.4	2.3	2.2	2.2	2.2	2.2	2.2	2.2	2.2
1963	3.0	2.9	2.9	3.0	2.9	2.8	2.9	2.7	2.8	2.6	2.4	2.4	2.5	2.3	2.2	2.1	2.3	2.3	2.3	2.2	2.2
1964	3.0	3.0	2.9	3.0	2.9	2.7	3.0	2.8	2.7	2.6	2.4	2.4	2.4	2.3	2.2	2.2	2.2	2.2	2.3	2.3	2.3
1965	3.0	2.9	2.9	3.0	2.8	2.7	2.9	2.7	2.7	2.6	2.4	2.4	2.4	2.3	2.2	2.2	2.2	2.2	2.2	2.2	2.2
1966	3.0	3.0	2.9	3.0	2.9	2.8	2.9	2.8	2.8	2.6	2.5	2.5	2.5	2.4	2.3	2.3	2.3	2.3	2.3	2.3	2.4
1967	3.0	2.9	2.9	2.9	2.9	2.7	2.9	2.7	2.8	2.6	2.4	2.4	2.4	2.3	2.2	2.2	2.3	2.3	2.4	2.3	2.3
1968	3.0	3.0	2.9	3.0	2.9	2.8	2.9	2.8	2.8	2.6	2.5	2.5	2.5	2.4	2.3	2.3	2.4	2.4	2.4	2.4	2.4
1969	2.9	2.9	2.8	2.9	2.8	2.7	2.8	2.7	2.7	2.5	2.4	2.4	2.4	2.3	2.2	2.2	2.2	2.3	2.2	2.3	2.3
1970	3.2	3.2	3.1	3.2	3.1	3.0	3.2	3.0	3.1	2.9	2.8	2.8	2.8	2.7	2.7	2.6	2.7	2.7	2.7	2.8	2.8
1971	3.3	3.3	3.3	3.3	3.3	3.2	3.3	3.2	3.2	3.1	2.9	2.9	3.0	2.9	2.8	2.8	2.9	2.9	3.0	3.0	3.0
1972	3.4	3.3	3.3	3.4	3.3	3.2	3.4	3.2	3.3	3.1	3.0	3.0	3.0	3.0	2.9	2.9	3.0	3.0	3.0	3.1	3.1
1973	3.4	3.4	3.4	3.4	3.3	3.3	3.4	3.3	3.3	3.1	3.1	3.0	3.1	3.1	3.0	3.0	3.1	3.1	3.1	3.1	3.2
1974	3.4	3.4	3.4	3.4	3.4	3.3	3.4	3.3	3.3	3.2	3.2	3.1	3.2	3.2	3.2	3.0	3.2	3.2	3.2	3.2	3.2
1975	3.5	3.5	3.5	3.5	3.5	3.4	3.5	3.4	3.5	3.3	3.2	3.2	3.3	3.4	3.4	3.2	3.3	3.3	3.3	3.4	3.4
1976	3.7	3.7	3.6	3.7	3.7	3.6	3.7	3.6	3.7	3.5	3.5	3.5	3.5	3.4	3.4	3.4	3.5	3.6	3.5	3.6	3.7
1977	3.7	3.7	3.6	3.7	3.7	3.5	3.7	3.6	3.6	3.5	3.4	3.4	3.5	3.4	3.4	3.4	3.5	3.5	3.5	3.6	3.6
1978	3.7	3.6	3.6	3.7	3.6	3.5	3.7	3.6	3.6	3.5	3.4	3.4	3.5	3.4	3.4	3.4	3.5	3.5	3.5	3.6	3.6
1979	3.7	3.7	3.6	3.7	3.6	3.6	3.7	3.6	3.6	3.5	3.4	3.4	3.5	3.4	3.4	3.4	3.5	3.5	3.5	3.6	3.6
1980	3.7	3.6	3.6	3.7	3.6	3.6	3.7	3.6	3.6	3.5	3.4	3.4	3.5	3.4	3.4	3.4	3.5	3.5	3.5	3.6	3.6
1981	3.8	3.7	3.7	3.8	3.7	3.7	3.8	3.7	3.7	3.6	3.6	3.6	3.6	3.6	3.5	3.6	3.6	3.7	3.7	3.7	3.8
1982	4.2	4.1	4.1	4.2	4.2	4.1	4.2	4.2	4.2	4.1	4.0	4.1	4.1	4.1	4.1	4.1	4.2	4.2	4.3	4.3	4.4
1983	4.2	4.2	4.2	4.3	4.2	4.2	4.3	4.2	4.2	4.1	4.1	4.1	4.1	4.2	4.1	4.2	4.3	4.3	4.4	4.4	4.5
1984	4.4	4.4	4.4	4.4	4.4	4.4	4.5	4.4	4.5	4.4	4.3	4.3	4.4	4.4	4.4	4.4	4.5	4.5	4.6	4.7	4.7
1985	4.6	4.6	4.6	4.7	4.7	4.6	4.8	4.7	4.7	4.7	4.6	4.6	4.7	4.7	4.7	4.7	4.8	4.9	4.9	5.0	5.1
1986	4.8	4.8	4.8	4.9	4.8	4.8	4.9	4.9	4.9	4.8	4.8	4.8	4.9	4.9	4.9	4.9	5.0	5.1	5.2	5.2	5.3
1987	4.8	4.8	4.8	4.8	4.8	4.8	4.9	4.8	4.9	4.8	4.8	4.8	4.9	4.8	4.8	4.9	5.0	5.1	5.1	5.2	5.3

EXHIBIT A-5 (Continued)

TO THE END OF	FROM THE BEGINNING OF 1947	1948	1949	1950	1951	1952	1953	1954	1955	1956	1957	1958	1959	1960	1961	1962	1963	1964	1965	1966	1967
1947	0.9																				
1948	1.4	1.8																			
1949	1.7	2.1	2.3																		
1950	1.4	1.6	1.5	0.7																	
1951	1.2	1.3	1.1	0.5	0.4																
1952	1.3	1.4	1.3	0.9	1.0	1.6															
1953	1.6	1.7	1.6	1.5	1.7	2.4	3.2														
1954	1.7	1.8	1.8	1.7	2.0	2.5	3.0	2.7													
1955	1.4	1.5	1.5	1.3	1.4	1.7	1.7	1.0	-0.7												
1956	1.3	1.3	1.2	1.1	1.1	1.3	1.2	0.5	-0.5	-0.4											
1957	1.8	1.9	1.9	1.9	2.1	2.3	2.5	2.3	2.2	3.6	7.8										
1958	1.6	1.6	1.6	1.5	1.6	1.8	1.8	1.6	1.3	2.0	3.2	-1.3									
1959	1.4	1.5	1.4	1.3	1.4	1.5	1.5	1.2	1.0	1.4	2.0	-0.8	-0.4								
1960	2.1	2.2	2.2	2.2	2.4	2.6	2.8	2.7	2.7	3.4	4.3	3.2	5.5	11.8							
1961	2.1	2.2	2.2	2.2	2.3	2.5	2.7	2.6	2.6	3.1	3.8	2.9	4.3	6.7	1.8						
1962	2.3	2.4	2.5	2.5	2.6	2.8	2.9	2.9	2.9	3.5	4.1	3.4	4.6	6.3	3.7	5.6					
1963	2.3	2.4	2.4	2.4	2.5	2.7	2.8	2.8	2.8	3.2	3.8	3.1	4.0	5.1	3.0	3.6	1.6				
1964	2.4	2.5	2.5	2.5	2.6	2.8	2.9	2.9	2.9	3.3	3.8	3.2	4.0	4.9	3.3	3.7	2.8	4.0			
1965	2.3	2.4	2.4	2.4	2.5	2.7	2.7	2.7	2.7	3.1	3.5	3.0	3.6	4.2	2.8	3.0	2.2	2.5	1.0		
1966	2.4	2.5	2.5	2.6	2.7	2.8	2.9	2.9	2.9	3.2	3.6	3.1	3.7	4.3	3.1	3.4	2.8	3.2	2.8	4.7	
1967	2.4	2.4	2.5	2.5	2.6	2.7	2.8	2.7	2.8	3.0	3.4	2.9	3.4	3.9	2.8	3.0	2.5	2.7	2.2	2.8	1.0
1968	2.5	2.5	2.6	2.6	2.7	2.8	2.9	2.9	2.9	3.2	3.5	3.1	3.5	4.0	3.0	3.2	2.8	3.0	2.8	3.4	2.8
1969	2.3	2.4	2.4	2.4	2.5	2.6	2.7	2.6	2.6	2.9	3.1	2.7	3.1	3.5	2.6	2.7	2.3	2.4	2.1	2.3	1.6
1970	2.9	3.0	3.0	3.0	3.2	3.3	3.4	3.4	3.5	3.8	4.1	3.8	4.2	4.6	3.9	4.2	4.0	4.4	4.4	5.1	5.2
1971	3.1	3.2	3.3	3.3	3.4	3.6	3.7	3.7	3.8	4.1	4.4	4.1	4.5	5.0	4.4	4.6	4.5	4.9	5.0	5.7	5.9
1972	3.2	3.3	3.3	3.4	3.5	3.7	3.8	3.8	3.8	4.1	4.4	4.2	4.6	5.0	4.4	4.7	4.6	4.9	5.0	5.6	5.8
1973	3.2	3.3	3.4	3.4	3.6	3.7	3.8	3.8	3.9	4.1	4.4	4.2	4.6	5.0	4.5	4.7	4.6	4.9	5.0	5.5	5.6
1974	3.3	3.4	3.4	3.5	3.6	3.8	3.9	3.9	4.0	4.2	4.5	4.3	4.7	5.0	4.5	4.7	4.7	5.0	5.1	5.7	5.6
1975	3.5	3.6	3.6	3.7	3.8	4.0	4.1	4.1	4.2	4.4	4.7	4.5	4.8	5.2	4.8	5.0	4.9	5.2	5.3	5.9	5.9
1976	3.8	3.9	3.9	4.0	4.1	4.3	4.4	4.5	4.5	4.8	5.1	4.9	5.3	5.6	5.2	5.5	5.5	5.8	5.9	6.4	6.5
1977	3.7	3.8	3.9	3.9	4.0	4.2	4.3	4.3	4.4	4.6	4.9	4.7	5.1	5.4	5.0	5.2	5.2	5.4	5.6	5.9	6.1
1978	3.7	3.8	3.8	3.9	4.0	4.2	4.3	4.3	4.4	4.6	4.8	4.7	5.0	5.3	4.9	5.1	5.1	5.3	5.4	5.8	5.8
1979	3.7	3.8	3.9	3.9	4.0	4.2	4.2	4.3	4.4	4.6	4.8	4.7	4.9	5.2	4.9	5.1	5.0	5.2	5.3	5.6	5.7
1980	3.7	3.8	3.9	3.9	4.0	4.1	4.2	4.3	4.3	4.5	4.8	4.6	4.9	5.2	4.8	5.0	5.0	5.2	5.2	5.5	5.6
1981	3.9	4.0	4.0	4.1	4.2	4.3	4.4	4.5	4.5	4.7	4.9	4.8	5.1	5.3	5.1	5.2	5.2	5.4	5.5	5.8	5.8
1982	4.5	4.6	4.7	4.8	4.9	5.0	5.2	5.2	5.3	5.5	5.8	5.7	6.0	6.3	6.0	6.2	6.3	6.5	6.7	7.0	7.2
1983	4.6	4.7	4.8	4.8	5.0	5.1	5.2	5.3	5.4	5.6	5.8	5.8	6.1	6.3	6.1	6.3	6.3	6.6	6.7	7.0	7.2
1984	4.8	4.9	5.0	5.1	5.2	5.4	5.5	5.6	5.7	5.9	6.1	6.1	6.3	6.6	6.4	6.6	6.7	6.9	7.1	7.4	7.5
1985	5.2	5.3	5.4	5.5	5.6	5.8	5.9	6.0	6.1	6.3	6.6	6.5	6.8	7.1	6.9	7.2	7.2	7.5	7.7	8.0	8.2
1986	5.4	5.5	5.6	5.7	5.9	6.0	6.2	6.3	6.4	6.6	6.9	6.8	7.1	7.4	7.2	7.5	7.5	7.8	8.0	8.3	8.5
1987	5.4	5.5	5.6	5.7	5.8	5.9	6.1	6.2	6.3	6.5	6.7	6.7	7.0	7.2	7.1	7.3	7.4	7.6	7.8	8.1	8.2

EXHIBIT A-5 (Continued)

TO THE END OF	FROM THE BEGINNING OF																			
	1968	1969	1970	1971	1972	1973	1974	1975	1976	1977	1978	1979	1980	1981	1982	1983	1984	1985	1986	1987
1968	4.5																			
1969	1.9	-0.7																		
1970	6.6	7.7	16.9																	
1971	7.2	8.0	12.7	8.7																
1972	6.8	7.3	10.1	6.9	5.2															
1973	6.4	6.8	8.7	6.1	4.9	4.6														
1974	6.3	6.6	8.1	6.0	5.1	5.1	5.7													
1975	6.5	6.8	8.1	6.4	5.8	6.0	6.8	7.8												
1976	7.2	7.5	8.7	7.4	7.2	7.7	8.8	10.3	12.9											
1977	6.6	6.8	7.8	6.6	6.2	6.4	6.9	7.3	7.0	1.4										
1978	6.3	6.5	7.3	6.2	5.8	5.9	6.2	6.3	5.8	2.4	3.5									
1979	6.1	6.3	7.0	5.9	5.6	5.7	5.8	5.9	5.4	3.0	3.8	4.1								
1980	5.9	6.1	6.7	5.7	5.4	5.4	5.6	5.5	5.1	3.2	3.8	4.0	3.9							
1981	6.2	6.3	6.9	6.1	5.8	5.9	6.0	6.1	5.8	4.4	5.2	5.8	6.6	9.5						
1982	7.6	7.8	8.5	7.8	7.7	8.0	8.4	8.7	8.8	8.2	9.6	11.2	13.7	18.9	29.1					
1983	7.6	7.8	8.4	7.8	7.7	7.9	8.3	8.6	8.7	8.1	9.2	10.4	12.1	14.9	17.8	7.4				
1984	7.9	8.2	8.8	8.2	8.2	8.4	8.8	9.1	9.2	8.8	9.9	11.0	12.4	14.7	16.5	10.7	14.0			
1985	8.6	8.8	9.5	9.0	9.0	9.3	9.7	10.1	10.3	10.0	11.2	12.3	13.7	15.8	17.4	13.8	17.1	20.3		
1986	8.9	9.2	9.8	9.4	9.4	9.7	10.1	10.5	10.7	10.5	11.6	12.6	13.9	15.7	17.0	14.1	16.5	17.7	15.1	
1987	8.6	8.8	9.4	9.0	9.0	9.2	9.6	9.9	10.1	9.8	10.7	11.5	12.5	13.8	14.5	11.8	12.9	12.5	8.8	2.9

179

EXHIBIT A-6
U.S. TREASURY BILLS: TOTAL RETURNS
RATES OF RETURN FOR ALL YEARLY HOLDING PERIODS FROM 1926 TO 1987
(Percent Per Annum Compounded Annually)

TO THE END OF	FROM THE BEGINNING OF																				
	1926	1927	1928	1929	1930	1931	1932	1933	1934	1935	1936	1937	1938	1939	1940	1941	1942	1943	1944	1945	1946
1926	3.3																				
1927	3.2	3.1																			
1928	3.2	3.2	3.2																		
1929	3.6	3.7	4.0	4.7																	
1930	3.4	3.4	3.5	3.6	2.4																
1931	3.0	2.9	2.9	2.7	1.7	1.1															
1932	2.7	2.6	2.5	2.3	1.5	1.0	1.0														
1933	2.4	2.3	2.1	1.9	1.2	0.8	0.6	0.3													
1934	2.1	2.0	1.8	1.6	1.0	0.6	0.5	0.2	0.2												
1935	1.9	1.8	1.6	1.4	0.8	0.5	0.4	0.2	0.2	0.2											
1936	1.8	1.6	1.5	1.2	0.7	0.5	0.4	0.2	0.2	0.2	0.2										
1937	1.6	1.5	1.3	1.1	0.7	0.4	0.4	0.2	0.2	0.2	0.2	0.3									
1938	1.5	1.4	1.2	1.0	0.6	0.4	0.3	0.2	0.2	0.2	0.2	0.1	-0.0								
1939	1.4	1.3	1.1	0.9	0.6	0.3	0.3	0.2	0.1	0.1	0.1	0.1	0.0	0.0							
1940	1.3	1.2	1.0	0.9	0.5	0.3	0.2	0.1	0.1	0.1	0.1	0.1	0.0	0.0	0.0						
1941	1.2	1.1	1.0	0.8	0.5	0.3	0.2	0.1	0.1	0.1	0.1	0.1	0.0	0.0	0.0	0.1					
1942	1.2	1.1	0.9	0.8	0.5	0.3	0.2	0.1	0.1	0.1	0.1	0.1	0.1	0.1	0.1	0.2	0.3				
1943	1.1	1.0	0.9	0.7	0.4	0.3	0.2	0.2	0.2	0.1	0.1	0.1	0.1	0.1	0.1	0.2	0.3	0.3			
1944	1.1	1.0	0.8	0.7	0.4	0.3	0.2	0.2	0.2	0.1	0.2	0.1	0.1	0.2	0.2	0.3	0.3	0.3	0.3		
1945	1.1	0.9	0.8	0.7	0.4	0.3	0.2	0.2	0.2	0.2	0.2	0.2	0.2	0.2	0.2	0.3	0.3	0.3	0.3	0.3	
1946	1.0	0.9	0.8	0.7	0.4	0.3	0.3	0.2	0.2	0.2	0.2	0.2	0.2	0.2	0.2	0.3	0.3	0.3	0.3	0.3	0.4
1947	1.0	0.9	0.8	0.7	0.4	0.3	0.3	0.2	0.2	0.2	0.2	0.2	0.2	0.2	0.3	0.3	0.3	0.3	0.4	0.4	0.4
1948	1.0	0.9	0.8	0.7	0.4	0.3	0.3	0.3	0.3	0.3	0.3	0.3	0.3	0.3	0.3	0.4	0.4	0.4	0.5	0.5	0.6
1949	1.0	0.9	0.8	0.7	0.5	0.4	0.3	0.3	0.3	0.3	0.3	0.3	0.3	0.4	0.4	0.5	0.5	0.5	0.6	0.6	0.7
1950	1.0	0.9	0.8	0.7	0.5	0.4	0.4	0.4	0.4	0.4	0.4	0.4	0.4	0.4	0.5	0.5	0.6	0.6	0.6	0.7	0.8
1951	1.0	0.9	0.8	0.7	0.6	0.5	0.4	0.4	0.4	0.4	0.5	0.5	0.5	0.5	0.6	0.6	0.7	0.7	0.7	0.8	0.9
1952	1.0	1.0	0.9	0.8	0.6	0.5	0.5	0.5	0.5	0.5	0.5	0.5	0.6	0.6	0.6	0.7	0.8	0.8	0.9	0.9	1.0
1953	1.1	1.0	0.9	0.8	0.7	0.6	0.6	0.5	0.6	0.6	0.6	0.6	0.6	0.7	0.7	0.8	0.8	0.9	1.0	1.0	1.1
1954	1.1	1.0	0.9	0.8	0.7	0.6	0.6	0.6	0.6	0.6	0.6	0.6	0.7	0.7	0.7	0.8	0.8	0.9	0.9	1.0	1.1
1955	1.1	1.0	1.0	0.9	0.7	0.6	0.6	0.6	0.6	0.6	0.7	0.7	0.7	0.7	0.8	0.8	0.9	1.0	1.0	1.1	1.1
1956	1.1	1.1	1.0	0.9	0.8	0.7	0.7	0.7	0.7	0.7	0.7	0.8	0.8	0.8	0.9	0.9	1.0	1.0	1.1	1.2	1.3
1957	1.2	1.1	1.1	1.0	0.8	0.7	0.8	0.8	0.8	0.8	0.9	0.9	0.9	1.0	1.0	1.1	1.1	1.2	1.3	1.3	1.4
1958	1.2	1.1	1.1	1.0	0.9	0.8	0.8	0.8	0.8	0.9	0.9	0.9	0.9	1.0	1.0	1.1	1.2	1.2	1.3	1.3	1.4
1959	1.3	1.2	1.1	1.1	0.9	0.9	0.9	0.9	0.9	0.9	1.0	1.0	1.0	1.1	1.1	1.2	1.3	1.3	1.4	1.4	1.5

EXHIBIT A-6 (Continued)

FROM THE BEGINNING OF

TO THE END OF	1926	1927	1928	1929	1930	1931	1932	1933	1934	1935	1936	1937	1938	1939	1940	1941	1942	1943	1944	1945	1946
1960	1.3	1.2	1.2	1.1	1.0	1.0	0.9	0.9	1.0	1.0	1.0	1.1	1.1	1.2	1.2	1.3	1.3	1.4	1.5	1.5	1.6
1961	1.3	1.3	1.2	1.1	1.0	1.0	1.0	1.0	1.0	1.0	1.1	1.1	1.1	1.2	1.3	1.3	1.4	1.4	1.5	1.6	1.6
1962	1.4	1.3	1.2	1.2	1.1	1.0	1.0	1.0	1.1	1.1	1.1	1.2	1.2	1.3	1.3	1.4	1.4	1.5	1.6	1.6	1.7
1963	1.4	1.3	1.3	1.2	1.1	1.1	1.1	1.1	1.1	1.2	1.2	1.2	1.3	1.3	1.4	1.4	1.5	1.6	1.6	1.7	1.8
1964	1.5	1.4	1.4	1.3	1.2	1.2	1.2	1.2	1.2	1.3	1.3	1.3	1.4	1.4	1.5	1.5	1.6	1.7	1.7	1.8	1.9
1965	1.5	1.5	1.4	1.4	1.3	1.3	1.3	1.3	1.3	1.3	1.4	1.4	1.5	1.5	1.6	1.6	1.7	1.8	1.8	1.9	2.0
1966	1.6	1.5	1.5	1.5	1.4	1.4	1.4	1.4	1.4	1.5	1.5	1.5	1.6	1.6	1.7	1.7	1.8	1.9	1.9	2.0	2.1
1967	1.7	1.6	1.6	1.5	1.5	1.4	1.4	1.5	1.5	1.6	1.6	1.6	1.7	1.7	1.8	1.8	1.9	2.0	2.0	2.1	2.2
1968	1.7	1.7	1.7	1.6	1.5	1.5	1.5	1.6	1.6	1.6	1.7	1.7	1.8	1.8	1.9	2.0	2.0	2.1	2.2	2.2	2.3
1969	1.8	1.8	1.8	1.7	1.7	1.6	1.7	1.7	1.7	1.8	1.8	1.9	1.9	2.0	2.0	2.1	2.2	2.3	2.3	2.4	2.5
1970	1.9	1.9	1.9	1.9	1.8	1.8	1.8	1.8	1.8	1.9	1.9	2.0	2.1	2.1	2.2	2.3	2.3	2.4	2.5	2.6	2.7
1971	2.0	2.0	1.9	1.9	1.8	1.8	1.9	1.9	1.9	2.0	2.0	2.1	2.1	2.2	2.3	2.3	2.4	2.5	2.6	2.6	2.7
1972	2.0	2.1	2.0	2.0	1.9	1.9	1.9	1.9	2.0	2.0	2.1	2.1	2.2	2.2	2.3	2.4	2.4	2.5	2.6	2.7	2.8
1973	2.1	2.1	2.1	2.1	2.0	2.0	2.0	2.0	2.1	2.1	2.2	2.2	2.3	2.4	2.4	2.5	2.6	2.7	2.7	2.8	2.9
1974	2.3	2.2	2.2	2.2	2.1	2.1	2.2	2.2	2.2	2.3	2.3	2.4	2.4	2.5	2.6	2.7	2.7	2.8	2.9	3.0	3.1
1975	2.3	2.3	2.3	2.3	2.2	2.2	2.2	2.3	2.3	2.4	2.4	2.5	2.5	2.6	2.7	2.8	2.8	2.9	3.0	3.1	3.2
1976	2.4	2.4	2.4	2.3	2.3	2.3	2.3	2.4	2.4	2.4	2.5	2.5	2.6	2.7	2.7	2.8	2.9	3.0	3.0	3.1	3.2
1977	2.4	2.4	2.3	2.4	2.3	2.3	2.4	2.4	2.5	2.5	2.5	2.6	2.7	2.7	2.8	2.9	3.0	3.0	3.1	3.2	3.3
1978	2.5	2.5	2.5	2.5	2.4	2.4	2.5	2.5	2.5	2.6	2.6	2.7	2.8	2.8	2.9	3.0	3.1	3.1	3.2	3.3	3.4
1979	2.7	2.6	2.6	2.6	2.6	2.6	2.6	2.7	2.7	2.8	2.8	2.9	2.9	3.0	3.1	3.2	3.3	3.3	3.4	3.5	3.6
1980	2.8	2.8	2.8	2.8	2.7	2.7	2.8	2.8	2.9	2.9	3.0	3.1	3.1	3.2	3.3	3.4	3.5	3.5	3.6	3.7	3.8
1981	3.0	3.0	3.0	3.0	3.0	3.0	3.0	3.1	3.1	3.2	3.2	3.3	3.4	3.5	3.5	3.6	3.7	3.8	3.9	4.0	4.1
1982	3.1	3.1	3.1	3.1	3.1	3.1	3.2	3.2	3.3	3.3	3.4	3.5	3.5	3.6	3.7	3.8	3.9	4.0	4.1	4.2	4.3
1983	3.2	3.2	3.2	3.2	3.2	3.2	3.3	3.3	3.4	3.4	3.5	3.6	3.6	3.7	3.8	3.9	4.0	4.1	4.2	4.3	4.4
1984	3.3	3.3	3.3	3.3	3.3	3.3	3.4	3.4	3.5	3.6	3.6	3.7	3.8	3.9	3.9	4.0	4.1	4.2	4.3	4.4	4.5
1985	3.4	3.4	3.4	3.4	3.4	3.4	3.5	3.5	3.6	3.6	3.7	3.8	3.9	3.9	4.0	4.1	4.2	4.3	4.4	4.5	4.6
1986	3.5	3.5	3.5	3.5	3.4	3.5	3.5	3.6	3.6	3.7	3.8	3.8	3.9	4.0	4.1	4.2	4.3	4.3	4.4	4.5	4.6
1987	3.5	3.5	3.5	3.5	3.5	3.5	3.5	3.6	3.7	3.7	3.8	3.9	3.9	4.0	4.1	4.2	4.3	4.4	4.5	4.6	4.7

EXHIBIT A-6 (Continued)

TO THE END OF	| FROM THE BEGINNING OF																				
	1967	1966	1965	1964	1963	1962	1961	1960	1959	1958	1957	1956	1955	1954	1953	1952	1951	1950	1949	1948	1947
1947																					0.5
1948																				0.8	0.7
1949																			1.1	1.0	0.8
1950																		1.2	1.1	1.0	0.9
1951																	1.5	1.3	1.3	1.1	1.0
1952																1.7	1.6	1.4	1.4	1.3	1.1
1953															1.8	1.7	1.7	1.5	1.5	1.3	1.2
1954														0.9	1.3	1.4	1.5	1.4	1.4	1.3	1.2
1955													1.6	1.2	1.4	1.5	1.5	1.4	1.4	1.3	1.2
1956												2.5	2.0	1.6	1.7	1.7	1.6	1.6	1.5	1.4	1.3
1957											3.1	2.8	2.4	2.0	2.0	1.9	1.9	1.8	1.7	1.6	1.5
1958										1.5	2.3	2.4	2.2	1.9	1.9	1.9	1.8	1.7	1.7	1.6	1.5
1959									3.0	2.2	2.5	2.5	2.3	2.1	2.0	2.0	1.9	1.9	1.8	1.7	1.6
1960								2.7	2.8	2.4	2.6	2.5	2.4	2.2	2.1	2.1	2.0	1.9	1.9	1.8	1.7
1961							2.1	2.4	2.6	2.3	2.5	2.5	2.4	2.2	2.1	2.1	2.0	2.0	1.9	1.8	1.7
1962						2.7	2.4	2.5	2.6	2.4	2.5	2.5	2.4	2.2	2.2	2.1	2.1	2.0	1.9	1.9	1.8
1963					3.1	2.9	2.7	2.7	2.7	2.5	2.6	2.6	2.5	2.3	2.3	2.2	2.2	2.1	2.0	1.9	1.9
1964				3.5	3.3	3.1	2.9	2.8	2.9	2.7	2.7	2.7	2.6	2.4	2.4	2.3	2.3	2.2	2.1	2.0	2.0
1965			3.9	3.7	3.5	3.3	3.1	3.0	3.0	2.8	2.9	2.8	2.7	2.5	2.5	2.4	2.4	2.3	2.2	2.1	2.1
1966		4.8	4.3	4.1	3.8	3.6	3.4	3.3	3.2	3.0	3.0	3.0	2.9	2.7	2.7	2.6	2.5	2.4	2.4	2.3	2.2
1967	4.2	4.5	4.3	4.1	3.9	3.7	3.5	3.4	3.3	3.2	3.2	3.1	3.0	2.8	2.8	2.7	2.6	2.5	2.5	2.4	2.3
1968	4.7	4.7	4.5	4.3	4.1	3.9	3.7	3.6	3.5	3.3	3.3	3.3	3.1	3.0	2.9	2.8	2.8	2.7	2.6	2.5	2.4
1969	5.3	5.2	4.9	4.7	4.5	4.3	4.0	3.9	3.8	3.6	3.6	3.5	3.4	3.2	3.1	3.0	3.0	2.9	2.8	2.7	2.6
1970	5.6	5.5	5.2	5.0	4.7	4.5	4.3	4.1	4.0	3.8	3.8	3.7	3.6	3.4	3.3	3.2	3.1	3.0	3.0	2.9	2.8
1971	5.4	5.3	5.1	4.9	4.7	4.5	4.3	4.1	4.0	3.9	3.8	3.7	3.6	3.4	3.4	3.3	3.2	3.1	3.0	2.9	2.8
1972	5.1	5.1	4.9	4.8	4.6	4.4	4.2	4.1	4.0	3.9	3.8	3.7	3.6	3.5	3.4	3.3	3.2	3.1	3.0	3.0	2.9
1973	5.4	5.3	5.1	5.0	4.8	4.6	4.4	4.3	4.2	4.1	4.0	3.9	3.8	3.6	3.6	3.5	3.4	3.3	3.2	3.1	3.0
1974	5.7	5.6	5.4	5.3	5.1	4.9	4.7	4.6	4.5	4.3	4.2	4.1	4.0	3.8	3.8	3.7	3.6	3.5	3.4	3.3	3.2
1975	5.7	5.6	5.5	5.3	5.1	5.0	4.8	4.6	4.5	4.4	4.3	4.2	4.1	3.9	3.8	3.7	3.7	3.6	3.5	3.4	3.3
1976	5.7	5.6	5.4	5.3	5.1	5.0	4.8	4.7	4.6	4.4	4.3	4.3	4.1	4.0	3.9	3.8	3.7	3.6	3.5	3.4	3.3
1977	5.6	5.5	5.4	5.3	5.1	5.0	4.8	4.7	4.6	4.4	4.4	4.3	4.2	4.0	3.9	3.9	3.8	3.7	3.6	3.5	3.4
1978	5.7	5.7	5.5	5.4	5.3	5.1	4.9	4.8	4.7	4.6	4.5	4.4	4.3	4.2	4.1	4.0	3.9	3.8	3.7	3.6	3.5
1979	6.1	6.0	5.9	5.7	5.6	5.4	5.2	5.1	5.0	4.8	4.8	4.7	4.5	4.4	4.3	4.2	4.1	4.0	3.9	3.8	3.7
1980	6.4	6.3	6.2	6.0	5.9	5.7	5.5	5.4	5.3	5.1	5.0	4.9	4.8	4.6	4.5	4.4	4.3	4.2	4.1	4.0	3.9
1981	7.0	6.8	6.7	6.5	6.3	6.1	5.9	5.8	5.7	5.5	5.4	5.3	5.1	5.0	4.9	4.8	4.7	4.5	4.4	4.3	4.2
1982	7.2	7.1	6.9	6.7	6.5	6.3	6.1	6.0	5.9	5.7	5.6	5.5	5.3	5.2	5.1	4.9	4.8	4.7	4.6	4.5	4.4
1983	7.3	7.1	7.0	6.8	6.6	6.4	6.3	6.1	6.0	5.8	5.7	5.6	5.4	5.3	5.2	5.1	4.9	4.8	4.7	4.6	4.5
1984	7.4	7.3	7.1	6.9	6.8	6.6	6.4	6.2	6.1	5.9	5.8	5.7	5.6	5.4	5.3	5.2	5.1	5.0	4.9	4.8	4.6
1985	7.4	7.3	7.1	7.0	6.8	6.6	6.5	6.3	6.2	6.0	5.9	5.8	5.7	5.5	5.4	5.3	5.2	5.1	4.9	4.8	4.7
1986	7.4	7.3	7.1	6.9	6.8	6.6	6.4	6.3	6.2	6.0	5.9	5.8	5.7	5.5	5.4	5.3	5.2	5.1	5.0	4.9	4.8
1987	7.3	7.2	7.0	6.9	6.7	6.6	6.4	6.3	6.2	6.0	5.9	5.8	5.7	5.5	5.4	5.3	5.2	5.1	5.0	4.9	4.8

EXHIBIT A-6 (Continued)

TO THE END OF	FROM THE BEGINNING OF 1968	1969	1970	1971	1972	1973	1974	1975	1976	1977	1978	1979	1980	1981	1982	1983	1984	1985	1986	1987
1968	5.2																			
1969	5.9	6.6																		
1970	6.1	6.6	6.5																	
1971	5.7	5.8	5.5	4.4																
1972	5.3	5.3	4.9	4.1	3.8															
1973	5.6	5.6	5.4	5.0	5.4	6.9														
1974	5.9	6.0	5.9	5.8	6.2	7.5	8.0													
1975	5.9	6.0	5.9	5.8	6.1	6.9	6.9	5.8												
1976	5.8	5.9	5.8	5.7	5.9	6.4	6.3	5.4	5.1											
1977	5.7	5.8	5.7	5.6	5.8	6.2	6.0	5.3	5.1	5.1										
1978	5.9	5.9	5.9	5.8	6.0	6.3	6.2	5.8	5.8	6.1	7.2									
1979	6.2	6.3	6.3	6.3	6.5	6.9	6.9	6.7	6.9	7.5	8.8	10.4								
1980	6.6	6.7	6.7	6.8	7.0	7.4	7.5	7.4	7.8	8.5	9.6	10.8	11.2							
1981	7.2	7.3	7.4	7.5	7.8	8.2	8.4	8.4	8.9	9.7	10.8	12.1	13.0	14.7						
1982	7.4	7.6	7.6	7.7	8.0	8.5	8.6	8.7	9.1	9.8	10.8	11.7	12.1	12.6	10.5					
1983	7.5	7.6	7.7	7.8	8.1	8.5	8.6	8.7	9.1	9.7	10.4	11.1	11.3	11.3	9.7	8.8				
1984	7.6	7.8	7.9	7.9	8.2	8.6	8.8	8.8	9.2	9.7	10.4	13.9	11.0	11.0	9.7	9.3	9.8			
1985	7.6	7.8	7.8	7.9	8.2	8.5	8.7	8.7	9.0	9.5	10.0	10.4	10.5	10.3	9.2	8.8	8.8	7.7		
1986	7.5	7.7	7.7	7.8	8.1	8.4	8.5	8.5	8.8	9.1	9.6	9.9	9.8	9.6	8.6	8.1	7.9	6.9	6.2	
1987	7.4	7.6	7.6	7.7	7.9	8.2	8.3	8.3	8.5	8.8	9.2	9.4	9.3	9.0	8.1	7.6	7.3	6.4	5.8	5.5

EXHIBIT A-7
CONSUMER PRICE INDEX: INFLATION RATES
RATES OF RETURN FOR ALL YEARLY HOLDING PERIODS FROM 1926 TO 1987
(Percent Per Annum Compounded Annually)

TO THE END OF	1926	1927	1928	1929	1930	1931	1932	1933	1934	1935	1936	1937	1938	1939	1940	1941	1942	1943	1944	1945	1946
1926	-1.5																				
1927	-1.8	-2.1																			
1928	-1.5	-1.5	-1.0																		
1929	-1.1	-1.0	-0.4	0.2																	
1930	-2.1	-2.2	-2.3	-3.0	-6.0																
1931	-3.4	-3.7	-4.2	-5.2	-7.8	-9.5															
1932	-4.4	-4.9	-5.4	-6.5	-8.6	-9.9	-10.3														
1933	-3.8	-4.1	-4.5	-5.1	-6.4	-6.6	-5.0	0.5													
1934	-3.2	-3.4	-3.6	-4.0	-4.8	-4.5	-2.7	1.3	2.0												
1935	-2.6	-2.7	-2.8	-3.0	-3.5	-3.0	-1.3	1.8	2.5	3.0											
1936	-2.2	-2.3	-2.3	-2.5	-2.9	-2.3	-0.8	1.7	2.1	2.1	1.2										
1937	-1.8	-1.8	-1.8	-1.9	-2.1	-1.6	-0.2	2.0	2.3	2.4	2.2	3.1									
1938	-1.9	-1.9	-1.9	-2.0	-2.2	-1.7	-0.6	1.2	1.3	1.1	0.5	0.1	-2.8								
1939	-1.8	-1.8	-1.8	-1.8	-2.0	-1.6	-0.6	0.9	1.0	0.8	0.2	-0.1	-1.6	-0.5							
1940	-1.6	-1.6	-1.6	-1.6	-1.8	-1.3	-0.4	0.9	1.0	0.8	0.4	0.2	-0.8	0.2	1.0						
1941	-0.9	-0.9	-0.8	-0.8	-0.9	-0.4	0.6	1.9	2.0	2.0	1.9	2.0	1.7	3.3	5.2	9.7					
1942	-0.3	-0.3	-0.2	-0.1	-0.1	0.4	1.3	2.6	2.8	2.9	2.9	3.2	3.2	4.8	6.6	9.5	9.3				
1943	-0.2	-0.1	0.0	0.1	0.1	0.6	1.5	2.6	2.9	2.9	2.9	3.2	3.2	4.4	5.7	7.3	6.2	3.2			
1944	-0.0	0.0	0.2	0.2	0.2	0.7	1.5	2.6	2.8	2.9	2.8	3.1	3.0	4.1	5.0	6.0	4.8	2.6	2.1		
1945	0.1	0.2	0.3	0.4	0.4	0.8	1.6	2.6	2.7	2.8	2.8	3.0	2.9	3.8	4.5	5.2	4.2	2.5	2.2	2.3	
1946	0.9	1.0	1.2	1.3	1.3	1.8	2.6	3.6	3.9	4.0	4.1	4.4	4.5	5.5	6.4	7.3	6.8	6.2	7.3	9.9	18.2
1947	1.2	1.4	1.5	1.7	1.7	2.2	3.0	4.0	4.2	4.4	4.5	4.8	5.0	5.9	6.7	7.5	7.2	6.8	7.7	9.6	13.5
1948	1.3	1.4	1.6	1.7	1.8	2.3	3.0	3.9	4.1	4.3	4.4	4.6	4.8	5.6	6.2	6.9	6.5	6.1	6.7	7.8	9.8
1949	1.2	1.3	1.4	1.5	1.6	2.0	2.7	3.5	3.7	3.8	3.9	4.1	4.2	4.9	5.4	5.9	5.5	4.9	5.2	5.8	6.8
1950	1.3	1.5	1.6	1.7	1.8	2.2	2.9	3.7	3.9	4.0	4.0	4.2	4.3	4.9	5.4	5.9	5.5	5.0	5.3	5.8	6.6
1951	1.5	1.6	1.8	1.9	2.0	2.4	3.0	3.8	4.0	4.1	4.1	4.3	4.4	5.0	5.5	5.9	5.5	5.1	5.4	5.8	6.5
1952	1.5	1.6	1.8	1.9	1.9	2.3	2.9	3.6	3.8	3.9	4.0	4.1	4.2	4.7	5.1	5.5	5.1	4.7	4.9	5.2	5.6
1953	1.5	1.6	1.7	1.8	1.9	2.2	2.8	3.5	3.6	3.7	3.8	3.9	4.0	4.4	4.8	5.1	4.7	4.3	4.4	4.7	5.0
1954	1.4	1.5	1.6	1.7	1.8	2.1	2.7	3.3	3.4	3.5	3.5	3.7	3.7	4.1	4.4	4.7	4.3	3.9	4.0	4.2	4.4
1955	1.4	1.5	1.6	1.7	1.7	2.1	2.6	3.2	3.3	3.4	3.4	3.5	3.5	3.9	4.2	4.4	4.0	3.6	3.7	3.8	4.0
1956	1.4	1.5	1.5	1.7	1.8	2.1	2.6	3.2	3.3	3.3	3.4	3.5	3.5	3.8	4.1	4.3	3.9	3.6	3.6	3.7	3.9
1957	1.5	1.5	1.6	1.8	1.8	2.1	2.6	3.2	3.2	3.3	3.3	3.4	3.5	3.8	4.0	4.2	3.9	3.5	3.6	3.7	3.8
1958	1.5	1.6	1.7	1.8	1.8	2.1	2.6	3.1	3.2	3.3	3.3	3.4	3.4	3.7	3.9	4.1	3.8	3.4	3.4	3.5	3.6
1959	1.5	1.6	1.7	1.8	1.8	2.1	2.5	3.0	3.1	3.2	3.2	3.3	3.3	3.6	3.8	3.9	3.6	3.3	3.3	3.4	3.5

FROM THE BEGINNING OF

EXHIBIT A-7 (Continued)

TO THE END OF	FROM THE BEGINNING OF																				
	1926	1927	1928	1929	1930	1931	1932	1933	1934	1935	1936	1937	1938	1939	1940	1941	1942	1943	1944	1945	1946
1960	1.5	1.6	1.7	1.7	1.8	2.1	2.5	3.0	3.1	3.1	3.1	3.2	3.2	3.5	3.7	3.8	3.5	3.2	3.2	3.3	3.3
1961	1.4	1.5	1.6	1.7	1.8	2.0	2.4	2.9	3.0	3.0	3.0	3.1	3.1	3.4	3.5	3.7	3.4	3.1	3.1	3.1	3.2
1962	1.4	1.5	1.6	1.7	1.7	2.0	2.4	2.8	2.9	3.0	3.0	3.0	3.0	3.3	3.4	3.6	3.3	3.0	3.0	3.0	3.1
1963	1.4	1.5	1.6	1.7	1.7	2.0	2.4	2.8	2.8	2.9	2.9	3.0	3.0	3.2	3.4	3.5	3.2	2.9	2.9	2.9	3.0
1964	1.4	1.5	1.6	1.7	1.7	2.0	2.3	2.7	2.8	2.9	2.9	2.9	2.9	3.1	3.3	3.4	3.1	2.8	2.8	2.9	2.9
1965	1.4	1.5	1.6	1.7	1.7	2.0	2.3	2.8	2.8	2.8	2.8	2.9	2.9	3.1	3.2	3.3	3.1	2.8	2.8	2.8	2.8
1966	1.5	1.6	1.7	1.7	1.8	2.0	2.4	2.8	2.8	2.8	2.8	2.9	2.9	3.1	3.2	3.3	3.1	2.8	2.8	2.8	2.9
1967	1.5	1.6	1.7	1.7	1.8	2.0	2.4	2.8	2.9	2.9	2.9	2.9	2.9	3.1	3.2	3.3	3.1	2.8	2.8	2.8	2.9
1968	1.6	1.7	1.8	1.8	1.9	2.1	2.4	2.8	2.9	2.9	2.9	3.0	3.0	3.1	3.3	3.4	3.1	2.9	2.9	2.9	3.0
1969	1.7	1.8	1.9	1.9	2.0	2.2	2.5	2.9	3.0	3.0	3.0	3.0	3.0	3.2	3.4	3.5	3.2	3.0	3.0	3.0	3.1
1970	1.8	1.9	2.0	2.0	2.1	2.3	2.6	3.0	3.0	3.1	3.1	3.1	3.1	3.3	3.4	3.5	3.3	3.1	3.1	3.1	3.2
1971	1.8	1.9	2.0	2.1	2.1	2.3	2.6	3.0	3.0	3.1	3.1	3.1	3.1	3.3	3.4	3.5	3.3	3.1	3.1	3.1	3.2
1972	1.9	1.9	2.0	2.1	2.1	2.3	2.6	3.0	3.0	3.1	3.1	3.1	3.1	3.3	3.4	3.5	3.3	3.1	3.1	3.2	3.2
1973	2.0	2.1	2.1	2.2	2.3	2.5	2.8	3.1	3.2	3.2	3.2	3.3	3.3	3.5	3.6	3.7	3.5	3.3	3.3	3.3	3.4
1974	2.2	2.3	2.4	2.4	2.5	2.7	3.0	3.3	3.4	3.4	3.4	3.5	3.5	3.7	3.8	3.9	3.7	3.6	3.6	3.6	3.7
1975	2.3	2.4	2.5	2.5	2.6	2.8	3.1	3.4	3.5	3.5	3.5	3.6	3.6	3.8	3.9	4.0	3.8	3.7	3.7	3.7	3.8
1976	2.3	2.5	2.5	2.6	2.6	2.8	3.1	3.4	3.5	3.6	3.6	3.6	3.6	3.8	3.9	4.0	3.9	3.7	3.7	3.8	3.8
1977	2.4	2.5	2.6	2.7	2.7	2.9	3.2	3.5	3.6	3.6	3.6	3.7	3.7	3.9	4.0	4.1	3.9	3.8	3.8	3.9	3.9
1978	2.5	2.6	2.7	2.8	2.8	3.0	3.3	3.6	3.7	3.7	3.8	3.8	3.8	4.0	4.1	4.2	4.1	3.9	4.0	4.0	4.1
1979	2.7	2.8	2.9	3.0	3.0	3.2	3.5	3.8	3.9	4.0	4.0	4.0	4.1	4.2	4.4	4.4	4.3	4.2	4.2	4.3	4.3
1980	2.9	3.0	3.1	3.2	3.2	3.4	3.7	4.0	4.1	4.1	4.2	4.2	4.2	4.4	4.5	4.6	4.5	4.4	4.4	4.5	4.5
1981	3.0	3.1	3.2	3.3	3.3	3.5	3.8	4.1	4.2	4.2	4.3	4.3	4.4	4.5	4.6	4.7	4.6	4.5	4.5	4.6	4.7
1982	3.0	3.1	3.1	3.3	3.3	3.5	3.8	4.1	4.2	4.2	4.2	4.3	4.3	4.5	4.6	4.7	4.6	4.5	4.5	4.6	4.6
1983	3.0	3.1	3.2	3.3	3.3	3.5	3.8	4.1	4.2	4.2	4.2	4.3	4.3	4.5	4.6	4.7	4.6	4.5	4.5	4.6	4.6
1984	3.0	3.1	3.2	3.3	3.4	3.5	3.8	4.1	4.2	4.2	4.2	4.3	4.3	4.5	4.6	4.7	4.6	4.5	4.5	4.5	4.6
1985	3.1	3.1	3.2	3.3	3.4	3.5	3.8	4.1	4.2	4.2	4.2	4.3	4.3	4.5	4.6	4.7	4.5	4.4	4.5	4.5	4.6
1986	3.0	3.1	3.2	3.3	3.3	3.5	3.8	4.0	4.1	4.1	4.2	4.2	4.2	4.4	4.5	4.6	4.5	4.4	4.4	4.4	4.5
1987	3.0	3.1	3.2	3.3	3.3	3.5	3.8	4.0	4.1	4.1	4.2	4.2	4.2	4.4	4.5	4.6	4.5	4.4	4.4	4.4	4.5

185

EXHIBIT A-7 (Continued)

TO THE END OF	FROM THE BEGINNING OF 1947	1948	1949	1950	1951	1952	1953	1954	1955	1956	1957	1958	1959	1960	1961	1962	1963	1964	1965	1966	1967
1947	9.0																				
1948	5.8	2.7																			
1949	3.2	0.4	-1.8																		
1950	3.8	2.2	1.9	5.8																	
1951	4.3	3.1	3.2	5.8	5.9																
1952	3.7	2.6	2.6	4.2	3.3	0.9															
1953	3.2	2.3	2.2	3.3	2.4	0.8	0.6														
1954	2.8	1.9	1.8	2.5	1.7	0.3	0.1	-0.5													
1955	2.5	1.7	1.6	2.1	1.4	0.3	0.2	-0.1	0.4												
1956	2.5	1.8	1.7	2.2	1.7	0.8	0.8	0.9	1.6	2.9											
1957	2.6	2.0	1.9	2.3	1.9	1.2	1.3	1.4	2.1	2.9	3.0										
1958	2.5	1.9	1.9	2.3	1.8	1.3	1.3	1.5	2.0	2.5	2.4	1.8									
1959	2.4	1.9	1.8	2.2	1.8	1.3	1.4	1.5	1.9	2.3	2.1	1.6	1.5								
1960	2.4	1.8	1.8	2.1	1.8	1.3	1.4	1.5	1.8	2.1	1.9	1.6	1.5	1.5							
1961	2.2	1.8	1.7	2.0	1.7	1.3	1.3	1.4	1.7	1.9	1.7	1.4	1.2	1.1	0.7						
1962	2.2	1.7	1.7	1.9	1.6	1.3	1.3	1.4	1.6	1.8	1.6	1.3	1.2	1.1	0.9	1.2					
1963	2.2	1.7	1.7	1.9	1.6	1.3	1.3	1.4	1.6	1.7	1.6	1.4	1.2	1.3	1.2	1.4	1.6				
1964	2.1	1.7	1.6	1.9	1.6	1.3	1.3	1.4	1.6	1.7	1.6	1.4	1.3	1.2	1.3	1.4	1.4	1.2			
1965	2.1	1.7	1.7	1.9	1.6	1.3	1.4	1.4	1.6	1.7	1.6	1.4	1.4	1.4	1.3	1.5	1.6	1.6	1.9		
1966	2.2	1.8	1.8	2.0	1.7	1.5	1.5	1.6	1.7	1.9	1.8	1.6	1.6	1.6	1.7	1.9	2.0	2.2	2.6	3.4	
1967	2.2	1.9	1.8	2.0	1.8	1.6	1.6	1.7	1.8	2.0	1.8	1.8	1.8	1.8	1.9	2.1	2.2	2.4	2.8	3.2	3.0
1968	2.3	2.0	2.0	2.2	2.0	1.7	1.8	1.9	2.0	2.2	2.1	2.0	2.1	2.1	2.2	2.6	2.8	3.3	3.3	3.7	3.9
1969	2.5	2.2	2.2	2.4	2.2	2.0	2.0	2.1	2.3	2.5	2.4	2.4	2.5	2.5	2.6	2.9	3.1	3.4	3.8	4.3	4.6
1970	2.6	2.3	2.3	2.5	2.3	2.2	2.2	2.3	2.5	2.7	2.6	2.6	2.7	2.8	2.9	3.2	3.4	3.7	4.1	4.5	4.8
1971	2.6	2.4	2.4	2.5	2.4	2.2	2.3	2.4	2.6	2.7	2.7	2.7	2.7	2.8	3.0	3.2	3.4	3.6	4.0	4.3	4.5
1972	2.7	2.4	2.4	2.6	2.4	2.3	2.3	2.4	2.6	2.7	2.7	2.7	2.8	2.9	3.0	3.2	3.4	3.6	3.9	4.2	4.3
1973	2.9	2.6	2.6	2.8	2.7	2.6	2.6	2.8	2.9	3.1	3.1	3.1	3.2	3.3	3.4	3.7	3.9	4.1	4.4	4.8	5.0
1974	3.2	3.0	3.0	3.2	3.1	3.0	3.1	3.2	3.4	3.5	3.6	3.6	3.7	3.9	4.0	4.3	4.6	4.8	5.2	5.6	5.9
1975	3.3	3.1	3.1	3.3	3.2	3.1	3.2	3.4	3.5	3.7	3.7	3.8	3.9	4.1	4.2	4.5	4.7	5.0	5.4	5.7	6.0
1976	3.4	3.2	3.2	3.4	3.3	3.2	3.3	3.4	3.6	3.8	3.8	3.8	4.0	4.1	4.3	4.5	4.8	5.0	5.3	5.6	5.9
1977	3.5	3.3	3.3	3.5	3.4	3.3	3.4	3.6	3.7	3.9	3.9	4.0	4.1	4.2	4.4	4.7	4.9	5.1	5.4	5.7	5.9
1978	3.7	3.5	3.5	3.7	3.6	3.5	3.6	3.8	3.9	4.1	4.2	4.2	4.3	4.5	4.7	4.9	5.1	5.4	5.7	6.0	6.2
1979	3.9	3.8	3.8	4.0	3.9	3.9	4.0	4.1	4.3	4.5	4.5	4.6	4.8	4.9	5.1	5.4	5.6	5.9	6.2	6.5	6.7
1980	4.2	4.0	4.1	4.3	4.2	4.2	4.3	4.4	4.6	4.8	4.9	4.9	5.1	5.3	5.5	5.7	6.0	6.2	6.6	6.9	7.1
1981	4.3	4.2	4.2	4.4	4.4	4.3	4.4	4.6	4.8	4.9	5.0	5.1	5.3	5.4	5.6	5.9	6.1	6.4	6.7	7.0	7.2
1982	4.3	4.2	4.2	4.4	4.3	4.3	4.4	4.5	4.7	4.9	5.0	5.1	5.2	5.4	5.5	5.8	6.0	6.2	6.5	6.8	7.0
1983	4.3	4.2	4.2	4.4	4.3	4.3	4.4	4.5	4.7	4.9	4.9	5.0	5.1	5.3	5.5	5.7	5.9	6.1	6.4	6.6	6.8
1984	4.3	4.1	4.1	4.4	4.3	4.3	4.4	4.5	4.6	4.8	4.9	5.0	5.1	5.2	5.4	5.6	5.8	6.0	6.3	6.5	6.7
1985	4.3	4.1	4.2	4.3	4.3	4.3	4.4	4.5	4.6	4.8	4.9	4.9	5.0	5.2	5.3	5.5	5.7	5.9	6.1	6.4	6.5
1986	4.2	4.1	4.1	4.3	4.2	4.2	4.3	4.4	4.5	4.7	4.7	4.8	4.9	5.0	5.2	5.4	5.5	5.7	5.9	6.1	6.2
1987	4.2	4.1	4.1	4.3	4.2	4.2	4.3	4.4	4.5	4.7	4.7	4.8	4.9	5.0	5.1	5.3	5.5	5.6	5.8	6.0	6.2

EXHIBIT A-7 (Continued)

TO THE END OF	FROM THE BEGINNING OF 1968	1969	1970	1971	1972	1973	1974	1975	1976	1977	1978	1979	1980	1981	1982	1983	1984	1985	1986	1987
1968	4.7																			
1969	5.4	6.1																		
1970	5.4	5.8	5.5																	
1971	4.9	5.0	4.4	3.4																
1972	4.6	4.6	4.1	3.4	3.4															
1973	5.3	5.4	5.2	5.2	6.1	8.8														
1974	6.3	6.5	6.6	6.9	8.1	10.5	12.2													
1975	6.4	6.6	6.7	6.9	7.8	9.3	9.6	7.0												
1976	6.2	6.4	6.4	6.6	7.2	8.2	8.0	5.9	4.8											
1977	6.2	6.4	6.4	6.6	7.1	7.9	7.7	6.2	5.8	6.8										
1978	6.5	6.7	6.7	6.9	7.4	8.1	7.9	6.9	6.9	7.9	9.0									
1979	7.0	7.3	7.4	7.6	8.1	8.8	8.8	8.1	8.4	9.7	11.1	13.3								
1980	7.4	7.7	7.8	8.1	8.6	9.3	9.3	8.8	9.2	10.3	11.6	12.9	12.4							
1981	7.6	7.8	7.9	8.1	8.6	9.2	9.3	8.9	9.2	10.1	10.9	11.5	10.7	8.9						
1982	7.3	7.5	7.6	7.8	8.2	8.7	8.7	8.2	8.4	9.0	9.5	9.6	8.3	6.4	3.9					
1983	7.1	7.2	7.3	7.5	7.8	8.2	8.2	7.7	7.8	8.2	8.5	8.4	7.2	5.5	3.8	3.8				
1984	6.9	7.0	7.1	7.2	7.5	7.9	7.8	7.3	7.4	7.7	7.8	7.6	6.5	5.1	3.9	3.9	4.0			
1985	6.7	6.8	6.9	7.0	7.2	7.5	7.4	7.0	7.0	7.3	7.3	7.1	6.1	4.8	3.8	3.8	3.9	3.8		
1986	6.4	6.5	6.5	6.6	6.8	7.1	6.9	6.5	6.5	6.6	6.6	6.3	5.3	4.2	3.3	3.2	2.9	2.4	1.1	
1987	6.3	6.4	6.4	6.5	6.7	6.9	6.8	6.3	6.3	6.4	6.4	6.1	5.2	4.2	3.5	3.4	3.3	3.1	2.8	4.4

EXHIBIT A-8
EQUITY RISK PREMIUMS: COMMON STOCKS MINUS TREASURY BILLS
RATES OF RETURN FOR ALL YEARLY HOLDING PERIODS FROM 1926 TO 1987
(Percent Per Annum Compounded Annually)

TO THE END OF	1926	1927	1928	1929	1930	1931	1932	1933	1934	1935	1936	1937	1938	1939	1940	1941	1942	1943	1944	1945	1946
1926	8.1																				
1927	20.0	33.3																			
1928	26.1	36.2	39.1																		
1929	15.1	17.5	10.3	-12.6																	
1930	5.1	4.4	-3.7	-19.9	-26.7																
1931	-5.3	-7.8	-15.9	-28.9	-35.9	-43.9															
1932	-5.9	-8.0	-14.6	-24.4	-28.0	-28.6	-9.1														
1933	-0.1	-1.0	-5.8	-12.9	-13.0	-7.8	18.2	53.5													
1934	-0.1	-1.1	-5.2	-4.4	-3.0	-6.3	11.2	22.9	-1.6												
1935	3.9	3.4	0.2	-0.3	1.5	2.6	19.3	30.6	20.4	47.4											
1936	6.3	6.1	3.4	2.2	1.5	7.2	22.0	31.4	24.7	40.4	33.7										
1937	2.0	1.4	-1.3	-5.0	-4.0	-0.2	9.8	14.0	5.9	8.5	-6.9	-35.2									
1938	4.0	3.6	1.3	-1.9	-0.6	3.2	12.6	16.7	10.5	13.7	4.3	-7.8	31.1								
1939	3.6	3.3	1.1	-1.8	-0.6	2.8	10.9	14.1	8.6	10.8	3.1	-5.4	14.3	-0.4							
1940	2.7	2.3	0.2	-2.4	-1.5	1.5	8.4	10.8	5.8	7.0	0.4	-6.5	5.6	-5.2	-9.8						
1941	1.7	1.3	-0.7	-3.2	-2.4	0.2	6.2	8.0	3.4	4.1	-1.7	-7.6	1.0	-7.4	-10.7	-11.6					
1942	2.7	2.4	0.6	-1.7	-0.8	1.7	7.4	9.2	5.1	6.0	1.1	-3.5	4.5	-1.2	-1.5	3.0	20.0				
1943	3.9	3.6	2.0	-0.1	0.9	3.4	8.8	10.6	7.0	8.0	3.9	0.2	7.8	3.6	4.7	10.0	22.7	25.5			
1944	4.6	4.4	3.0	1.0	2.0	4.4	9.6	11.3	8.1	9.1	5.5	2.4	9.4	6.1	7.5	12.3	21.6	22.4	19.4		
1945	6.0	5.9	4.6	2.8	3.9	6.3	11.3	13.0	10.2	11.3	8.2	5.7	12.4	9.9	11.8	16.6	25.0	26.8	27.4	36.0	
1946	5.3	5.1	3.8	2.2	3.1	5.3	9.8	11.3	8.6	9.5	6.6	4.2	9.9	7.5	8.6	12.0	17.5	16.9	14.1	11.6	-8.4
1947	5.3	5.1	3.9	2.3	3.2	5.3	9.5	10.9	8.4	9.2	6.5	4.3	9.4	7.2	8.2	11.0	15.3	14.4	11.8	9.4	-1.8
1948	5.2	5.1	3.9	2.4	3.3	5.3	9.2	10.5	8.1	8.8	6.3	4.3	8.9	6.9	7.8	10.2	13.8	12.7	10.4	8.2	0.3
1949	5.7	5.6	4.5	3.1	4.0	5.9	9.7	10.9	8.7	9.4	7.1	5.3	9.6	7.9	8.7	11.0	14.2	13.4	11.5	10.0	4.3
1950	6.6	6.6	5.5	4.2	5.1	7.0	10.7	11.9	9.8	10.6	8.5	6.9	11.1	9.6	10.5	12.8	15.9	15.4	14.0	13.1	9.0
1951	7.2	7.1	6.2	4.9	5.8	7.7	11.2	12.4	10.5	11.2	9.3	7.8	11.8	10.5	11.4	13.6	16.5	16.1	15.0	14.4	11.1
1952	7.5	7.5	6.6	5.4	6.2	8.0	11.5	12.6	10.8	11.5	9.7	8.4	12.1	10.9	11.8	13.8	16.5	16.1	15.2	14.6	11.9
1953	7.1	7.1	6.2	5.0	5.8	7.6	10.8	11.8	10.1	10.7	9.0	7.7	11.1	9.9	10.7	12.5	14.8	14.3	13.2	12.6	9.9
1954	8.4	8.4	7.6	6.5	7.4	9.1	12.3	13.4	11.8	12.5	10.9	9.7	13.2	12.1	13.0	14.9	17.2	17.0	16.2	15.9	13.9
1955	9.0	9.1	8.3	7.3	8.2	9.8	13.0	14.0	12.5	13.2	11.7	10.7	14.0	13.1	14.0	15.8	18.1	17.9	17.3	17.1	15.4
1956	8.9	8.9	8.1	7.2	8.0	9.6	12.6	13.6	12.1	12.8	11.4	10.3	13.5	12.6	13.4	15.0	17.1	16.9	16.2	16.0	14.3
1957	8.1	8.1	7.3	6.4	7.1	8.7	11.5	12.4	10.9	11.5	10.1	9.1	12.0	11.0	11.7	13.1	14.9	14.5	13.8	13.4	11.7
1958	9.0	9.0	8.3	7.4	8.2	9.7	12.4	13.4	12.0	12.6	11.3	10.4	13.2	12.4	13.1	14.5	16.3	16.0	15.4	15.2	13.7
1959	9.0	9.0	8.3	7.4	8.2	9.6	12.3	13.2	11.9	12.4	11.2	10.3	13.0	12.2	12.9	14.2	15.8	15.6	15.0	14.7	13.3

FROM THE BEGINNING OF

EXHIBIT A-8 (Continued)

TO THE END OF	FROM THE BEGINNING OF																				
	1926	1927	1928	1929	1930	1931	1932	1933	1934	1935	1936	1937	1938	1939	1940	1941	1942	1943	1944	1945	1946
1960	8.6	8.7	8.0	7.1	7.8	9.2	11.8	12.6	11.3	11.8	10.6	9.7	12.3	11.5	12.1	13.3	14.8	14.5	13.9	13.6	12.2
1961	9.0	9.1	8.4	7.6	8.3	9.7	12.2	13.0	11.8	12.3	11.1	10.3	12.8	12.0	12.6	13.8	15.3	15.0	14.5	14.2	13.0
1962	8.4	8.5	7.8	7.0	7.7	9.0	11.3	12.1	10.9	11.3	10.2	9.4	11.7	10.9	11.5	12.5	13.9	13.6	13.0	12.6	11.4
1963	8.7	8.7	8.1	7.3	8.0	9.3	11.6	12.3	11.1	11.6	10.5	9.7	12.0	11.3	11.8	12.8	14.1	13.8	13.3	12.9	11.8
1964	8.8	8.8	8.2	7.5	8.1	9.4	11.6	12.3	11.2	11.6	10.5	9.8	11.9	11.3	11.8	12.8	14.0	13.8	13.2	12.9	11.8
1965	8.8	8.8	8.2	7.5	8.1	9.3	11.5	12.2	11.1	11.5	10.5	9.8	11.9	11.2	11.7	12.6	13.8	13.5	13.0	12.7	11.6
1966	8.2	8.2	7.6	6.9	7.4	8.6	10.7	11.3	10.2	10.6	9.6	8.9	10.8	10.2	10.6	11.5	12.5	12.2	11.6	11.3	10.3
1967	8.4	8.4	7.9	7.2	7.7	8.9	10.9	11.5	10.5	10.9	9.9	9.2	11.1	10.5	10.9	11.7	12.7	12.5	11.9	11.6	10.6
1968	8.3	8.3	7.8	7.1	7.7	8.8	10.7	11.3	10.3	10.7	9.7	9.1	10.9	10.3	10.7	11.5	12.5	12.2	11.7	11.4	10.4
1969	7.8	7.8	7.2	6.5	7.1	8.1	10.0	10.6	9.6	9.9	9.0	8.3	10.0	9.4	9.8	10.5	11.4	11.1	10.6	10.2	9.3
1970	7.5	7.5	7.0	6.3	6.8	7.8	9.7	10.2	9.2	9.5	8.6	7.9	9.6	9.0	9.3	10.0	10.9	10.6	10.0	9.7	8.8
1971	7.6	7.6	7.0	6.4	6.9	7.9	9.7	10.2	9.2	9.5	8.6	8.0	9.6	9.0	9.3	10.0	10.8	10.5	10.0	9.7	8.8
1972	7.7	7.7	7.2	6.6	7.1	8.0	9.8	10.3	9.4	9.7	8.8	8.2	9.8	9.2	9.5	10.2	11.0	10.7	10.2	9.9	9.0
1973	7.0	7.0	6.5	5.9	6.3	7.3	8.9	9.4	8.5	8.8	7.9	7.3	8.8	8.2	8.5	9.1	9.8	9.5	9.0	8.7	7.8
1974	6.1	6.0	5.5	4.9	5.3	6.2	7.8	8.2	7.3	7.5	6.6	6.0	7.4	6.8	7.1	7.6	8.2	7.9	7.4	7.0	6.1
1975	6.5	6.5	6.0	5.4	5.8	6.6	8.2	8.7	7.8	8.0	7.2	6.6	8.0	7.4	7.6	8.2	8.8	8.5	8.0	7.6	6.8
1976	6.7	6.7	6.2	5.6	6.0	6.9	8.4	8.9	8.0	8.2	7.4	6.8	8.2	7.7	7.9	8.4	9.1	8.8	8.3	8.0	7.2
1977	6.3	6.3	5.8	5.2	5.6	6.4	7.9	8.3	7.5	7.7	6.5	6.3	7.7	7.1	7.3	7.8	8.4	8.1	7.6	7.3	6.5
1978	6.2	6.1	5.7	5.1	5.5	6.3	7.7	8.1	7.3	7.5	6.7	6.2	7.4	6.9	7.1	7.6	8.2	7.9	7.4	7.1	6.3
1979	6.2	6.2	5.7	5.1	5.5	6.3	7.7	8.1	7.3	7.5	6.7	6.2	7.4	6.9	7.1	7.6	8.1	7.8	7.4	7.1	6.3
1980	6.4	6.4	5.9	5.4	5.8	6.6	8.0	8.3	7.5	7.8	7.0	6.5	7.7	7.2	7.4	7.9	8.4	8.1	7.7	7.4	6.7
1981	5.9	5.9	5.5	4.9	5.3	6.0	7.4	7.8	7.0	7.2	6.4	5.9	7.1	6.6	6.7	7.2	7.7	7.4	6.9	6.6	5.9
1982	6.0	6.0	5.5	5.0	5.4	6.1	7.4	7.8	7.0	7.2	6.5	6.0	7.1	6.6	6.8	7.2	7.7	7.4	7.0	6.7	6.0
1983	6.1	6.1	5.7	5.1	5.5	6.2	7.5	7.9	7.1	7.3	6.6	6.1	7.2	6.8	6.9	7.4	7.9	7.6	7.2	6.9	6.2
1984	6.0	5.9	5.5	5.0	5.3	6.0	7.3	7.7	6.9	7.1	6.4	5.9	7.0	6.5	6.7	7.1	7.6	7.3	6.9	6.6	5.9
1985	6.2	6.2	5.8	5.3	5.6	6.3	7.6	7.9	7.2	7.4	6.7	6.2	7.3	6.9	7.0	7.4	7.9	7.6	7.2	7.0	6.3
1986	6.3	6.3	5.9	5.4	5.7	6.4	7.7	8.0	7.3	7.5	6.8	6.3	7.4	6.9	7.1	7.5	8.0	7.7	7.3	7.1	6.4
1987	6.2	6.2	5.8	5.3	5.6	6.3	7.5	7.8	7.1	7.3	6.7	6.2	7.2	6.8	7.0	7.3	7.8	7.5	7.2	6.9	6.3

EXHIBIT A-8 (Continued)

FROM THE BEGINNING OF

TO THE END OF	1947	1948	1949	1950	1951	1952	1953	1954	1955	1956	1957	1958	1959	1960	1961	1962	1963	1964	1965	1966	1967
1947	5.2																				
1948	4.9	4.7																			
1949	9.0	10.9	17.5																		
1950	13.9	17.0	23.7	30.2																	
1951	15.5	18.3	23.2	26.1	22.2																
1952	15.7	17.9	21.5	22.8	19.3	16.4															
1953	12.8	14.2	16.2	15.8	11.4	6.4	-2.8														
1954	17.1	18.9	21.4	22.2	20.3	19.7	21.3	51.3													
1955	18.4	20.1	22.5	23.4	22.1	22.1	24.0	40.0	29.5												
1956	16.9	18.2	20.0	20.4	18.9	18.2	18.7	26.8	16.1	4.0											
1957	13.7	14.6	15.8	15.5	13.6	12.2	11.4	15.2	5.2	-5.2	-13.5										
1958	15.8	16.8	18.1	18.1	16.7	16.0	15.9	20.0	13.3	8.3	10.5	41.2									
1959	15.2	16.1	17.2	17.2	15.8	15.0	14.8	18.1	12.3	8.4	9.9	23.9	8.7								
1960	13.9	14.6	15.4	15.3	13.9	13.0	12.6	14.9	9.8	6.2	6.8	14.5	3.2	-2.1							
1961	14.5	15.2	16.1	16.0	14.8	14.1	13.8	16.1	11.7	9.0	10.1	16.9	9.8	10.3	24.2						
1962	12.7	13.3	13.9	13.6	12.4	11.5	11.0	12.7	8.6	5.9	6.2	10.6	4.1	2.6	5.1	-11.2					
1963	13.1	13.6	14.2	14.0	12.9	12.1	11.7	13.3	9.7	7.5	8.0	12.0	6.9	6.5	9.5	2.9	19.1				
1964	13.1	13.6	14.1	13.9	12.8	12.1	11.8	13.2	10.0	8.0	8.5	12.1	7.9	7.7	10.3	6.0	15.8	12.5			
1965	12.8	13.2	13.8	13.5	12.5	11.9	11.5	12.8	9.8	8.0	8.5	11.6	7.9	7.8	9.9	6.5	13.2	10.3	8.2		
1966	11.3	11.6	12.0	11.7	10.6	9.9	9.4	10.4	7.6	5.8	6.0	8.4	4.9	4.3	5.4	2.0	5.6	1.5	-3.6	-14.1	
1967	11.6	12.0	12.4	12.1	11.1	10.4	10.1	11.0	8.4	6.8	7.1	9.4	6.3	6.0	7.3	4.7	8.2	5.6	3.4	1.1	19.0
1968	11.3	11.7	12.0	11.7	10.8	10.2	9.8	10.7	8.2	6.7	7.0	9.0	6.3	6.0	7.1	4.8	7.7	5.6	3.9	2.5	12.1
1969	10.1	10.3	10.6	10.3	9.3	8.6	8.2	8.9	6.6	5.1	5.2	6.9	4.2	3.8	4.5	2.2	4.3	2.0	0.0	-1.9	2.5
1970	9.5	9.7	10.0	9.6	8.7	8.0	7.6	8.2	6.0	4.6	4.6	6.2	3.7	3.2	3.8	1.7	3.4	1.4	-0.4	-2.0	1.3
1971	9.5	9.7	10.0	9.6	8.7	8.1	7.7	8.3	6.2	4.9	4.9	6.4	4.1	3.7	4.3	2.5	4.1	2.4	1.0	-0.2	2.9
1972	9.7	9.9	10.1	9.8	9.0	8.4	8.0	8.6	6.6	5.4	5.5	6.9	4.8	4.5	5.1	3.5	5.1	3.6	2.6	1.8	4.7
1973	8.4	8.6	8.7	8.4	7.5	6.9	6.5	7.0	5.0	3.8	3.8	5.0	2.9	2.5	2.9	1.3	2.5	1.0	-0.2	-1.2	0.8
1974	6.7	6.7	6.8	6.4	5.5	4.8	4.3	4.7	2.8	1.5	1.4	2.3	0.3	-0.2	-0.1	-1.8	-0.9	-2.6	-4.0	-5.2	-4.1
1975	7.4	7.5	7.6	7.2	6.4	5.8	5.3	5.7	3.9	2.8	2.7	3.7	1.8	1.4	1.7	0.2	1.1	-0.2	-1.3	-2.2	-0.8
1976	7.7	7.8	7.9	7.6	6.8	6.2	5.8	6.2	4.5	3.4	3.4	4.4	2.7	2.3	2.6	1.3	2.2	1.1	0.1	-0.5	0.9
1977	7.0	7.1	7.2	6.8	6.0	5.5	5.1	5.4	3.7	2.7	2.6	3.5	1.8	1.5	1.7	0.4	1.3	0.1	-0.8	-1.5	-0.3
1978	6.8	6.8	6.9	6.6	5.8	5.2	4.8	5.1	3.6	2.6	2.5	3.3	1.7	1.4	1.6	0.4	1.1	0.0	-0.8	-1.5	-0.3
1979	6.8	6.8	6.9	6.6	5.9	5.3	4.9	5.2	3.7	2.8	2.7	3.5	2.0	1.7	1.9	0.7	1.5	0.5	-0.3	-0.9	0.3
1980	7.1	7.2	7.3	7.0	6.3	5.8	5.4	5.7	4.3	3.4	3.3	4.1	2.7	2.4	2.7	1.6	2.4	1.5	0.8	0.4	1.5
1981	6.4	6.4	6.4	6.1	5.4	4.9	4.5	4.8	3.4	2.5	2.4	3.1	1.8	1.4	1.6	0.6	1.3	0.4	-0.3	-0.8	0.1
1982	6.5	6.5	6.5	6.2	5.6	5.1	4.7	5.0	3.6	2.7	2.7	3.4	2.1	1.8	2.0	1.0	1.7	0.8	0.2	-0.2	0.7
1983	6.6	6.7	6.7	6.4	5.8	5.3	4.9	5.2	3.9	3.1	3.1	3.7	2.5	2.2	2.4	1.5	2.2	1.4	0.8	0.4	1.4
1984	6.3	6.4	6.4	6.1	5.5	5.0	4.7	4.9	3.7	2.9	2.8	3.5	2.2	2.0	2.2	1.3	1.9	1.2	0.6	0.2	1.1
1985	6.7	6.8	6.8	6.5	5.9	5.5	5.2	5.4	4.2	3.5	3.4	4.1	2.9	2.7	2.9	2.1	2.7	2.1	1.6	1.3	2.1
1986	6.8	6.9	7.0	6.7	6.1	5.7	5.4	5.6	4.4	3.7	3.7	4.4	3.2	3.0	3.2	2.5	3.1	2.5	2.0	1.7	2.6
1987	6.7	6.7	6.8	6.5	5.9	5.5	5.2	5.4	4.3	3.6	3.6	4.2	3.1	2.9	3.1	2.4	3.0	2.3	1.9	1.6	2.5

EXHIBIT A-8 (Continued)

TO THE END OF	FROM THE BEGINNING OF																			
	1968	1969	1970	1971	1972	1973	1974	1975	1976	1977	1978	1979	1980	1981	1982	1983	1984	1985	1986	1987
1968	5.6																			
1969	-4.8	-14.2																		
1970	-4.0	-8.5	-2.4																	
1971	-0.8	-2.8	3.4	9.5																
1972	2.1	1.3	7.0	12.0	14.6															
1973	-2.0	-3.4	-0.6	0.0	-4.4	-20.2														
1974	-7.0	-8.9	-7.8	-9.1	-14.6	-26.3	-31.9													
1975	-3.0	-4.2	-2.4	-2.4	-5.2	-11.0	-6.0	29.7												
1976	-0.9	-1.7	0.2	0.7	-1.0	-4.5	1.3	23.6	17.9											
1977	-2.0	-2.8	-1.3	-1.2	-2.9	-6.0	-2.1	10.5	2.0	-11.7										
1978	-1.9	-2.6	-1.2	-1.1	-2.5	-5.1	-1.8	7.6	1.1	-6.3	-0.6									
1979	-1.2	-1.8	-0.4	-0.2	-1.4	-3.4	-0.3	7.6	2.6	-2.0	3.3	7.3								
1980	0.3	-0.2	1.2	1.6	0.7	-0.9	2.2	9.4	5.7	2.9	8.3	13.0	19.0							
1981	-1.1	-1.6	-0.5	-0.3	-1.2	-2.8	-0.4	5.1	1.5	-1.4	1.3	1.9	-0.7	-17.1						
1982	-0.4	-0.8	0.3	0.5	-0.3	-1.6	0.7	5.7	2.7	0.3	2.9	3.8	2.7	-4.6	9.8					
1983	0.4	0.0	1.1	1.4	0.8	-0.4	1.8	6.5	3.9	2.0	4.5	5.5	5.1	0.8	11.2	12.6				
1984	0.1	-0.2	0.8	1.1	0.4	-0.7	1.3	5.4	3.1	1.3	3.4	4.0	3.4	-0.2	6.2	4.4	-3.3			
1985	1.3	1.0	2.1	2.4	1.9	1.0	3.0	6.9	4.9	3.5	5.6	6.5	6.4	4.0	10.1	10.1	8.9	22.7		
1986	1.8	1.6	2.6	2.9	2.5	1.7	3.6	7.3	5.5	4.3	6.2	7.1	7.1	5.2	10.4	10.5	9.8	17.0	11.6	
1987	1.7	1.5	2.4	2.7	2.3	1.6	3.3	6.7	5.0	3.9	5.6	6.3	6.2	4.4	8.5	8.3	7.2	11.0	5.5	-0.2

EXHIBIT A-9
REAL INTEREST RATES: TREASURY BILLS MINUS INFLATION
RATES OF RETURN FOR ALL YEARLY HOLDING PERIODS FROM 1926 TO 1987
(Percent Per Annum Compounded Annually)

FROM THE BEGINNING OF

TO THE END OF	1926	1927	1928	1929	1930	1931	1932	1933	1934	1935	1936	1937	1938	1939	1940	1941	1942	1943	1944	1945	1946
1926	4.8																				
1927	5.1	5.3																			
1928	4.8	4.8	4.2																		
1929	4.7	4.7	4.4	4.5																	
1930	5.6	5.8	5.9	6.7	9.0																
1931	6.6	6.9	7.3	8.4	10.3	11.7															
1932	7.4	7.8	8.4	9.4	11.1	12.1	12.6														
1933	6.4	6.7	6.9	7.4	8.1	7.9	6.0	-0.2													
1934	5.5	5.6	5.6	5.8	6.1	5.3	3.3	-1.0	-1.8												
1935	4.6	4.6	4.5	4.5	3.7	3.7	1.8	-1.6	-2.3	-2.7											
1936	4.1	4.0	3.9	3.8	3.7	2.9	1.2	-1.5	-1.9	-1.9	-1.0										
1937	3.5	3.4	3.2	3.1	2.9	2.1	0.5	-1.7	-2.1	-2.2	-1.9	-2.7									
1938	3.5	3.3	3.2	3.1	2.9	2.2	0.9	-1.0	-1.1	-0.9	-0.3	0.0	2.8								
1939	3.2	3.1	2.9	2.8	2.7	2.0	0.8	-0.8	-0.8	-0.6	-0.1	0.2	1.7	0.5							
1940	3.0	2.8	2.6	2.5	2.3	1.7	0.6	-0.8	-0.9	-0.7	-0.3	-0.1	0.8	-0.2	-0.9						
1941	2.2	2.0	1.8	1.6	1.3	0.7	-0.4	-1.7	-1.9	-1.9	-1.8	-1.9	-1.7	-3.2	-5.0	-8.8					
1942	1.5	1.3	1.1	0.9	0.6	-0.1	-1.1	-2.4	-2.6	-2.7	-2.7	-3.0	-3.0	-4.5	-6.1	-8.5	-8.3				
1943	1.3	1.1	0.8	0.6	0.3	-0.3	-1.2	-2.4	-2.6	-2.7	-2.7	-3.0	-3.0	-4.1	-5.2	-6.6	-5.5	-2.7			
1944	1.1	0.9	0.7	0.5	0.2	-0.4	-1.3	-2.4	-2.5	-2.6	-2.6	-2.8	-2.8	-3.7	-4.6	-5.4	-4.3	-2.2	-1.7		
1945	1.0	0.8	0.5	0.3	0.1	-0.5	-1.3	-2.3	-2.5	-2.6	-2.5	-2.7	-2.7	-3.5	-4.1	-4.7	-3.7	-2.1	-1.8	-1.9	
1946	0.2	-0.1	-0.4	-0.6	-0.9	-1.5	-2.3	-3.3	-3.5	-3.7	-3.7	-4.0	-4.2	-5.0	-5.8	-6.5	-6.1	-5.5	-6.4	-8.7	-15.1
1947	-0.2	-0.5	-0.7	-1.0	-1.3	-1.9	-2.7	-3.6	-3.8	-4.0	-4.1	-4.4	-4.5	-5.3	-6.0	-6.7	-6.4	-6.0	-6.8	-8.4	-11.5
1948	-0.3	-0.5	-0.8	-1.0	-1.3	-1.9	-2.6	-3.5	-3.7	-3.8	-3.9	-4.2	-4.3	-5.0	-5.6	-6.1	-5.7	-5.3	-5.8	-6.8	-8.4
1949	-0.2	-0.4	-0.6	-0.9	-1.1	-1.6	-2.3	-3.1	-3.3	-3.4	-3.4	-3.6	-3.7	-4.3	-4.7	-5.2	-4.7	-4.2	-4.4	-4.9	-5.7
1950	-0.3	-0.5	-0.8	-1.0	-1.3	-1.8	-2.4	-3.2	-3.4	-3.5	-3.5	-3.7	-3.8	-4.3	-4.7	-5.1	-4.7	-4.2	-4.4	-4.8	-5.4
1951	-0.5	-0.7	-0.9	-1.2	-1.4	-1.9	-2.5	-3.2	-3.4	-3.5	-3.5	-3.7	-3.8	-4.3	-4.7	-5.0	-4.6	-4.2	-4.4	-4.7	-5.2
1952	-0.4	-0.6	-0.9	-1.1	-1.3	-1.8	-2.4	-3.0	-3.2	-3.3	-3.3	-3.4	-3.5	-3.9	-4.3	-4.5	-4.1	-3.7	-3.8	-4.1	-4.4
1953	-0.4	-0.6	-0.8	-1.0	-1.2	-1.6	-2.2	-2.8	-3.0	-3.0	-3.1	-3.2	-3.2	-3.6	-3.9	-4.1	-3.7	-3.3	-3.3	-3.5	-3.7
1954	-0.3	-0.5	-0.7	-0.9	-1.1	-1.5	-2.0	-2.7	-2.8	-2.8	-2.8	-2.9	-2.9	-3.3	-3.5	-3.7	-3.3	-2.9	-2.9	-3.0	-3.1
1955	-0.3	-0.4	-0.6	-0.8	-1.0	-1.4	-1.9	-2.5	-2.6	-2.6	-2.6	-2.7	-2.7	-3.0	-3.2	-3.4	-3.0	-2.6	-2.6	-2.6	-2.7
1956	-0.3	-0.4	-0.6	-0.8	-1.0	-1.4	-1.8	-2.4	-2.5	-2.5	-2.5	-2.6	-2.6	-2.9	-3.1	-3.2	-2.8	-2.4	-2.4	-2.5	-2.5
1957	-0.3	-0.4	-0.6	-0.8	-1.0	-1.3	-1.8	-2.3	-2.4	-2.4	-2.4	-2.5	-2.5	-2.7	-2.9	-3.0	-2.6	-2.3	-2.2	-2.3	-2.3
1958	-0.3	-0.4	-0.6	-0.8	-0.9	-1.3	-1.7	-2.2	-2.3	-2.3	-2.3	-2.4	-2.4	-2.6	-2.8	-2.9	-2.5	-2.1	-2.2	-2.1	-2.1
1959	-0.2	-0.4	-0.5	-0.7	-0.9	-1.2	-1.6	-2.1	-2.2	-2.2	-2.2	-2.2	-2.2	-2.4	-2.6	-2.6	-2.3	-1.9	-1.9	-1.9	-1.9

EXHIBIT A-9 (Continued)

FROM THE BEGINNING OF

TO THE END OF	1926	1927	1928	1929	1930	1931	1932	1933	1934	1935	1936	1937	1938	1939	1940	1941	1942	1943	1944	1945	1946
1960	0.2	-0.3	-0.5	-0.6	-0.8	-1.1	-1.5	-2.0	-2.0	-2.1	-2.0	-2.1	-2.0	-2.3	-2.4	-2.5	-2.1	-1.8	-1.7	-1.7	-1.7
1961	0.1	-0.3	-0.4	-0.6	-0.7	-1.0	-1.4	-1.9	-1.9	-1.9	-1.9	-1.9	-1.9	-2.1	-2.2	-2.3	-1.9	-1.6	-1.5	-1.5	-1.5
1962	0.1	-0.2	-0.4	-0.5	-0.7	-0.9	-1.3	-1.8	-1.8	-1.8	-1.8	-1.8	-1.8	-2.0	-2.1	-2.1	-1.8	-1.5	-1.4	-1.4	-1.3
1963	0.0	-0.2	-0.3	-0.4	-0.6	-0.9	-1.2	-1.7	-1.6	-1.7	-1.7	-1.7	-1.6	-1.8	-1.9	-2.0	-1.6	-1.3	-1.2	-1.2	-1.2
1964	0.1	-0.1	-0.2	-0.4	-0.5	-0.8	-1.1	-1.5	-1.6	-1.6	-1.5	-1.5	-1.5	-1.7	-1.7	-1.8	-1.5	-1.1	-1.1	-1.0	-1.0
1965	0.1	-0.1	-0.2	-0.3	-0.4	-0.7	-1.0	-1.4	-1.5	-1.5	-1.4	-1.4	-1.4	-1.5	-1.6	-1.6	-1.3	-1.0	-0.9	-0.9	-0.8
1966	0.1	-0.0	-0.2	-0.3	-0.4	-0.6	-1.0	-1.3	-1.4	-1.4	-1.3	-1.3	-1.3	-1.4	-1.5	-1.5	-1.2	-0.8	-0.8	-0.8	-0.7
1967	0.1	0.0	-0.1	-0.2	-0.4	-0.6	-0.9	-1.2	-1.3	-1.3	-1.2	-1.2	-1.2	-1.3	-1.4	-1.4	-1.1	-0.8	-0.7	-0.7	-0.7
1968	0.1	0.0	-0.1	-0.2	-0.3	-0.6	-0.9	-1.2	-1.3	-1.2	-1.2	-1.2	-1.2	-1.3	-1.3	-1.4	-1.1	-0.8	-0.7	-0.7	-0.6
1969	0.1	0.0	-0.1	-0.2	-0.3	-0.5	-0.8	-1.2	-1.2	-1.2	-1.1	-1.1	-1.1	-1.2	-1.3	-1.3	-1.0	-0.7	-0.7	-0.6	-0.6
1970	0.2	0.1	-0.1	-0.2	-0.3	-0.5	-0.8	-1.1	-1.2	-1.1	-1.1	-1.1	-1.0	-1.2	-1.2	-1.2	-0.9	-0.7	-0.6	-0.6	-0.5
1971	0.2	0.1	-0.0	-0.1	-0.3	-0.5	-0.8	-1.1	-1.1	-1.1	-1.0	-1.0	-0.9	-1.1	-1.1	-1.1	-0.9	-0.6	-0.5	-0.5	-0.4
1972	0.2	0.1	-0.0	-0.1	-0.2	-0.4	-0.7	-1.0	-1.1	-1.0	-1.0	-1.0	-1.0	-1.0	-1.1	-1.1	-0.8	-0.6	-0.5	-0.5	-0.4
1973	0.1	0.0	-0.1	-0.2	-0.3	-0.5	-0.7	-1.1	-1.1	-1.1	-1.0	-1.0	-1.0	-1.1	-1.2	-1.1	-0.9	-0.6	-0.5	-0.5	-0.5
1974	0.1	0.0	-0.2	-0.2	-0.3	-0.6	-0.8	-1.1	-1.1	-1.1	-1.1	-1.1	-1.0	-1.1	-1.2	-1.2	-1.0	-0.7	-0.7	-0.6	-0.6
1975	0.0	-0.1	-0.2	-0.3	-0.4	-0.5	-0.8	-1.1	-1.1	-1.1	-1.1	-1.1	-1.0	-1.1	-1.2	-1.2	-1.0	-0.7	-0.6	-0.6	-0.6
1976	0.0	-0.1	-0.2	-0.3	-0.4	-0.6	-0.8	-1.1	-1.1	-1.1	-1.0	-1.1	-1.0	-1.1	-1.2	-1.2	-0.9	-0.7	-0.6	-0.6	-0.6
1977	0.0	-0.1	-0.2	-0.3	-0.4	-0.5	-0.8	-1.1	-1.1	-1.1	-1.1	-1.1	-1.0	-1.1	-1.2	-1.2	-0.9	-0.7	-0.7	-0.6	-0.6
1978	0.0	-0.1	-0.2	-0.3	-0.4	-0.6	-0.8	-1.1	-1.1	-1.1	-1.1	-1.1	-1.0	-1.1	-1.2	-1.2	-1.0	-0.8	-0.7	-0.7	-0.6
1979	0.1	0.2	-0.3	-0.4	-0.4	-0.6	-0.9	-1.1	-1.2	-1.1	-1.1	-1.1	-1.1	-1.2	-1.2	-1.2	-1.0	-0.8	-0.8	-0.7	-0.7
1980	0.1	-0.2	-0.3	-0.4	-0.5	-0.6	-0.9	-1.1	-1.2	-1.1	-1.1	-1.1	-1.1	-1.2	-1.2	-1.2	-1.0	-0.8	-0.8	-0.7	-0.7
1981	0.0	-0.1	-0.2	-0.3	-0.4	-0.5	-0.8	-1.0	-1.0	-1.0	-1.0	-1.0	-0.9	-1.0	-1.1	-1.1	-0.9	-0.7	-0.6	-0.5	-0.5
1982	0.1	0.0	-0.1	-0.1	-0.2	-0.4	-0.6	-0.8	-0.9	-0.9	-0.8	-0.8	-0.8	-0.9	-0.9	-0.9	-0.7	-0.5	-0.4	-0.4	-0.4
1983	0.2	0.1	0.0	-0.1	-0.1	-0.3	-0.5	-0.8	-0.8	-0.7	-0.7	-0.7	-0.7	-0.7	-0.8	-0.8	-0.6	-0.4	-0.3	-0.3	-0.2
1984	0.3	0.2	0.1	0.0	0.0	-0.2	-0.4	-0.6	-0.6	-0.6	-0.6	-0.6	-0.5	-0.6	-0.6	-0.6	-0.4	-0.2	-0.2	-0.1	-0.1
1985	0.3	0.3	0.2	0.1	0.0	-0.1	-0.3	-0.5	-0.6	-0.5	-0.5	-0.5	-0.4	-0.5	-0.5	-0.5	-0.3	-0.1	-0.1	-0.0	0.0
1986	0.4	0.3	0.2	0.1	0.1	-0.0	-0.2	-0.5	-0.5	-0.4	-0.4	-0.4	-0.3	-0.4	-0.4	-0.4	-0.2	-0.0	0.0	0.1	0.1
1987	0.4	0.4	0.3	0.2	0.1	-0.0	-0.2	-0.4	-0.4	-0.4	-0.4	-0.4	-0.3	-0.4	-0.4	-0.4	-0.2	0.0	0.1	0.1	0.2

EXHIBIT A-9 (Continued)

TO THE END OF	* 1947	1948	1949	1950	1951	1952	1953	1954	1955	1956	1957	1958	1959	1960	1961	1962	1963	1964	1965	1966	1967
1947	-7.8																				
1948	-4.9	-1.8																			
1949	-2.3	0.5	3.0																		
1950	-2.8	-1.1	-0.8	-4.3																	
1951	-3.1	-1.9	-1.9	-4.2	-4.1																
1952	-2.5	-1.4	-1.2	-2.6	-1.7	0.8															
1953	-2.0	-0.9	-0.8	-1.7	-0.8	1.0	1.2														
1954	-1.5	-0.6	-0.4	-1.1	-0.2	1.1	1.3	1.4													
1955	-1.2	-0.4	-0.2	-0.7	0.1	1.1	1.3	1.3	1.2												
1956	-1.2	-0.4	-0.2	-0.6	-0.0	0.8	0.8	0.7	0.4	-0.4											
1957	-1.0	-0.3	-0.2	-0.6	0.0	0.7	0.7	0.6	0.3	-0.1	0.1										
1958	-1.0	-0.3	-0.2	-0.5	0.0	0.6	0.5	0.4	0.2	-0.2	-0.1	-0.2									
1959	-0.8	-0.2	-0.0	-0.3	0.1	0.7	0.7	0.6	0.4	0.2	0.4	0.6	1.4								
1960	-0.7	-0.1	0.1	-0.2	0.2	0.7	0.7	0.7	0.5	0.4	0.6	0.8	1.3	1.2							
1961	-0.5	0.0	0.2	-0.1	0.3	0.8	0.8	0.8	0.7	0.6	0.8	1.0	1.3	1.3	1.4						
1962	-0.4	0.1	0.3	0.1	0.4	0.9	0.9	0.8	0.8	0.7	0.9	1.1	1.4	1.4	1.5	1.5					
1963	-0.3	0.2	0.3	0.2	0.5	0.9	0.9	0.9	0.9	0.8	1.0	1.1	1.4	1.4	1.5	1.5	1.4				
1964	-0.1	0.3	0.5	0.3	0.6	1.0	1.0	1.0	1.0	1.0	1.1	1.3	1.5	1.6	1.7	1.8	1.9	2.3			
1965	-0.0	0.4	0.6	0.4	0.7	1.1	1.1	1.1	1.1	1.1	1.2	1.4	1.6	1.6	1.7	1.7	1.8	2.1	2.0		
1966	0.0	0.5	0.6	0.5	0.8	1.1	1.1	1.1	1.1	1.1	1.2	1.4	1.6	1.6	1.7	1.7	1.6	1.9	1.7	1.4	
1967	0.1	0.5	0.6	0.5	0.8	1.1	1.1	1.1	1.1	1.1	1.2	1.4	1.5	1.5	1.6	1.6	1.4	1.7	1.5	1.2	1.1
1968	0.1	0.5	0.6	0.5	0.8	1.1	1.1	1.1	1.1	1.1	1.2	1.3	1.5	1.5	1.5	1.5	1.4	1.4	1.2	1.0	0.8
1969	0.1	0.5	0.6	0.5	0.8	1.0	1.1	1.0	1.0	1.0	1.1	1.2	1.3	1.3	1.3	1.3	1.3	1.3	1.1	0.8	0.7
1970	0.2	0.5	0.6	0.5	0.8	1.0	1.0	1.0	1.0	1.0	1.1	1.2	1.3	1.3	1.3	1.3	1.3	1.2	1.1	0.9	0.8
1971	0.2	0.5	0.6	0.5	0.8	1.0	1.0	1.0	1.0	1.0	1.1	1.2	1.3	1.3	1.3	1.3	1.2	1.2	1.0	0.9	0.8
1972	0.2	0.5	0.6	0.5	0.8	1.0	0.9	1.0	1.0	1.0	1.1	1.1	1.2	1.2	1.2	1.2	1.1	1.1	1.0	0.8	0.7
1973	0.1	0.4	0.5	0.4	0.7	0.9	0.9	0.9	0.8	0.8	0.9	0.9	1.0	1.0	1.0	0.9	0.9	0.8	0.7	0.5	0.4
1974	-0.0	0.3	0.4	0.3	0.5	0.7	0.7	0.6	0.6	0.6	0.6	0.7	0.7	0.7	0.6	0.6	0.5	0.4	0.2	0.0	-0.1
1975	-0.1	0.2	0.3	0.2	0.4	0.6	0.6	0.6	0.5	0.5	0.5	0.6	0.6	0.6	0.5	0.4	0.4	0.3	0.1	-0.1	-0.3
1976	-0.0	0.2	0.3	0.2	0.4	0.6	0.6	0.5	0.5	0.5	0.5	0.5	0.6	0.5	0.5	0.4	0.4	0.3	0.1	-0.1	-0.2
1977	-0.1	0.2	0.2	0.2	0.3	0.6	0.5	0.5	0.4	0.4	0.4	0.4	0.4	0.4	0.3	0.3	0.2	0.3	-0.0	-0.2	-0.3
1978	-0.1	0.1	0.2	0.1	0.3	0.5	0.4	0.4	0.3	0.3	0.3	0.3	0.4	0.3	0.3	0.2	0.1	0.0	-0.1	-0.3	-0.4
1979	-0.2	0.0	0.1	0.0	0.2	0.3	0.3	0.3	0.2	0.2	0.2	0.2	0.2	0.2	0.1	0.0	-0.1	-0.1	-0.3	-0.5	-0.6
1980	-0.2	0.0	0.1	-0.0	0.1	0.3	0.2	0.2	0.2	0.1	0.1	0.1	0.2	0.1	0.0	-0.0	-0.1	-0.2	-0.4	-0.5	-0.6
1981	-0.1	0.2	0.2	0.1	0.3	0.4	0.4	0.4	0.4	0.3	0.3	0.4	0.4	0.3	0.3	0.2	0.2	0.1	-0.0	-0.2	-0.3
1982	0.1	0.3	0.4	0.3	0.5	0.6	0.6	0.6	0.6	0.5	0.6	0.6	0.6	0.6	0.6	0.5	0.5	0.4	0.3	0.2	0.2
1983	0.2	0.4	0.5	0.4	0.6	0.7	0.7	0.7	0.7	0.7	0.7	0.8	0.8	0.8	0.7	0.7	0.7	0.6	0.6	0.5	0.4
1984	0.4	0.6	0.7	0.6	0.7	0.9	0.9	0.9	0.9	0.9	0.9	0.9	1.0	1.0	0.9	0.9	0.9	0.9	0.8	0.7	0.7
1985	0.4	0.7	0.7	0.7	0.8	1.0	1.0	1.0	1.0	1.0	1.0	1.0	1.1	1.1	1.1	1.0	1.0	1.0	0.9	0.9	0.9
1986	0.6	0.8	0.8	0.8	0.9	1.1	1.1	1.1	1.1	1.1	1.1	1.2	1.2	1.2	1.2	1.2	1.2	1.2	1.1	1.1	1.1
1987	0.6	0.8	0.9	0.8	0.9	1.1	1.1	1.1	1.1	1.1	1.1	1.2	1.2	1.2	1.2	1.2	1.2	1.2	1.1	1.1	1.1

* FROM THE BEGINNING OF

EXHIBIT A-9 (Continued)

TO THE END OF	FROM THE BEGINNING OF																			
	1968	1969	1970	1971	1972	1973	1974	1975	1976	1977	1978	1979	1980	1981	1982	1983	1984	1985	1986	1987
1968	0.5																			
1969	0.5	0.4																		
1970	0.6	0.7	1.0																	
1971	0.7	0.8	1.0	1.0																
1972	0.7	0.7	0.8	0.7	0.4															
1973	0.3	0.2	0.2	-0.1	-0.7	-1.7														
1974	-0.3	-0.5	-0.6	-1.0	-1.7	-2.7	-3.7													
1975	-0.4	-0.5	-0.7	-1.1	-1.6	-2.2	-2.4	-1.1												
1976	-0.3	-0.4	-0.6	-0.8	-1.2	-1.6	-1.6	-0.4	0.3											
1977	-0.5	-0.6	-0.7	-0.9	-1.3	-1.6	-1.6	-0.8	-0.6	-1.5										
1978	-0.6	-0.7	-0.8	-1.0	-1.3	-1.6	-1.6	-1.0	-1.0	-1.6	-1.7									
1979	-0.7	-0.9	-1.0	-1.2	-1.5	-1.7	-1.7	-1.3	-1.4	-1.9	-2.1	-2.6								
1980	-0.8	-0.9	-1.0	-1.2	-1.4	-1.7	-1.6	-1.3	-1.3	-1.7	-1.8	-1.8	-1.0							
1981	-0.3	-0.4	-0.5	-0.6	-0.8	-0.9	-0.8	-0.4	-0.3	-0.4	-0.1	0.5	2.1	5.3						
1982	0.1	0.1	0.0	-0.0	-0.1	-0.2	-0.0	0.4	0.7	0.7	1.2	2.0	3.5	5.9	6.4					
1983	0.4	0.4	0.4	0.3	0.3	0.2	0.4	0.9	1.2	1.3	1.8	2.5	3.8	5.5	5.6	4.8				
1984	0.7	0.7	0.7	0.7	0.7	0.7	0.9	1.4	1.7	1.9	2.3	3.0	4.2	5.6	5.6	5.2	5.7			
1985	0.9	0.9	0.9	0.9	0.9	0.9	1.2	1.6	1.9	2.1	2.5	3.1	4.1	5.2	5.2	4.8	4.7	3.8		
1986	1.1	1.1	1.1	1.1	1.2	1.2	1.4	1.9	2.2	2.4	2.8	3.4	4.3	5.2	5.1	4.8	4.8	4.4	5.0	
1987	1.1	1.1	1.1	1.1	1.1	1.2	1.4	1.8	2.1	2.2	2.6	3.1	3.8	4.6	4.4	4.0	3.9	3.3	3.0	1.0

EXHIBIT A-10
LONG-HORIZON EQUITY RISK PREMIUMS
RATES OF RETURN FOR ALL YEARLY HOLDING PERIODS FROM 1926 TO 1987
(Percent Per Annum Compounded Annually)

FROM THE BEGINNING OF

TO THE END OF	1926	1927	1928	1929	1930	1931	1932	1933	1934	1935	1936	1937	1938	1939	1940	1941	1942	1943	1944	1945	1946
1926	7.6																				
1927	19.6	33.0																			
1928	25.8	36.0	39.1																		
1929	15.2	17.9	11.0	-11.5																	
1930	5.1	4.4	-3.6	-19.8	-27.3																
1931	-5.7	-8.2	-16.3	-29.3	-36.9	-45.2															
1932	-6.6	-8.7	-15.4	-25.2	-29.3	-30.3	-11.5														
1933	-0.9	-2.1	-7.0	-14.1	-14.8	-10.2	15.0	49.3													
1934	-1.3	-2.4	-6.6	-12.6	-12.8	-8.8	8.1	19.4	-4.5												
1935	2.5	1.9	-1.4	-6.2	-5.3	-0.1	16.1	27.0	17.1	43.6											
1936	4.7	4.4	1.7	-2.2	-0.8	4.4	18.8	27.8	21.4	36.8	30.3										
1937	0.4	-0.2	-3.0	-6.9	-6.3	-2.8	6.9	11.1	3.1	5.8	-9.2	-36.7									
1938	2.3	1.9	-0.6	-3.9	-6.3	0.6	9.7	13.7	7.6	5.8	1.8	-10.1	27.7								
1939	1.9	1.5	-0.8	-3.8	-3.0	0.2	8.1	11.2	5.8	8.0	0.6	-7.7	11.5	-2.7							
1940	0.9	0.5	-1.7	-4.5	-3.8	-1.1	5.7	8.0	3.1	4.5	-2.0	-8.7	3.1	-7.4	-11.8						
1941	0.0	-0.5	-2.5	-5.2	-4.6	-2.2	3.6	5.4	0.9	1.7	-4.0	-9.7	-1.3	-9.4	-12.5	-13.3					
1942	0.9	0.5	-1.3	-3.7	-3.1	-0.7	4.8	6.6	2.6	3.6	-1.2	-5.6	2.2	-3.3	-3.5	0.9	17.5				
1943	2.1	1.7	0.0	-2.1	-1.4	0.9	6.2	7.9	4.5	5.5	1.6	-2.0	5.4	1.4	2.5	7.8	20.1	22.9			
1944	2.8	2.5	1.0	-1.0	-0.3	2.0	7.0	8.7	5.6	6.6	3.2	0.2	7.0	3.9	5.2	10.0	19.0	19.8	16.9		
1945	4.1	4.0	2.5	0.7	1.5	3.8	8.7	10.4	8.8	8.8	5.8	3.4	10.0	7.6	9.5	14.3	22.5	24.2	24.8	33.3	
1946	3.4	3.2	1.8	0.1	0.8	2.9	7.3	8.8	7.1	7.1	4.3	2.0	7.6	5.3	6.5	9.9	15.2	14.6	12.0	9.6	-9.9
1947	3.4	3.2	1.9	0.3	1.0	2.9	7.1	8.4	6.0	6.8	4.2	2.1	7.1	5.1	6.1	8.9	13.1	12.3	9.8	7.5	-3.4
1948	3.4	3.2	2.0	0.4	1.1	2.9	6.8	8.1	5.8	6.6	4.1	2.2	6.8	4.9	5.7	8.2	13.1	10.7	8.4	6.4	-1.3
1949	3.9	3.7	2.6	1.1	1.8	3.6	7.3	8.5	6.4	7.2	5.0	3.2	7.5	5.8	6.7	9.0	12.2	11.5	9.7	8.3	2.8
1950	4.8	4.7	3.6	2.2	2.9	4.7	8.4	9.6	7.6	8.4	6.4	4.9	9.0	7.6	8.6	10.9	13.9	13.5	12.2	11.5	7.6
1951	5.4	5.3	4.3	3.0	3.7	5.5	9.0	10.2	8.3	9.1	7.3	5.9	9.9	8.6	9.6	11.8	14.6	14.3	13.3	12.8	9.7
1952	5.7	5.7	4.7	3.5	4.2	5.9	9.3	10.4	8.7	9.5	7.7	6.5	10.2	9.1	10.0	12.1	14.7	14.4	13.5	13.1	10.5
1953	5.4	5.3	4.4	3.2	3.8	5.5	8.6	9.7	8.0	8.7	7.1	5.8	9.3	8.2	9.0	10.8	12.6	12.6	11.7	11.1	8.6
1954	6.6	6.6	5.7	4.6	5.3	7.0	10.1	11.2	9.7	10.4	8.9	7.8	11.3	10.3	11.2	13.1	15.4	15.3	14.6	14.4	12.4
1955	7.3	7.3	6.5	5.4	6.1	7.7	10.8	11.9	10.5	11.2	9.8	8.8	12.1	11.3	12.2	14.0	16.3	16.2	15.7	15.6	13.9
1956	7.2	7.2	6.4	5.3	6.0	7.6	10.5	11.5	10.1	10.9	9.5	8.5	11.7	10.8	11.7	13.4	15.4	15.2	14.7	14.5	12.9
1957	6.4	6.4	5.6	4.6	5.2	6.7	9.5	10.4	9.0	9.6	8.3	7.4	10.2	9.4	10.1	11.5	13.3	13.0	12.4	12.0	10.4
1958	7.3	7.3	6.6	5.6	6.3	7.7	10.4	11.4	10.1	10.7	9.5	8.6	11.5	10.7	11.5	12.9	14.7	14.5	14.0	13.8	12.4
1959	7.3	7.3	6.6	5.7	6.3	7.7	10.3	11.2	10.0	10.6	9.4	8.6	11.3	10.5	11.3	12.6	14.3	14.1	13.6	13.3	12.0

EXHIBIT A-10 (Continued)

FROM THE BEGINNING OF

TO THE END OF	1926	1927	1928	1929	1930	1931	1932	1933	1934	1935	1936	1937	1938	1939	1940	1941	1942	1943	1944	1945	1946
1960	7.0	7.0	6.3	5.4	6.0	7.3	9.8	10.7	9.4	10.0	8.9	8.0	10.6	9.9	10.5	11.7	13.3	13.0	12.5	12.2	10.9
1961	7.4	7.4	6.7	5.8	6.4	7.8	10.2	11.0	9.9	10.5	9.3	8.6	11.0	10.4	11.0	12.2	13.7	13.5	13.0	12.8	11.6
1962	6.8	6.8	6.1	5.3	5.8	7.1	9.4	10.2	9.0	9.5	8.5	7.7	10.0	9.3	9.9	11.0	12.3	12.0	11.5	11.2	10.0
1963	7.1	7.1	6.4	5.6	6.2	7.4	9.7	10.4	9.3	9.8	8.8	8.1	10.3	9.7	10.2	11.3	12.6	12.3	11.8	11.6	10.5
1964	7.2	7.2	6.6	5.8	6.3	7.5	9.7	10.5	9.4	9.9	8.9	8.2	10.4	9.7	10.2	11.3	12.5	12.3	11.8	11.6	10.5
1965	7.2	7.2	6.6	5.8	6.4	7.5	9.7	10.4	9.4	9.8	8.9	8.2	10.3	9.7	10.2	11.2	12.3	12.1	11.6	11.4	10.4
1966	6.6	6.6	6.0	5.3	5.8	6.9	8.9	9.6	8.6	9.0	8.0	7.4	9.3	8.7	9.2	10.1	11.1	10.9	10.4	10.1	9.1
1967	6.9	6.9	6.3	5.6	6.1	7.2	9.2	9.8	8.8	9.3	8.4	7.7	9.6	9.1	9.5	10.4	11.4	11.2	10.7	10.5	9.5
1968	6.9	6.9	6.3	5.6	6.1	7.1	9.1	9.7	8.7	9.2	8.3	7.6	9.5	8.9	9.4	10.2	11.2	10.9	10.5	10.2	9.3
1969	6.4	6.3	5.8	5.1	5.5	6.5	8.4	9.0	8.1	8.4	7.5	6.9	8.7	8.1	8.5	9.3	10.2	9.9	9.4	9.2	8.3
1970	6.2	6.1	5.6	4.9	5.3	6.3	8.1	8.7	7.7	8.1	7.2	6.6	8.3	7.8	8.1	8.9	9.7	9.4	9.0	8.7	7.8
1971	6.2	6.2	5.6	4.9	5.4	6.3	8.1	8.6	7.7	8.1	7.2	6.6	8.3	7.8	8.1	8.8	9.6	9.4	8.9	8.6	7.8
1972	6.3	6.3	5.8	5.1	5.5	6.5	8.2	8.7	7.9	8.2	7.4	6.8	8.4	7.9	8.2	8.9	9.7	9.5	9.0	8.8	8.0
1973	5.7	5.6	5.1	4.5	4.9	5.8	7.4	7.9	7.1	7.4	6.6	6.0	7.5	7.0	7.3	7.9	8.7	8.4	7.9	7.6	6.8
1974	4.8	4.7	4.2	3.5	3.9	4.7	6.3	6.8	5.9	6.2	5.4	4.8	6.2	5.7	5.9	6.5	7.1	6.8	6.4	6.0	5.2
1975	5.2	5.1	4.6	4.0	4.3	5.2	6.7	7.2	6.4	6.6	5.9	5.3	6.7	6.2	6.5	7.0	7.7	7.4	7.0	6.6	5.9
1976	5.3	5.3	4.8	4.2	4.5	5.4	6.9	7.4	6.6	6.8	6.1	5.5	6.9	6.4	6.7	7.2	7.9	7.6	7.2	6.9	6.1
1977	4.9	4.9	4.4	3.8	4.1	4.9	6.4	6.9	6.0	6.3	5.5	5.0	6.3	5.8	6.1	6.6	7.2	6.9	6.5	6.2	5.5
1978	4.8	4.8	4.3	3.7	4.0	4.8	6.3	6.7	5.9	6.1	5.4	4.9	6.2	5.7	5.9	6.4	7.0	6.9	6.5	6.0	5.2
1979	4.9	4.8	4.4	3.8	4.1	4.9	6.3	6.7	5.9	6.2	5.5	4.9	6.2	5.7	6.0	6.5	7.0	6.8	6.3	6.1	5.4
1980	5.2	5.1	4.7	4.1	4.4	5.2	6.6	7.0	6.2	6.5	5.8	5.3	6.5	6.1	6.3	6.8	7.4	7.1	6.7	6.4	5.8
1981	4.8	4.7	4.3	3.7	4.0	4.7	6.1	6.5	5.8	6.0	5.3	4.8	6.0	5.5	5.7	6.2	6.7	6.5	6.1	5.8	5.1
1982	4.8	4.8	4.3	3.8	4.1	4.8	6.1	6.5	5.8	6.0	5.3	4.8	6.0	5.6	5.8	6.2	6.7	6.5	6.1	5.8	5.2
1983	4.9	4.9	4.4	3.9	4.2	4.9	6.2	6.6	5.9	6.1	5.4	5.0	6.1	5.7	5.9	6.3	6.8	6.6	6.2	6.0	5.3
1984	4.7	4.7	4.2	3.7	4.0	4.7	6.0	6.4	5.7	5.9	5.2	4.7	5.9	5.4	5.6	6.1	6.6	6.3	5.9	5.7	5.0
1985	5.0	5.0	4.5	4.0	4.3	4.9	6.2	6.6	5.9	6.1	5.5	5.0	6.1	5.7	5.9	6.3	6.8	6.6	6.2	6.0	5.4
1986	5.0	5.0	4.6	4.0	4.3	5.0	6.3	6.6	5.9	6.2	5.5	5.1	6.2	5.8	6.0	6.4	6.9	6.6	6.3	6.0	5.5
1987	4.9	4.8	4.4	3.9	4.2	4.9	6.1	6.4	5.8	6.0	5.4	4.9	6.0	5.6	5.8	6.2	6.7	6.4	6.1	5.8	5.3

EXHIBIT A-10 (Continued)

FROM THE BEGINNING OF

TO THE END OF	1967	1966	1965	1964	1963	1962	1961	1960	1959	1958	1957	1956	1955	1954	1953	1952	1951	1950	1949	1948	1947
1947																					3.5
1948																				3.0	3.3
1949																			16.2	9.4	7.4
1950																		29.0	22.4	15.6	12.4
1951																	21.1	25.0	22.0	16.9	14.1
1952																15.3	18.2	21.7	20.3	16.6	14.3
1953															-3.7	5.4	10.4	14.8	15.0	12.9	11.5
1954														48.5	19.6	18.1	18.9	20.8	20.0	17.4	15.6
1955													28.0	37.9	22.3	20.5	20.7	22.0	21.2	18.7	16.9
1956												3.5	15.1	25.3	17.3	16.9	17.6	19.2	18.8	16.9	15.5
1957											-13.7	-5.5	4.5	14.1	10.3	11.1	12.5	14.4	14.6	13.4	12.5
1958										38.8	9.4	7.4	12.2	18.7	14.6	14.7	15.5	16.9	16.9	15.5	14.5
1959									7.6	22.2	8.8	7.5	11.3	16.8	13.6	13.8	14.6	16.0	16.0	14.8	13.9
1960								-3.6	1.8	12.9	5.6	5.1	8.7	13.6	11.3	11.7	12.6	14.0	14.2	13.3	12.6
1961							22.2	8.5	8.2	15.2	8.7	7.8	10.5	14.7	12.4	12.7	13.5	14.7	14.8	13.9	13.2
1962						-12.2	3.6	1.1	2.7	9.1	4.9	4.7	7.4	11.3	9.7	10.2	11.1	12.4	12.6	12.0	11.4
1963					18.2	1.9	8.2	5.1	5.6	10.6	6.7	6.3	8.5	12.0	10.4	10.8	11.6	12.7	13.0	12.3	11.8
1964				11.8	15.0	5.1	9.1	6.4	6.6	10.7	7.3	6.9	8.8	12.0	10.6	10.9	11.6	12.4	12.9	12.1	11.6
1965			7.9	9.9	12.6	5.8	8.9	6.7	6.8	10.4	7.4	7.0	8.8	11.6	10.4	10.7	11.4	12.4	12.6	12.1	11.6
1966		-13.9	-3.6	1.3	5.3	1.5	4.7	3.5	4.0	7.4	5.0	4.9	6.7	9.4	8.4	8.9	9.6	10.6	10.9	10.5	10.2
1967	18.5	1.0	3.3	5.3	7.8	4.2	6.6	5.2	5.5	8.4	6.2	6.0	7.5	10.0	9.1	9.4	10.1	11.1	11.3	10.5	10.5
1968	11.7	2.4	3.8	5.3	7.4	4.3	6.4	5.2	5.5	8.1	6.1	5.9	7.4	9.7	8.8	9.2	9.8	10.8	11.0	10.6	10.3
1969	2.5	-1.9	0.0	1.9	4.1	1.9	4.0	3.2	3.6	6.1	4.5	4.4	5.8	8.1	7.3	7.8	8.4	9.4	9.7	9.4	9.1
1970	1.2	-2.0	-0.4	1.3	3.2	1.4	3.3	2.6	3.1	5.4	3.9	3.9	5.3	7.4	6.8	7.2	7.9	8.8	9.1	8.8	8.6
1971	2.5	-0.5	0.7	2.0	3.7	2.0	3.7	3.0	3.4	5.6	4.2	4.1	5.4	7.4	6.8	7.2	7.8	8.7	9.0	8.8	8.6
1972	4.0	1.3	2.1	3.1	4.5	2.9	4.4	3.7	4.0	6.0	4.7	4.6	5.8	7.7	7.1	7.5	8.0	8.9	9.2	8.9	8.7
1973	0.2	-1.7	-0.6	0.5	2.0	0.8	2.3	1.8	2.2	4.2	3.0	3.1	4.2	6.1	5.6	6.0	6.7	7.5	7.8	7.6	7.5
1974	-4.4	-5.5	-4.3	-2.9	-1.3	-2.2	-0.6	-0.8	-0.3	1.7	0.7	0.9	2.1	3.9	3.6	4.0	4.7	5.6	6.0	5.9	5.8
1975	-1.3	-2.7	-1.8	-0.7	0.6	-0.3	1.0	0.7	1.1	2.9	2.0	2.0	3.2	4.9	4.5	4.9	5.5	6.3	6.7	6.6	6.4
1976	0.2	-1.2	-0.5	0.4	1.6	0.6	1.8	1.5	1.8	3.5	2.6	2.6	3.7	5.3	4.9	5.3	5.9	6.6	7.0	6.8	6.7
1977	0.2	-2.3	-1.5	-0.6	0.5	-0.3	0.9	0.6	1.0	2.6	1.7	1.8	2.8	4.4	4.1	4.5	5.1	5.8	6.2	6.1	6.0
1978	-1.2	-2.2	-2.3	-0.7	0.4	-0.4	0.7	0.5	0.9	2.4	1.6	1.7	2.7	4.2	3.9	4.3	4.8	5.6	5.9	5.8	5.8
1979	-0.4	-1.5	-0.9	-0.1	0.9	0.1	1.2	0.9	1.2	2.7	1.9	2.0	2.9	4.4	4.1	4.4	5.0	5.7	6.0	5.9	5.9
1980	0.9	-0.1	0.4	1.0	1.9	1.1	2.1	1.8	2.0	3.4	2.6	2.7	3.5	4.9	4.6	5.0	5.5	6.2	6.5	6.3	6.3
1981	-0.2	-1.1	-0.6	0.1	0.9	0.2	1.2	1.0	1.2	2.6	1.9	1.9	2.8	4.2	3.9	4.2	4.7	5.4	5.7	5.7	5.6
1982	0.2	-0.7	-0.2	0.4	1.2	0.5	1.4	1.2	1.5	2.7	2.1	2.1	2.9	4.2	4.0	4.3	4.8	5.5	5.8	5.7	5.6
1983	0.8	-0.0	0.4	0.9	1.7	1.0	1.8	1.6	1.8	3.1	2.4	2.4	3.2	4.5	4.2	4.5	5.0	5.6	5.9	5.8	5.8
1984	0.5	-0.3	0.1	0.6	1.4	0.7	1.5	1.3	1.6	2.7	2.1	2.2	2.9	4.1	3.9	4.2	4.7	5.3	5.6	5.5	5.5
1985	1.4	0.6	0.9	1.4	2.1	1.4	2.2	1.9	2.2	3.3	2.6	2.7	3.4	4.6	4.3	4.6	5.1	5.7	5.9	5.9	5.8
1986	1.8	0.9	1.3	1.7	2.3	1.7	2.4	2.2	2.4	3.5	2.8	2.9	3.6	4.7	4.4	4.7	5.2	5.7	6.0	5.9	5.9
1987	1.5	0.8	1.1	1.5	2.1	1.5	2.2	2.0	2.2	3.3	2.7	2.7	3.4	4.5	4.2	4.5	4.9	5.5	5.8	5.7	5.7

EXHIBIT A-10 (Continued)

TO THE END OF	FROM THE BEGINNING OF 1968	1969	1970	1971	1972	1973	1974	1975	1976	1977	1978	1979	1980	1981	1982	1983	1984	1985	1986	1987
1968	5.3																			
1969	-4.7	-13.6																		
1970	-4.0	-8.3	-2.6																	
1971	-1.2	-3.3	2.4	7.5																
1972	1.4	0.4	5.6	9.9	12.4															
1973	-2.5	-4.0	-1.4	-1.1	-5.1	-19.9														
1974	-7.3	-9.3	-8.4	-9.7	-14.9	-25.9	-31.4													
1975	-3.6	-4.8	-3.2	-3.4	-5.9	-11.3	-6.7	27.0												
1976	-1.7	-2.5	-0.8	-0.5	-2.1	-5.4	0.0	20.8	14.8											
1977	-2.9	-3.8	-2.5	-2.5	-4.1	-7.1	-3.6	8.1	-0.3	-13.5										
1978	-2.8	-3.6	-2.4	-2.3	-3.7	-6.1	-3.1	5.7	-0.6	-7.6	-1.3									
1979	-1.9	-2.5	-1.3	-1.2	-2.2	-4.1	-1.2	6.3	1.6	-2.4	3.6	8.8								
1980	-0.3	-0.7	0.5	0.8	0.1	-1.3	1.7	8.6	5.2	2.9	9.0	14.6	20.7							
1981	-1.4	-1.9	-0.9	-0.7	-1.5	-2.9	-0.6	4.9	1.6	-0.9	2.5	3.8	1.4	-14.8						
1982	-0.9	-1.3	-0.3	-0.1	-0.8	-2.0	0.2	5.1	2.3	0.4	3.4	4.6	3.2	-4.6	6.9					
1983	-0.2	-0.5	0.5	0.7	0.2	-0.9	1.3	5.7	3.3	1.8	4.6	5.8	5.1	0.3	8.9	10.9				
1984	-0.5	-0.8	0.1	0.3	-0.2	-1.2	0.7	4.6	2.4	0.9	3.2	3.9	3.0	-1.0	4.1	2.7	-4.9			
1985	0.5	0.2	1.2	1.4	1.0	0.2	2.1	5.8	3.9	2.8	5.0	5.9	5.5	2.7	7.6	7.8	6.3	18.8		
1986	0.9	0.7	1.6	1.9	1.5	0.8	2.6	6.1	4.4	3.4	5.4	6.3	5.9	3.7	7.8	8.1	7.1	13.7	8.9	
1987	0.8	0.5	1.4	1.6	1.3	0.6	2.2	5.4	3.8	2.8	4.6	5.3	4.9	2.8	6.0	5.9	4.6	8.0	3.0	-2.5

REFERENCES

Banz, Rolf W. "The Relationship Between Returns and Market Value of Common Stocks." *Journal of Financial Economics* 9 (1981): 3-18.

Chen, Nai-Fu, Richard Roll, and Stephen A. Ross. "Economic Forces and the Stock Market." *Journal of Business* 59 (1986): 383-403.

Coleman, Thomas S., Lawrence Fisher, and Roger G. Ibbotson. *U.S. Treasury Yield Curves: 1926 through 1987.* New York: Moody's Investors Service, 1988.

Gordon, Myron J. and Eli Shapiro. "Capital Equipment Analysis: The Required Rate of Profit." *Management Science* 3 (1956): 102-10.

Ibbotson, Roger G., Jeffrey J. Diermeier, and Laurence B. Siegel. "The Demand for Capital Market Returns: A New Equilibrium Theory." *Financial Analysts Journal* 40 (1984): 22-23.

Ibbotson, Roger G., and Rex A. Sinquefield. *Stocks, Bonds, Bills, and Inflation. Historical Returns (1926-1978).* Charlottesville, Virginia: The Financial Analysts Research Foundation, 1979.

Ibbotson, Roger G., and Rex A. Sinquefield. *Stocks, Bonds, Bills, and Inflation. The Past and The Future,* 1982 ed. Charlottesville, Virginia: The Financial Analysts Research Foundation, 1982.

Ibbotson, Roger G., and Rex A. Sinquefield. *Stocks, Bonds, Bills, and Inflation. The Past (1926-1976) and The Future (1977-2000)*. 1977 ed. Charlottesville, Virginia: The Financial Analysts Research Foundation, 1977.

Ibbotson, Roger G., and Rex A. Sinquefield. "Stocks, Bonds, Bills, and Inflation. Simulations of the Future (1976-2000)." *Journal of Business* 49 (1976): 313-38.

Ibbotson, Roger G., and Rex A. Sinquefield. "Stocks, Bonds, Bills, and Inflation. Year-by-Year Historical Returns (1926-1974)." *Journal of Business* 49 (1976): 11-47.

Keim, Donald B. "Size-Related Anomalies and Stock Return Seasonality: Further Empirical Evidence." *Journal of Financial Economics* 12 (1983): 13-32.

Roll, Richard and Stephen A. Ross. "The Arbitrage Pricing Theory Approach to Strategic Portfolio Planning." *Financial Analysts Journal* 40 (1984): 14-26.

Ross, Stephen A. "The Arbitrage Theory of Capital Asset Pricing," *Journal of Economic Theory* 13 (1976): 341-60.

Ross, Stephen A. "Return, Risk, and Arbitrage," in Friend and Bicklser, eds., *Risk and Return in Finance*. Cambridge, Massachusetts: Ballinger, 1976.

Ross, Stephen A. and Randolph W. Westerfield. "Level-Coupon Bonds." *Corporate Finance*. St. Louis: Times Mirror/Mosby, 1988, 97.

Stocks, Bonds, Bills, and Inflation Yearbook, annual. Chicago, Illinois: Ibbotson Associates, Inc., 1984, 1985, 1986, 1987, 1988, 1989.

Van Horne, James C. *Financial Management and Policy.* 8th edition. Englewood Cliffs, New Jersey: Prentice-Hall, Inc., 1989.

Williams, John B. *The Theory of Investment Value.* Cambridge, Massachusetts: Harvard University Press, 1938.